Michael Devitt is a distinguished philosopher of language. In this new book he takes up foundational issues in semantics.

Three important questions lie at the core of this book: What are the main objectives of semantics? Why are they worthwhile? How should we accomplish them? Devitt answers these "methodological" questions naturalistically and explores what semantic program arises from the answers. The approach is anti-Cartesian, rejecting the idea that linguistic or conceptual competence yields any privileged access to meanings.

This new methodology is used first against holism. Devitt argues for a truth-referential localism and in the process rejects direct-reference, two-factor, and verificationist theories. The book concludes by arguing against revisionism, eliminativism, and the idea that we should ascribe narrow meanings to explain behavior.

A substantial contribution to the literature on meaning and intentionality, this important study will be of particular interest to philosophers of language and mind and could be used in graduate-level seminars in these areas. The book will also appeal to readers in linguistics and the other cognitive sciences.

CAMBRIDGE STUDIES IN PHILOSOPHY

Coming to Our Senses

CAMBRIDGE STUDIES IN PHILOSOPHY

General editor Ernest Sosa

Advisory editors

Jonathan Dancy – University of Keele
Gilbert Harman – Princeton University
Frank Jackson – University of Melbourne
William G. Lycan – University of North Carolina, Chapel Hill
Sidney Shoemaker – Cornell University
Judith J. Thomson – Massachusetts Institute of Technology

RECENT TITLES

Coming to Our Senses

A Naturalistic Program for Semantic Localism

Michael Devitt
University of Maryland

CAMBRIDGE
UNIVERSITY PRESS

Published by the Press Syndicate of the University of Cambridge
The Pitt Building, Trumpington Street, Cambridge CB2 1RP
40 West 20th Street, New York, NY 10011–4211, USA
10 Stamford Road, Oakleigh, Melbourne 3166, Australia

First published 1996

Printed in the United States of America

Library of Congress Cataloging-in-Publication Data
Devitt, Michael, 1938–

Coming to our senses : a naturalistic program for semantic
localism / Michael Devitt.

p.   cm. – (Cambridge studies in philosophy)

Includes bibliograpical references and index.

ISBN 0-521-49543-1. – ISBN 0-521-49887-2 (pbk.)

1. Semantics.   2. Semantics (Philosophy).   3. Holism.   I. Title.
II. Series.
P325.D47 1996
121'.68–20   95-6275
                                                                     CIP

A catalog record for this book is available from the British Library.

ISBN 0-521-49543-1 hardback
ISBN 0-521-49887-2 paperback

Contents

v

Preface

Two things led to this book. The more immediate, but less important, cause was my concern about semantic, or meaning, holism. Holism has, as Jerry Fodor says, "something of the status of the received doctrine in the philosophy of language" (1987: 57). And it is urged, or taken for granted, in psychology and artificial intelligence. Yet it seemed to me, as it did to Fodor, clearly false ("crazy" was his word). So, in 1989, I set out to show this.

First, I had to show that the arguments for holism were no good. The main argument stems from Quine: The localist idea that *some but not all* inferential properties of a token constitute its meaning (or content) is alleged to yield an analytic-synthetic distinction with epistemologically objectionable consequences. You can accept this argument without becoming a holist, of course, if you are prepared to adopt an "atomistic" localism according to which *no* inferential property *ever* constitutes the meaning of a token. That is Fodor's path. However, atomism strikes me as implausibly extreme. Very likely, the meanings of some tokens are atomistic, but surely the meanings of others – perhaps 'bachelor' is an example – are not. I want to defend a "molecular" localism, according to which *a few* of the inferential properties of a token *may* constitute its meaning. I think that I can have what I want because I reject the Quinean argument: Molecular localism does *not* have epistemologically objectionable consequences unless it is saddled, gratuitously, with an epistemic thesis. I also reject other arguments against there being a "principled basis" for the molecular localist's distinction among inferential properties.

It is one thing to reject arguments against there being a principled basis, it is another to show that there is one. This was the second thing I had to do to refute holism and establish localism. I found doing this much harder than I expected.

Attempting to do it soon raised some very general questions. What are the semantic tasks? Why are they worthwhile? How should we accomplish them? I have been bothered by these "methodological" questions from my semantic beginnings, long before holism marred my horizon. Signs of this bother are to be found scattered through my earlier writings.

That brings me to the less immediate, but more important, cause of this book: my desire to confront the methodological questions directly and thoroughly and to see what semantic program would follow from my answers. This cause is largely independent of the one arising from holism but, as I have indicated, not entirely so. My first use of my methodology is to show that localism has the principled basis it needs. So the program I urge is localistic.

Some parts of my semantic program – for example, truth-referentialism – are common enough. Some parts – for example, molecular localism – are not common at all (although I am here, unusually, in agreement with Michael Dummett). Some parts – for example, the view that a token has more than one meaning – are positively rare. I think that the main interest of this book lies not so much in these substantive theses as in its proposal of a novel methodology and in its use of this to support those theses.

I had a problem finding a title. A straightforwardly descriptive title using some combination of such well-worn terms as 'meaning', 'mind', 'semantic', 'reference', 'representation', 'content', 'truth', even 'holism' or 'localism', and certainly 'realism' or 'reality' would make the eyes glaze (and likely raise the question, "Wasn't that one of Putnam's books?"). I sought the help of my colleague, Michael Slote. In describing the book to him, I said that it proposes a methodology that it then uses against some popular but, in my view, very implausible views in semantics. Among these are holism, "two-factor" theories, and verificationism. Among them also is the " 'Fido'-Fido," or "Millian," theory of names, recently resurrected by "direct-reference" philosophers. According to this theory, a name lacks a sense, its meaning being simply its property of referring to its bearer. Finally, I emphasized to Slote that the semantic program proposed in the book was intended to be naturalistic and hence "derived from experience." Putting all this together, in a divine moment of inspiration while "in the bathroom," he thought of the nice pun "Coming to Our Senses." (I should add that the senses I come to for names are not Fregean; they are nondescriptive senses made up of causal modes of reference.) The subtitle was easy and all my own work.

Work on the book led to two "unpublications," "Meaning Localism" and "What Did Quine Show Us about Meaning Holism?," and then to several publications. These are "Localism and Analyticity" (1993a), which is a brief early version of some ideas in Chapters 1 and 3; "A Critique of the Case for Semantic Holism" (1993b), of which Chapter 1 is a modified version; "Semantic Localism: Who Needs a Principled Basis?" (1994a), which is a brief early version of some ideas in Chapters 2 and 3; and "The Methodology of Naturalistic Semantics" (1994b), of which Chapter 2 is a modified version.

These papers, as well as draft chapters, have been delivered at many conferences and universities over the last five years. The book has benefitted from the ensuing discussions. It has also benefitted from the comments on some of these items of at least the following (my apologies to those omitted): Louise Antony, Ned Block, David Braun, Alex Byrne, Fiona Cowie, Rey Elugardo, Hartry Field, Jerry Fodor, Peter Godfrey-Smith, Dorothy Grover, Gil Harman, David Lewis, Eric Lormand, Peter Ludlow, Bill Lycan, Graham Oppy, Greg Ray, Michael Slote, Kim Sterelny, Corliss Swain, Ken Taylor, and, especially, Georges Rey.

I am grateful to the University of Maryland for giving me time off from teaching in the following ways: a Semester Research Award from the General Research Board of Graduate Studies and

Research in fall 1989; a Fellowship at the Research Center for Arts and Humanities in fall 1990; and a sabbatical leave in spring 1994. I am also grateful to the Australian National University for a Visiting Fellowship, March–June 1994.

Introduction

Three important questions get insufficient attention in semantics. What are the semantic tasks? Why are they worthwhile? How should we accomplish them? The central purpose of this book is to answer these "methodological" questions and to see what semantic program follows from the answers.

It is troubling that much semantic theorizing proceeds with inexplicit reliance on apparently ad hoc views of the semantic tasks. Thus it is common to take for granted that semantics is concerned with truth and reference. I think that this view is right, but *why* is it right? What can we say to someone who disagrees, claiming that semantics should be concerned with, say, warranted assertability or "use"? Furthermore, it is troubling that, in attempting to accomplish the semantic task, we all go in for "intuition mongering," even those of us who are naturalistically inclined and skeptical of the practice (e.g., Jerry Fodor 1990: 169). Broadly, it is troubling that we seem to lack a scientifically appealing method for settling the disputes that bedevil semantics. In Chapter 2, I propose a view of the semantic tasks by looking at the purposes we attempt to serve in ascribing meanings. And I propose a way of accomplishing them. This methodology has a place for intuitions, but it is the same limited place that they have elsewhere in science. I think that applying this methodology will help with all semantic issues. In this book I shall use it in the hope of settling some, including some of the most notorious.

A by-product of this methodological discussion is a naturalistic account of the thought experiments characteristic of "armchair" philosophy.

1

In approaching the methodological questions, I make three important and related assumptions. First, I assume anti-Cartesianism. It is common to think that linguistic-conceptual competence brings "privileged access" to meanings (or contents). One example of this is the widespread view that semantic competence consists in knowledge of truth conditions. Another is the received Fregean view that two expressions that differ in informativeness must differ in meaning. I argue briefly against such Cartesianism here (secs. 1.7, 1.8, 2.2) and have argued against it at much greater length elsewhere (1981a: 95–110; 1983: 674–5; 1991b: 270–5; Devitt and Sterelny 1989). In any case, I think that the onus lies very much on the other side. The supposition that someone who has a thought, or uses an expression, that has a certain meaning *thereby has knowledge about that meaning* is a strong one requiring much more support than it has ever been given (even if the knowledge is described as only "tacit"). I think that we should be skeptical of the supposition that semantic competence alone yields semantic propositional knowledge. My aim is for a semantics that does not make these suppositions.

My second assumption is already obvious. It is naturalism: that there is only one way of knowing, the empirical way that is the basis of science (whatever that way may be). So I reject "a priori knowledge." I do not give a detailed argument for my rejection but I do give two reasons (2.2): Briefly, first, with the recognition of the holistic nature of confirmation, we lack a strong motivation for thinking that mathematics and logic are immune from empirical revision; and, second, the idea of a priori knowledge is deeply obscure, as the history of failed attempts to explain it shows.

My third assumption is implicit but nonetheless important. It is realism about the external world: that the physical world posited by science and common sense objectively exists independently of the mental. The chances that discoveries about meaning will cast doubt on this realism are, in my view, just about nil. I have argued for this at length elsewhere (1991b). I take realism so much for granted in this work that I hardly mention it.

My methodological discussion was one natural way to start this book. But I have a particular concern with semantic (or meaning) holism, and I do not need either the methodology or the previous three assumptions for my critique of the case *for* this holism. So I decided to make this critique Chapter 1 and the methodological discussion Chapter 2.

My aim in Chapter 1 is not to defend an "atomistic" localism like Fodor's according to which *no* inferential property of a token constitutes its meaning. It is to defend a more moderate, "molecular," localism according to which *a few* of the inferential properties of a token *may* constitute its meaning. And I expect that we shall discover that many meanings *are* indeed constituted by inferential properties. In leaving open this possibility, I challenge the conventional wisdom that molecular localism is untenable because there is "no principled basis" for its distinction among inferential properties.

My first use of the methodology is in Chapter 3 to argue a case *against* semantic holism and *for* molecular localism. Chapter 1 rejects the arguments against there being a principled basis for distinguishing inferential properties alleged to constitute a token's meaning from its other inferential properties. Chapter 3 argues that, insofar as we need a principled basis, we have one.

I use the methodology next, in Chapter 4, to present a program for a *particular* localistic semantics. This program is "Representationalist": It holds that the meanings of sentences are entirely constituted by the properties that go into determining their truth conditions and that the meanings of words are entirely constituted by properties that go into determining their references. (So Representationalism is in the spirit of the slogan "The meaning of a sentence is its truth condition.") Arguing for this program requires rejecting two-factor, functional- (conceptual-) role, verificationist, and "use" theories. I use the methodology finally, in Chapter 5, to reject "narrow"-meaning theories and other forms of revisionism and eliminativism.

Representationalism is, of course, common in semantics. The most notable thing about my program is *the argument for it* based on the proposed methodology. Also notable is the claim that a

3

token has more than one meaning. With this claim goes partial acceptance and partial rejection of two influential views of singular terms: first, the " 'Fido'-Fido," or "Millian," view, recently resurrected by direct-reference theorists, that a term's only meaning is its property of referring to its bearer; second, the Fregean view that a term's only meaning is its "mode of presenting" its bearer. I argue that a term has both meanings. I agree with Frege that the meaning that is a mode *may* be descriptive, involving inferential links to other terms; that is my molecularism. I disagree with Frege, and just about everybody else, in arguing that some meanings are nondescriptive causal modes of reference.

I mostly call what I propose a "program" rather than a "theory" because I do not go into a lot of semantic details; in particular, although I talk about reference all the time, I say very little to explain it. This does not reflect any lack of interest in these details (see my 1981a, for example). Rather, my present aim is to focus attention on the more general question: Which way should semantics go in future?

Chapters 1 and 3 are on the holism-localism issue. Chapter 3 presupposes the methodological Chapter 2. A reader interested only in arguments to do with that issue should read only those three chapters. On the other hand, a reader who does not care about the holism–localism issue but is interested in other aspects of the semantic program can skip Chapters 1 and 3 and focus on Chapters 2, 4, and 5.

SUMMARY OF CHAPTERS

At its most extreme, semantic holism is the doctrine that all of the inferential properties of a token in language or thought constitute its meaning. Holism is supported by the consideration that there is no principled basis for molecular localism's distinction among these properties. In Chapter 1, I reject four arguments for this consideration. The first, the argument from confirmation holism, is dismissed quickly because it rests on verificationism, which the localist need not accept. The second, the argument from the rejection of analyticity, is more popular and is discussed at some length. I argue that it fails because it saddles the localist, gratuitously, with epistemic assumptions; in particular, with the Cartesian thesis that if the meaning of a word depends on its inferential relations to other words then a competent speaker must know about this. Localism is a *semantic* doctrine that need not be committed to any particular epistemological thesis. So it need not be committed to a priori knowledge or to knowledge that is in any interesting sense unrevisable. The third is the argument from psychological explanation. I discuss a version of it due to Ned Block, based on Hilary Putnam's "Ruritania" example. I reject the argument because it begs the question. The fourth, the argument from functionalism, needs to be accompanied by a further argument that functionalism is *essentially* holistic. In any case, it could only establish a very mild holism.

In Chapter 2, I address the methodological questions that began this introduction. I define three semantic tasks by focusing on the purposes for which we ascribe meanings: in particular, the purposes of explaining behavior and using thoughts and utterances as guides to reality. I then propose a methodology for accomplishing these tasks. We should tackle the "basic" task of explaining the nature of meanings by tackling the "normative" one of explaining the properties that we ought to ascribe for semantic purposes ("first proposal"). Our ordinary attitude ascriptions attribute certain properties for semantic purposes. These properties are *putative* meanings. Given the apparent success of the ascriptions it is likely that these putative meanings are *real* ones. So we should look to the "descriptive" task of explaining putative meanings for evidence for the normative/basic one ("second proposal"). Because we approach the descriptive task pretty much from scratch, we should use the "ultimate" method ("third proposal"). The preliminary first stage of this method identifies examples for a straightforwardly scientific examination in the second stage. Intuitions and thought experiments of the sort that dominate semantics are important in the first stage. However, they are empirical responses to the phenomena and are open to revision at the second stage.

5

Finally, in doing semantics, we should "put metaphysics first" ("fourth proposal").

In Chapter 3, I present a case for semantic localism. It is generally thought that the molecular localist must show that there is a principled basis for distinguishing any inferential properties of a token that she alleges constitute its meaning from its other inferential properties. I begin the chapter by responding to this demand. We must distinguish two ways of construing it. (*a*) If the demand were making a "descriptive" point, it would require that we distinguish the inferential properties that constitute any property that we do ascribe to a token for semantic purposes from the other inferential properties of the token. A consideration of analogous demands elsewhere shows that this demand should be dismissed. A property may be constituted localistically out of some properties and not out of others. That may be the way the world is and nothing more needs to be said. (*b*) It is more likely that the demand for a principled basis is making a "basic" point. It raises the question: What makes a property that we ascribe for semantic purposes – a particular set of inferential properties – *a meaning?* We must distinguish the inferential properties of a token that are *meaning* constituters from the other inferential properties of the token. We do need a principled basis here. And we have one. A property – hence the inferential properties that constitute it – is a meaning if and only if it plays a semantic role and so is one we should ascribe for semantic purposes.

We are left with an epistemic problem: *showing* that localistic properties not holistic ones meet this criterion and are meanings. Three arguments are urged in the rest of the chapter. First, applying the "ultimate" method, all the properties we do ascribe for semantic purposes are in fact localistic. So, given the success of our current ascriptions in serving those purposes, we have good reason to suppose that the properties we ought to ascribe are localistic. Second, *in general,* whether our purposes are explanatory, practical, or perhaps even frivolous, we tend to ascribe properties that are localistic because only localistic properties have the sort of generality we are interested in; localistic properties are likely to be shared by many things. This yields the simplest, least theory-laden, argument against semantic holism: We ought to ascribe localistic properties because only such properties have the generality that will serve our semantic purposes. Hence, only localistic properties play semantic roles. Hence, all meanings are localistic. Third, the popular, overarching theory, "Representationalism," that word meanings are entirely constituted by referential properties, provides a further argument, for no such meaning is holistic.

In Chapter 4, I argue for a certain Representationalist program. Applying the "ultimate" method, we find the descriptive version of that doctrine confirmed by the classic discussion, generated by Quine, of transparent and opaque ascriptions. The folk seem to ascribe at least three different sorts of putative referential meaning to a definite singular term: the property of referring to a specified object under a specified mode (opaque ascription); the property of referring to a specified object ("simply-transparent" ascription); the property of referring en rapport to a specified object ("rapport-transparent" ascription). Given the success of ordinary ascriptions in serving our semantic purposes, this is evidence that we ought to ascribe these properties and, hence, that Representationalism is correct as a normative/basic doctrine too. Exploration of the ways in which these ascriptions serve those purposes confirms this.

What we most need in order to explain these referential meanings are theories of reference. I argue that three sorts of theory of reference are possible. "Description" theories are one sort, but they could not be true for all words. Some words must be covered by "causal" theories – historical, reliablist, or teleological – explaining reference not in terms of the reference of other words but in terms of direct noninferential relations to reality. And some words may be covered by "descriptive-causal" theories.

I argue that the meanings (opaquely) ascribed to words may be constituted by descriptive modes of reference: This is a familiar molecularism. But I also argue for the apparently radical thesis that some such meanings must be *causal* modes of reference. I illustrate this with a historical-causal theory of names and other singular terms.

I reject rival programs. 'Fido'-Fido theories, hence direct-reference theories, of names fail because of well-known problems, particularly the identity problem: The true identities '$a = a$' and '$a = b$' differ in meaning. I do not argue for this difference in the usual way, by appealing to the differing informativeness of the identities, for that argument assumes Cartesian access to meanings. I argue for it by applying the methodology: We distinguish 'a' from 'b' in serving our semantic purposes, and we are right to do so. The evidence does not support "semi-Representationalist" two-factor theories as descriptive theories and counts against "anti-Representationalist" verificationist, use, and one-factor functional-role theories. The burden of showing that theories of these sorts are nevertheless normatively correct is very great.

I consider the meanings of attitude ascriptions – "second-level" meanings. I reject the view that these are extremely context dependent. I find support for an "intimate link," usually identity, between the meaning ascribed and a meaning of the ascribing content sentence. I argue that we should "put metaphysics first" in discussing ascriptions and hence take them to concern concrete thoughts and utterances rather than Platonic propositions. Finally, I develop the program to handle various puzzles including those due to Richard, Castañeda, and Kripke.

Chapter 5 is concerned with eliminativism and revisionism. Eliminativism is the view that nothing has a meaning. I take this to be an empirical doctrine that is not open to dismissal by popular transcendental arguments to the effect that the doctrine is "incoherent." Nevertheless, I think that its evidential support is weak.

Revisionism rejects the status quo: We ought to ascribe for semantic purposes properties other than the ones we do ascribe. Given the arguments in Chapter 4, I take the status quo to be Representationalist. I defend this position from two arguments, the argument from the computer analogy and the argument from methodological solipsism. Neither argument supports the view that psychology should ascribe only syntactic properties, strictly understood, to mental states. The mind is not purely syntactic at any level. The argument from methodological solipsism may seem to support the view that psychology should ascribe only narrow meanings.

To assess this support we need to distinguish two views of narrow meaning. According to one, the narrow meaning of a sentence is a function taking an external context as argument to yield a wide meaning as value. According to the other, the narrow meaning is a functional role involving other sentences, proximal sensory inputs, and proximal behavioral outputs. Narrow meanings as functions must be acceptable to someone who believes in wide meaning. And they would yield explanations of behavior. I argue, however, that the moderately revisionist idea that we should ascribe these meanings instead of wide ones is mistaken; in particular, the meanings, and the behavior they would explain, are too coarse grained to serve our purposes. I am much more critical of the more popular functional-role narrow meanings. I argue that they are unexplained and mysterious. Even if they were not, we have been given no idea how such meanings *could* explain intentional behaviors. If they do not explain these behaviors, then revisionism requires that intentional behaviors be denied altogether. We have been given no reason to believe such a denial. These failings are very bad news for the highly revisionist doctrine that psychology should ascribe these putative meanings. That doctrine has a heavy onus arising from the apparently striking success of our present practice of ascribing wide meanings to explain behavior.

1

A critique of the
case for semantic holism

I. INTRODUCTION

1.1. Semantic Holism and Semantic Localism

At its most extreme, semantic, or meaning, holism is the doctrine that all of the inferential properties of a token in language or thought constitute its meaning. This doctrine is opposed by semantic localism, which, at its most extreme, denies that any of the inferential properties of a token constitute its meaning.

Despite its prima facie implausibility, semantic holism is ubiquitous. It has, as Jerry Fodor says, "something of the status of the received doctrine in the philosophy of language" (1987: 57). And it is urged, or taken for granted, in psychology and artificial intelligence. In this chapter, I shall look critically at the case for semantic holism.

The case can always be made to fit the following "basic" argument:

(1) Some of a token's inferential properties constitute its meaning.
(2) If some of a token's inferential properties constitute its meaning then they all do.
(3) So, all of a token's inferential properties constitute its meaning.

Fodor is an extreme "atomistic" localist: He resists this argument by rejecting premise (1) (pp. 73–95). Fodor's major reason for rejecting (1) is quite clear: He thinks that it leads inexorably to holism, which he regards as "a *crazy* doctrine" (p. 60) threatening Life As We Know It. He thinks that (1) has this unfortunate consequence because he accepts (2). Indeed, he is as committed to (2) as the most fervent holist.

I agree with Fodor's view of the holistic conclusion but think that he is quite wrong about (2). My aim in this chapter is to reject the case for (2). This aim is very important if we are to be safe from holism. First, the total rejection of (1) is difficult to sustain. Even if it is plausible that some tokens do not depend for their meanings on inferential properties, it is surely also plausible that some tokens do so depend; the likes of 'bachelor' spring to mind. If a significant proportion do so depend, and (2) is accepted, we still face a disagreeably holistic future. Second, we lack any persuasive argument against (1).[1] Finally, the localist should not put all her eggs in the one basket of rejecting (1). So I shall be defending a moderate "molecular" localism according to which *a few* of the inferential properties of a token *may* constitute its meaning.[2]

Why do people believe (2)? Premise (2) is accompanied by thinking along the following lines:

There is no principled basis for the molecular localist's distinction between the few inferential properties of a token alleged to constitute its meaning and all its other inferential properties. Only a token that shared all the inferential properties of the original token would really share a meaning with it.[3]

---

1 Fodor and Lepore (1992), in effect, offer an argument against *the case for* (1), but that is not of course the same as offering an argument against (1). (The qualification "in effect" is made necessary by their unusual presentation of the basic argument in terms of their notion *anatomistic*.)

2 It is worth noting that a "cluster" localist (see sec. 3.4) might accept (1) without thinking that any one inferential property is *essential* to the meaning: What is essential is (a weighted) most of a small set of such properties.

3 If this sort of thinking were supported by a "slippery-slope" or "sorites" argument it could perhaps be swiftly dismissed. But it is not obvious that any of the arguments I shall consider are slippery slopes: It is not obvious that they rest on the claim that there is no distinction *because no sharp line can be drawn between the properties that count and the properties that do not* (cf. Fodor and Lepore 1992: 25). (Thanks to Ned Block and Georges Rey.)

11

So, to understand why people are semantic holists, we need to discover why this "no-principled-basis consideration," offered in support of (2), seems plausible. I shall discuss and reject four arguments for the consideration: the argument from confirmation holism (part II), the argument from the rejection of analyticity (III), the argument from psychological explanation (IV), and the argument from functionalism (V).

Rejecting arguments that there is no principled basis does not of course establish that there *is* a principled basis. Some people are drawn to holism because they think "no one has provided a convincing reason for including some inferences and excluding others" (Block 1991: 40). I shall not be addressing this concern in this chapter; my arguments here are against the *arguments for* holism. I argue against holism itself in Chapter 3, where I claim that the demand for a principled basis is partly misconceived and that, insofar as a basis is needed, we have it.

Some preliminaries are necessary before considering the arguments.

1.2. Preliminaries

1. Two points about usage. (i) We need a convenient term to refer to the linguistic and the mental items that concern the dispute over semantic holism. I have chosen to use 'token' rather than 'representation' because it is less theory laden. (ii) The "meaning" of a token is the same as its "content."

2. A thought is an attitude toward a mental token. I assume that the meaning of this token, like the meaning of a sentence, is complex. Furthermore, I assume that the mental token is also like a sentence in being itself complex: It has its meaning in virtue of its parts having meanings.[4] Neither of these assumptions is

---

4   This is a further assumption because something without this complexity can have a complex meaning; for example, a yellow flag on a ship used to mean **THIS SHIP HAS YELLOW FEVER.** (I shall follow the convention of using uppercase bold words to refer to meanings and concepts.)

controversial in the holism dispute that concerns me. It would be a little controversial to go still further, however, and assume that the mental token is complex *in the way that a sentence is* (rather than, say, in the way a map is). This would assume the "language-of-thought" hypothesis. I shall argue for this assumption later (sec. 4.4), but it is no part of my argument against holism. Nevertheless, I shall apply the term 'sentence' to the full mental token in a thought, and 'word' to its meaningful parts, through lack of any better terminology.

3. A sentence could have a holistic meaning in virtue of having a holistic structure or holistic word meanings. I shall be criticizing the arguments for semantic holism about words.

4. I have located the difference between the holist and the localist in their views of the extent to which the *inferential properties* of a token contribute to its meaning. Sometimes the difference is located in the extent to which *beliefs* associated with the expression contribute to its meaning. Although these two versions of the dispute are in fact distinct, as we shall see (1.8), they are usually treated as equivalent. My purpose is to reject the case for both versions of holism. However, I shall mostly discuss "the inference version" and treat "the belief version" separately only when that is called for. The inference version of localism is close to the sort of semantics I shall defend.

5. The tokens we are concerned with are datable, placeable mental states, inscriptions, sounds, and so on. These tokens are, of course, *meaningful,* differing from meaningless ones (e.g., tokens written in the sand by the wind) in their historically given causal relations to speakers and hence to other meaningful tokens and the world. So they should not be thought of as if they were stripped of these relations and "uninterpreted." By talking of meaningful tokens, we can avoid talk of "propositions." This is an advantage not simply because propositions are creatures of darkness but also because talk of propositions in this context is explanatorily unhelpful (4.12). However, at one place I shall apply the discussion to propositions (1.10).

6. A mental sentence token has its inferential properties in

virtue of its actual and potential inferential relations to other sentences. These inferential relations are causal (and nonnormative) relations of a certain sort. The inferential properties of a mental word token are those that the sentence containing it has in virtue of that word (rather than in virtue of other words or solely in virtue of structure). The inferential properties of a linguistic token are derived from the properties of the mental token that caused it. It is likely that every word is related by inferential properties to every other word.

7. According to atomistic localism, a word's meaning is constituted not by its inferential properties but only by its links to the world (or to proximal sensory inputs and/or behavioral outputs).[5] We shall see that such links must have *something* to do with the word's meaning, either directly, or indirectly via inferential relations to other words, in *any* plausible theory (4.5). So we should not take the holist as proposing that all meanings are *fully* constituted by inferential properties. The idea that the external relations of language have nothing to do with meaning is absurd (despite its popularity in the structuralist tradition).[6]

8. Talk of "the meaning" of a token is vague. I think that this vagueness plays an important role in the holist's misconception of the issue. In particular, the implication that a token has just one meaning is very misleading. A defense of localism will require our being much more precise in the next chapter, particularly about the purposes for which we attribute meanings. Nevertheless, in assessing the arguments for holism in this chapter, we can leave the talk of meaning vague.

5 The links will be to the world if the meaning is "wide," but they will be to proximal inputs and outputs if the meaning is "narrow," supervening on what is internal to the organism.
6 Fiona Cowie (1987) points out that holists are extremely casual about the place of extralinguistic links in constituting meaning, often writing as if the links had no place, as if meaning is constituted solely by the relations between tokens. The casualness she points to is part of a general tendency in the philosophy of psychology to ignore inputs and outputs (5.6–5.8).

9. Two of the four arguments for holism that I shall consider are due to Quine. However, I shall not consider his famous argument for the indeterminacy of translation (1960). Nor shall I consider arguments that start from a "principle of charity."[7] I have argued against such principles elsewhere.[8]

1.3. A Straw Man?

The conclusion of the basic argument is that all of the inferential properties of a token constitute its meaning. This is a startlingly "individualistic" doctrine (in a non-Burgean sense). For a token in my head to have the same meaning as one in yours there must be not the smallest difference in their inferential relations; in that respect, we must be functional duplicates. Indeed, for a token in my head this week to mean the same as a token in my head last week I must be a functional duplicate of my earlier self. As a result, it is almost certain that no person ever shares a single thought with any other person nor even with himself at a different time.

The individualistic aspect of this extreme holism may seem *so* startling as to raise doubts that anyone subscribes to it. Indeed, consider the recent response of Todd Jones, Edmond Mulaire, and Stephen Stich to Fodor's individualistic characterization of holism:

We can't think of anyone who has explicitly endorsed this very rad-ical version of Holism. Nor is Fodor much help on this score; he

---

7   E.g., Davidson 1980: 239; 1984: 199–201; Harman 1973: 14; Putnam 1983: 149–50; 1988: 8–9. See Fodor and Lepore (1992: 59–104) for a criticism of such arguments. Sometimes the arguments seem not to be for semantic holism. They seem, rather, to presuppose semantic eliminativism (nihilism) – that there is (near enough) no fact of the matter about meaning – and to be for a holistic account *of our practice of ascribing meanings* (see, e.g., Putnam 1983: xiii). See section 2.7 for more on this.
8   1981a: 115–8; 1991b: 192–9; Devitt and Sterelny 1987: 244–9.

offers no references.... Fodor's Meaning Holist is a straw man. (1991: 69)

Are they right?

A problem with semantic holism is that it is seldom stated clearly and explicitly. Fodor complains of this (1987: 55), and Jones, Mulaire, and Stich concede the point (1991: 69). Nevertheless, sometimes we find fairly explicit statements of an individualistic doctrine like extreme holism:

What our words mean depends on *everything* we believe, on *all* the assumptions we are making. (Harman 1973: 14)

every theoretical difference between individuals creates differences in the identities of their concepts and threatens reference failure whenever those theories are faulty. (Papineau 1987: 98)

the holistically individuated conceptual role of 'polio' in some world-view can not only be altered by finding out about the nature of the underlying etiology of the disease, but also by finding that, say, my Aunt Sally had it as a young girl. (McClamrock 1989: 260; the conceptual role is the "meaning" of 'polio')

if I say "Water is more greenish than bluish," and you say "Water is more bluish than greenish," then we have different narrow contents for "water." . . . in the real world we can expect no two cases to be subsumed by the same law of content. (Block 1991: 40–1)

Apart from what is explicit, something close to the extreme doctrine is implicit in most holist writings.[9] One persuasive reason for thinking this is that if the arguments for holism were good then, with the exception of the argument from functionalism (V), they would establish an extreme doctrine.

Anything close to the extreme doctrine alarms Fodor and should alarm us all. However, my rejection of the arguments for holism does not depend on taking their conclusions as extreme. The arguments are not good in any case.

9 If not something more extreme: Many seem to take even differences of affective tone to be relevant to meaning.

II. THE ARGUMENT FROM CONFIRMATION HOLISM

1.4. The Argument

One cause of the inexplicitness of holism is the idea that Quine somehow established the doctrine years ago in "Two Dogmas" (1953: 20–46). What Quine established in "Two Dogmas" and elsewhere, to my satisfaction at least, was the *epistemological* view, confirmation holism: Put extremely, perhaps too extremely, the justification of a sentence depends on the justification of every other sentence. Combining this with the *semantic* view, verificationism, does indeed yield a simple argument for semantic holism. For, according to verificationism, the meaning of a sentence is its method of justification. So if that justification depends on every sentence then the meaning does as well.[10]

This combination of confirmation holism and verificationism can be related to the basic argument as follows. Consider the first premise of the argument:

(1) Some of a token's inferential properties constitute its meaning.

Why should we believe this? The verificationist has an easy answer: because it is (partly) in virtue of its inferential properties that a sentence is justified. If this is the reason for believing the first premise then confirmation holism leads to the second:

(2) If some of a token's inferential properties constitute its meaning then they all do.

There can be no principled basis for distinguishing the inferential properties that count toward meaning from those that do not.

Despite its evident appeal, verificationism is not supported by

---

10 Quine 1960: 12–13; 1969: 80–1; 1981: 70–1. (Quine regrets the suggestion in "Two Dogmas" that the unit of significance is the whole of science: A substantial body of theory is sufficient; see 1991: 268.) There are signs of the argument in Putnam 1983: 144–7. Fodor summarizes the argument (1987: 62–3); so does Loar (1982: 273), attributing it to Harman.

any compelling argument and is, in my view, false (4.10). That it leads to semantic holism is a compelling reason to reject it (cf. Quine 1969: 81).[11]

III. THE ARGUMENT FROM THE REJECTION OF ANALYTICITY

1.5. Analyticity and the Fregean Assumption

Independent of any verificationist assumptions, Quine is usually thought to have supported (2) and the no-principled-basis consideration in his attack on the analytic-synthetic distinction.[12] It is claimed that to reject (2) (after accepting (1)) is to support this distinction. As a result, some sentences would be known a priori; they could not conceivably be false; they would be unrevisable in that they must be held true come what may in experience; there would be privileged knowledge. Furthermore, the analytic-synthetic distinction would require principled distinctions between "change of belief and change of meaning,"[13] between "collateral information and the determinants of content,"[14] between "what properly belongs in a dictionary and what properly belongs in an encyclopedia."[15] Quine is supposed to have shown us that there is no such privileged knowledge and that there are no such distinctions.

An analytically true sentence is often said to be one that is true solely in virtue of meaning. A synthetically true sentence, in contrast, is one that is not true solely in virtue of meaning. What

---

11   Fodor and Lepore (1992: 37–58) argue that there is another crucial flaw in Quine's argument: Confirmation holism *presupposes* semantic localism.

12   See, e.g., P. M. Churchland 1979: 46–54; P. S. Churchland 1986: 265–7; Putnam 1988: 8–11.

13   See Harman 1973: 108–9.

14   See Block 1986: 629.

15   Wilson 1967: 63. Wilson credits the formulation to Jerrold Katz. See also Harman 1973: 97–100; Block 1991.

has this distinction to do with the rejection of (2)? Suppose that a molecular localist rejects (2) while accepting (1) for some token of, say, 'bachelor'. This has the consequence that the meaning of the token is constituted by its inferential links to tokens of some words[16] – for example, 'unmarried'- but not to others – for example, 'frustrated'. It may then look as though the sentence 'All bachelors are unmarried' is true solely in virtue of this fact about meaning and hence is analytic in the sense just noted.[17] In contrast, 'All bachelors are frustrated' is not true solely in virtue of meaning and hence, if true at all, is synthetically so.

Appearances are deceptive. First, it has been insufficiently noted that *this line of reasoning depends crucially on the following "Fregean assumption": that inferential properties constitute meaning only insofar as they determine reference.*[18] From this assumption it follows that the meaning-determining link of 'bachelor' to 'unmarried' is also *reference* determining, and so 'bachelor' can refer only to objects that 'unmarried' refers to, that is, to unmarried objects. This is what makes 'All bachelors are unmarried' appear analytic. Without this assumption the meaning-determining link would be quite compatible with the sentence's falsity.[19]

I agree with the Fregean assumption (Chaps. 4 and 5). As a

16 I shall mostly not be as pedantic as this about the type-token distinction.

17 What would appear to be analytic for a "cluster localist" (n. 2) would be something of the form 'All *F*'s have (a weighted) most of the properties, *G*, *H*, ...' And the same goes for the "cluster holist." Cluster holism differs from cluster localism simply in the size of the set of properties in the cluster. I ignore cluster views in this chapter (but see Chap. 3). Taking account of them would require heavy qualifications in the discussion in this and the next section.

18 Note that inferential properties *could not* (fully) constitute the meanings, hence determine the references, of *all* words. Direct links to the world must (at least partly) do this job for some words (1.2, point 7; 4.5).

19 Putnam's theory of "stereotypes" (1975: 139–52) provides a nice example of a semantics that rejects the Fregean assumption. Putnam thinks that an association with 'yellow' is part of the stereotype, and hence meaning, of 'lemon' even though 'all lemons are yellow' is not analytic or even true.

result, I think that a truth-referential semantics will explain the contribution of inferential properties to meaning at the same time that it explains reference. However, many disagree. They think that the inferential properties constitute one factor of meaning, and reference and truth constitute another. These two relatively independent factors require distinct semantics, a "narrow" functional-role (or "conceptual-" or "inferential-" role)[20] semantics *as well as* a "wide" truth-referential semantics.[21] In this "two-factor" theory, the rejection of (2) does not imply any doctrine of analyticity, for that rejection is concerned with the inferential factor of meaning, whereas analyticity, being a doctrine of truth, is concerned with the other factor.

Paul Boghossian, however, has pointed out that we would miss the Quinean point if we concluded simply that the argument against analyticity has no holistic consequences for a non-truth-referential semantics.[22] Any such semantics must explain meaning *some* way. So, it will be committed to some *analogue* of the Fregean assumption leading, apparently, to the view that some sentences have some *analogue* of analyticity. Thus, suppose that the semantics explains meaning not in terms of truth but in terms of warrant. Then it will be committed to the assumption that inferential properties constitute meaning only insofar as they determine warrant. So, for example, the meaning-determining link of 'bachelor' to 'unmarried' is also warrant determining. Then, the application of 'bachelor' is warranted only if the application of

---

20 I prefer "functional-role" for the reasons indicated later (4.9; 5.6–5.8).

21 See, e.g., Field 1977; Loar 1982; McGinn 1982; Block 1986. Earlier, Putnam had split the meaning of a word into one external component, the referent, and three internal components, one of which was a stereotype (1975: 269).

22 1993: 34. Boghossian is responding to Block's claim, along the lines of the preceding paragraph, that narrow functional-role meanings are not analytic (1993: 18). My 1993b is mistaken in its handling of this matter (although, with Bill Lycan's help, it went some of the way toward Boghossian's point in n. 18).

'unmarried' is. It may then look as though 'All bachelors are unmarried' is warranted solely in virtue of meaning.

So it seems, after all, as if the molecular localist in rejecting (2) is committed via the Fregean assumption or an analogue to analyticity or an analogue. Two further points are worth making before moving to the second way in which appearances are deceptive.

I choose to defend a molecular localism committed to the Fregean assumption, but this is not an assumption that the holist should accept. For, consider its consequences for the reference of a word. According to the localist, if, through some error in a person's theory, the conjunction of her word's few reference-determining words fails to refer, so also does the original word; for example, if 'adult unmarried male' failed to refer, so would 'bachelor'. According to the holist, *the slightest error in the person's theory threatens general reference failure* (as David Papineau notes in the passage quoted in 1.3); the reference of each word depends on so many others in the theory. Given such truisms as "If 'cat' does not refer then there are no cats," this loss of reference threatens *loss of the world*. Many holists resist this threat by claiming that we all "live in different worlds" of our theories' making. Sensible holists will simply drop the assumption.

Whether we adopt the Fregean assumption or an analogue, it is odd to see the argument from the rejection of analyticity as an argument *for holism*. Suppose that the localist's view that there is a meaning-determining relation between 'F' and 'G' commits her to the view that 'All F's are G' is analytic (or an analogue). Then the holist should also be committed to this view. For the holist also thinks that there is that meaning-determining relation between 'F' and 'G'. He differs from the localist in thinking that there are *many more* such relations: to 'H', 'I', 'J', and so on (some, presumably, yielding nonuniversal sentences). His disagreement with the localist should be simply over the *size* of the group of analytic (or analogue) statements. If commitment to analyticity (or analogue) posed a problem for the localist, it would pose a much worse one for the holist. I shall return to this.

1.6. Analyticity and Logical Truth

Appearances are deceptive in a second way because, even with the Fregean assumption, the sentence 'All bachelors are unmarried' is not true *solely* in virtue of meaning and so is not analytic in the sense discussed earlier. The sentence is indeed true partly in virtue of the fact that 'unmarried' must refer to anything that 'bachelor' refers to, but *it is also true partly in virtue of the truth of 'All unmarrieds are unmarried'*. The latter sentence is what Quine calls a "logical truth." So the molecular localist is committed to the sentence being analytic in another, perhaps less popular, sense: It can be "reduced by definition" to a logical truth. But her rejection of (2) does not commit her to the view that logical truths are true solely in virtue of meaning. So she is not committed to the sentence being analytic in the original sense.

In virtue of what is 'All unmarrieds are unmarried' true? The localist could, and I think should, answer as follows: It is true partly in virtue of what it means and partly in virtue of the way the world is, in virtue of all unmarrieds *being* unmarried. And because the truth of 'All bachelors are unmarried' depends on this logical truth, its truth *also* depends partly on the world.[23] So our localist can go along with the general Quinean dictum that the truth of every sentence depends partly on its meaning and partly on the world. Hence she does not believe that some sentences are true *solely* in virtue of meaning. She believes that they are true in virtue of meaning *given the logical truths*; they are analytic only in this weak sense.

'All bachelors are unmarried', logical truths, and mathematical truths are often thought to be *logically necessary*. The attempt to explain this necessity was a major motivation for doctrines of analyticity. It is important to note that the localist's rejection of (2) does not commit her to any doctrine with such pretensions.

---

23 I emphasize that this is not the uninteresting dependence of a sentence on the world for its *meaning*. With its meaning already fixed (1.2, point 5), the sentence depends on the world for its *truth*.

22

She might not accept that the truths are necessary. If she does think that they are, she need not accept any particular theory of that necessity.[24]

1.7. The Argument from "Two Dogmas"

I have agreed that, in accepting (1) and rejecting (2) while accepting the Fregean assumption, the molecular localist is committed to a weak sort of analyticity. What has "Two Dogmas" got to do with this? The paper has two sorts of argument against analyticity. The first sort are arguments against attempts – mostly Rudolf Carnap's – to explain analyticity in terms of notions of *synonymy, state description, definition,* and *semantic rule.* Quine argues that the explanations do not break out of the intensional circle. But *these* arguments cannot, of course, prejudge *all* attempts to break out of the circle. They must leave it as an open empirical question whether a scientifically respectable account of meaning can be given, and whether a theory that gives this will be a molecular localist one with weak analyticity of the sort just noted. So I shall say no more of these arguments.

The second sort of argument has been more influential. It establishes certain *epistemological* views, in particular, confirmation holism and empirical revisability. A consequence is that no belief, not even a law of logic or mathematics, is immune to revision in the face of experience; the web of belief is "seamless." The contrasting view – that the web is seamed – supplied the other major motivation for traditional doctrines of analyticity. According to those doctrines, analytic beliefs have a privileged epistemic status; they are known a priori and are empirically unrevisable. So Quine's "Two Dogmas" stands clearly opposed to the epistemo-

---

24 Cf. Lepore and Fodor who argue (against my 1993a) as if I *must* use analyticity to explain my modal talk (1993: 674). If this point had been sound, it would have been much more effective against them: Their own modal talk would have committed them to analyticity, something they dread almost as much as holism.

23

logical aspects of traditional doctrines of analyticity. *But localism's rejection of (2) does not commit it to any of these epistemological aspects.*

The rejection of (2) is simply a *semantic* matter, making no epistemic claims at all. Insofar as the considerations just cited provide a route from this rejection to a doctrine worthy of the name "analyticity," it is a route to a nonepistemic doctrine.[25] This

25 Of course the doctrine *is about* inferential properties, which are clearly epistemic: Inferential properties are significant in belief formation. But the doctrine *is not itself* epistemic: It does not entail that the difference between inferential properties that constitute a meaning and ones that do not has epistemic significance; it does not entail anything about the epistemic status of sentences – for example, that some are known a priori.

This distinction between *being about* something epistemic and *being* something epistemic is important in assessing Fodor and Lepore's rejection of molecularism. Their official position is that Quine undermined doctrines with "an epistemic criterion like aprioricity or unrevisability" for analyticity (1992: 58), doctrines that *are* epistemic in the respect just noted. Despite this, they frequently argue as if Quine has *thereby* undermined doctrines that are merely *about* something epistemic, hence undermined *any* sort of molecularism (e.g., p. 57). This conclusion is in direct contrast to what I am arguing here. I made this argument against Fodor and Lepore briefly before (1993a). In their reply, they persist:

> On our view, Quine brought into question the possibility of *any* reconstruction of 'meaning constituting inferences' in terms of 'inferences accepted'. The crucial point is that there is, according to Quine, no way of distinguishing the inferences X accepts *because of what he believes* from those he accepts *because of what he means*; . . . (Lepore and Fodor 1993: 673; see also Fodor and Lepore 1993b: 309)

But "the crucial point" is aimed at a doctrine that *is* epistemic – analyticity implying something like aprioricity about *the conditions under which* inferences are accepted – whereas the possibility allegedly "brought into question" is a doctrine that might be merely *about* something epistemic – a doctrine about meanings explained in terms of inferences accepted. So their point is not relevant, let alone crucial. The molecular localist who accepts (1) but rejects (2) is committed to nothing whatever about *why* inferences are accepted. Why do Fodor and Lepore think otherwise? The answer is clear: They are *totally* convinced that a nonepistemic criterion for analyticity cannot be found (see, e.g., the passage quoted in sec. 3.1). But a conviction is not an argument. They are entitled to demand that the molecular localist

doctrine will yield a privileged epistemic status to the sentence 'All bachelors are unmarried' *only if we add assumptions about our knowledge of meanings and about our knowledge of logical truths.* There is no compelling reason for the localist to make any assumptions contrary to Quine's naturalized epistemology.

Consider logical truths. The localist may think that these, like any other, are true partly in virtue of their meaning and partly in virtue of the way the world is. The logical truths do of course enjoy a privileged epistemic status of some sort, but there need be no more to this than Quine indicated: A sentence earns its place on the list of logical truths by having a certain centrality in our web of belief.

Consider meanings. Cartesianism is still rife in this realm. Linguistic (conceptual) competence is thought to give "privileged access" to meanings. Merely understanding the words 'bachelor' and 'unmarried' (merely having the concepts **BACHELOR** and **UNMARRIED**) yields propositional knowledge of their meanings, including the relations these meanings have to each other. And this knowledge can be brought before the conscious mind by "analysis." The localist need not go along with this Cartesianism. She can see competence not as semantic propositional knowledge but as an *ability or skill:* It is knowledge-how not knowledge-that. Not only can she have this view of competence, I shall argue that she should have this view (Chap. 2).

Once (1) is accepted, we have seen that the rejection of (2), which is so important to stopping holism, commits the Fregean molecular localist to the doctrine that some sentences can be "reduced by definition" to logical truths. This doctrine does not pretend to explain either logical necessity or aprioricity.[26] Perhaps, therefore, it is not worthy of the name "analyticity." That is of no

produce a nonepistemic criterion. I shall attempt to meet this demand in Chapter 3. But, if my present argument is correct, they are not entitled to give the impression that Quine has *already shown* that there can be no such criterion.

26 This weak doctrine is in the spirit of Putnam (1975: 33–40). See also Antony 1987.

concern to the localist. Her concern is simply to reject (2), not to resurrect a traditional doctrine of analyticity. I shall now draw out in more detail how this rejection is perfectly compatible with a Quinean epistemology. I shall consider the matter of a priori knowledge first, the matter of revisability second, and the matter of the unprincipled distinctions third.

1.8. A Priori Knowledge

A priori knowledge is often claimed to be *knowledge not derived from experience,* knowledge that is, or could be, justified without any appeal to experience. The Fregean molecular localist is not committed to such knowledge.

Suppose that Joe believes tokens of

(A) All F's are G
(S) All F's are H

– they are in his "belief box." Suppose further that the meaning of 'F' depends on its inferential links to 'G' but not on its links to 'H'. On the strength of this, let us say that (A) is, but (S) is not, "weakly analytic." Suppose that Joe not only believes these sentences but *knows* them. *Must* the localist think that there is a difference in the way Joe knows, or could know, them? No. She may think that the processes by which they get into the belief box and are maintained there must both meet the same standard of justification, whatever that may be. The story for both sentences can be fully in accord with confirmation holism.

Of course, there is a route to knowledge of (A) that is not available for (S). If Joe knows (i) that the reference of 'F' in his belief box is (partly) determined by the reference of 'G', and (ii) that 'All G's are G' is true, then he can infer (A). However, this route need not be *interestingly* different from the route for the nonanalytic (S). Both (i), which is an application of theoretical semantic knowledge, and (ii), which is a logical truth, may be arrived at in the usual empirical way.

Consider (i) in particular. The Cartesian view is that, as a result

26

of his linguistic competence, Joe (tacitly) *knows that* 'G' stands in the meaning-determining relation to 'F.' By taking competence as an ability or skill, the localist can reject this. So, competence with 'F' consists (partly) in being disposed to infer tokens of 'x is G' from tokens of 'x is F'. It does not consist in knowing that 'F' is related in this way to 'G' nor in knowing that this relation (partly) constitutes the meaning of 'F'. That knowledge would be an application of a semantic theory. Joe may well be in a privileged position to apply this theory to his own thoughts, for he has ready access to those thoughts. But this does not give the theory or its application any special epistemic status (2.11).

However, suppose I were wrong about this. Suppose that we became convinced by the analyticity argument that molecular localism has epistemologically unacceptable consequences. Then we should also be convinced that holism has even worse ones: If localism yielded privileged knowledge of a few facts, holism would yield privileged knowledge of many.

The Fregean molecular localist's rejection of (2) gives no support to the idea that there can be knowledge that is not derived from experience. But there is another idea of a priori knowledge (or, perhaps, another way of understanding the first idea): It is knowledge of the world that *can be gained in the process of learning a word or concept.* Let us explore this idea.

Earlier (1.2, point 4), I distinguished two versions of the holism–localism dispute. According to the inference version the dispute is over the extent to which the *inferential properties* of a word constitute its meaning. According to the belief version the dispute is over the extent to which *beliefs* associated with the word constitute its meaning. So far, we have been discussing the inference version although the arguments could be adapted to the belief version. At this point, it is necessary to attend briefly to the difference between the two versions.

Clearly, if it were the case that a belief in (A) constituted the meaning of the word 'F', then it *would follow* that Joe could not gain the word without gaining the belief. In contrast, if it were the case that the inferential practice of inferring 'x is G' from 'x is

F' constituted the meaning, then it *would not follow*. To get from his inferential practice to the belief, Joe would need to go through a further process; for example, an inferential process involving the following three other beliefs: the belief that he followed the practice; the belief that the practice is good; and the logical belief that it would not be good unless (A) were true. This demonstrates that the two versions of the holism–localism dispute are not equivalent.

On the inference version, competence alone does not even require a *belief* in (A) and so there can be no question of it requiring knowledge of (A). On the belief version, competence does require the belief, but how could competence supply the justification that turns the belief into *knowledge?* Only, once again, by assuming a Cartesianism access to meanings and by taking knowledge of logical truths for granted. We have already seen that the localist need not accept that competence yields propositional knowledge about '*F*'s. No more must it yield propositional knowledge about *F*'s.[27]

1.9. Unrevisable Sentences

Here is a typical statement of a common worry:

> analyticity has obvious epistemological consequences: An analytic sentence would be *unrevisable,* in the sense that to deny or reject it would be *eo ipso* to abandon its standard meaning; one who called it false would be, as Quine says, not denying the doctrine but changing the subject. Thus nothing could count as evidence against the truth expressed by an analytic sentence, and more generally we could have no rational grounds for doubting that truth (we could be mistaken only about the meanings of the relevant words). (Lycan 1991: 112)

I think that the idea that analyticity leads to an unacceptable unrevisability is misguided.

We should first remind ourselves that the localist is not committed to the *logical necessity* of analytic sentences (1.6). So if there

27 This goes against Devitt and Sterelny 1987: 79–80.

is to be a relevant worry about revisability it must concern *our epistemic relations* to these sentences.

Consider the inference version of localism. For Joe to revise his opinion of (A) is for him to drop it from his belief box. Our discussion shows that Joe *can* drop (A) without changing the meaning of '*F*'. For, belief in (A) is *not constitutive* of understanding the meaning of '*F*'. Thus, Joe might drop the sentence because he is unaware that he follows the practice of inferring '*x* is *G*' from '*x* is *F*', or because he does not realize that this practice is meaning constituting, or because he does not realize that there is a logical link between the practice and the sentence.

Perhaps it is not *psychologically* possible for Joe to drop (A) from his belief box without changing meaning. But nothing interesting follows from this, and certainly nothing un-Quinean does. It is, for example, quite compatible with Quinean epistemology that it should be psychologically impossible for humans to abandon various logical truths.

Suppose that Joe *knew* that (A) was weakly analytic. Then he would know that he can drop it from his belief box only by changing its meaning or abandoning a logical truth. But, of course, his knowledge that (A) is weakly analytic is as revisable as can be: It is the result of the fallible application of a fallible theory; there need be no question of it being held come what may in experience.[28]

Revisability does not even *appear* to be a problem for the inference version of localism. However, it may appear to be a problem for the belief version. For, in that version, weakly analytic sentences are indeed not revisable without meaning change. I shall argue that this is not a problem. But suppose it were. It

28 Morton White pointed out years ago that "the statement ' 'All men are rational animals' is analytic' is itself empirical" (1950: 320). This point has not had the impact it deserves. Note that even if there *were* sentences that were *strongly* analytic in that they were true *solely* in virtue of meaning, hence not in virtue of anything about the extralinguistic world, they would still be revisable. For, one's opinion of the linguistic facts upon which such truths would depend would be revisable.

would be a worse problem for holism. For, where the localist makes a few beliefs unrevisable without meaning change, the holist makes many. *Worries about revisability provide no argument for holism.*

Here are some perfectly general considerations. A token is of a certain type – whether it be a cat, a pain, a hammer, a philosopher, a pawn, a capitalist, or whatever – in virtue of having certain properties. Those properties constitute its being of that type so that if something did not have those properties it would not be of that type. Often the constitutive properties are relational; they are ones an object has in virtue of its relations to other things.

Let us compare two tokens that are of relational types: a token that is a capitalist, and a token that means **BACHELOR.** The token capitalist has many relational properties that may change over time. Some of these changes, for example, ceasing to own a Volvo, do not affect the person's still being a capitalist. Others, for example, ceasing to own means of production, do affect this: If she loses that property, she ceases to be a capitalist. But there is nothing more in principle to stop her losing what is essential to being a capitalist from what is inessential. Similarly, a particular token in Joe's belief box that has the relational property of meaning **BACHELOR** may change over time. (Or, if the idea of such a token continuing through time is farfetched, think of it being replaced by another with different relations. I shall ignore this subtlety.) According to the localist, some of these changes do not affect the meaning of the token but others do. In the inference version, we have been supposing that ceasing to be inferentially related to tokens meaning **FRUSTRATED** does not affect meaning whereas ceasing to be inferentially related to tokens meaning **UNMARRIED** does. In the belief version, ceasing to be appropriately related to a token sentence in the belief box meaning **ALL BACHELORS ARE FRUSTRATED** does not affect meaning whereas ceasing to be appropriately related to one that means **ALL BACHELORS ARE UNMARRIED** does. But there is nothing more in principle to stop the token from losing what is essential to its meaning than from losing what is inessential. Something cannot cease to be appropriately related to means of production and still be a capitalist. Something cannot cease to be appropriately related to certain other tokens and still mean **BACHELOR.**

In general, the nature of a type constrains which tokens can have it. When the type is that of being a capitalist, the constraints are economic. When the type is that of meaning **BACHELOR,** the constraints are semantic. The latter constraints should be no more shocking or surprising than the former, even when they involve beliefs.

According to a semantic theory, dropping a token that means **ALL BACHELORS ARE UNMARRIED** changes meanings. According to an economic theory, ceasing to own means of production changes something from being a capitalist. The former fact is no more reason for abandoning the semantic theory than is the latter for abandoning the economic theory. *Such unrevisability is not epistemological; it is harmlessly "metaphysical."*

There may, of course, be good semantic reasons for doubting (as I do) that the meaning of a token is partly constituted by a certain belief. My point is simply that the worry about unrevisability should not be among those reasons.

My argument involves a distinction between the properties of a token that constitute its being of a certain type and the properties that do not. This may seem to result in an un-Quinean involvement in modalities. But it need not. The distinction and the modalities can be sustained by mere regularities; for example, the fact that all capitalists own means of production but they do not all own Volvos. This is acceptable even to Quine (1966: 50–1). Apart from that, this modal issue is quite general, having no special bearing on semantics or epistemology.

Neither version of localism conflicts in any way with confirmation holism, even in the extreme form in which I stated it. In the face of experience, each token in the belief box, with its meaning-determining relations, might have to be assessed against any other one, with its meaning-determining relations. As a result of this assessment, any token could be dropped from the belief

31

box. Linguistic or conceptual competence alone brings no knowledge and so does not prevent this revision.

Localism can accept that a person could be wrong about anything, that a person can believe any false sentence token and disbelieve any true one.[29] If it seems inconceivable that we could be wrong about some sentence, that needs explanation. If the weak analyticity of the sentence were to be part of the explanation, there would have to be a psychologicial link between that analyticity and the inconceivability. It is hard to see what this link could be without Cartesianism. And there are other possible explanations of inconceivability as Quine, Putnam, and others have shown. In any case, the inconceivability of error cannot establish truth; what was once inconceivable is often now taken for granted, as many familiar examples show.

In sum, the inference version of localism does not even appear to have a problem with revisability. The belief version may appear to have one but does not really: The unrevisability it is committed to has no consequences that are epistemologically or otherwise objectionable.

1.10. Unrevisable Propositions

So far I have avoided talk of propositions. Some will think that this misses the main point. They will object that it is a consequence of localism that some *propositions* are unrevisable and that this is dreadful. But they would be wrong. Our discussion now carries straight over to propositions.

On the basis of the inferential links between 'F' and 'G', and the logical truth of the proposition that all F's are F, we might say that the proposition that all F's are G is weakly analytic. Is this proposition unrevisable? We should start by reminding ourselves,

---

29 On the belief version, of course, a token of hers could not *both* be disbelieved by her *and* have a meaning that is weakly analytic (perhaps, e.g., the meaning **ALL BACHELORS ARE UNMARRIED**). But note the need for caution in the next section.

once again, that the localist is not committed to any logical necessities. So the worry about revisability must concern our epistemic relations to analytic propositions.

For Joe who believes the proposition that all *F*'s are *G*, to cease to believe it is to drop from his belief box any sentence that expresses the proposition. Obviously, Joe can do this. But suppose he *entertains* that proposition, then surely he must believe it? Not in the inference version of localism: Entertaining a sentence that expresses that proposition requires engaging in certain inferential practices, but it does not require any particular belief. In the belief version, in contrast, entertaining the proposition does indeed seem to require believing it. But Joe is no more prevented from revising his relation to the proposition than was our capitalist from revising her relation to the means of production. If Joe is to entertain the proposition he must believe it. If the person is to be a capitalist she must own means of production. In neither case is this "metaphysical" unrevisability objectionable.

Could Joe come to believe the proposition that some *F*'s are not *G*? Certainly he could in the inference version. In the belief version, the answer is not so clear. For Joe to have a token that means **SOME F'S ARE NOT G** in his belief box he would also have to have one that means **ALL F'S ARE G**. Perhaps the localist will answer that this is not possible. Or perhaps she will answer that in those circumstances Joe would believe neither the proposition that some *F*'s are not *G* nor the proposition that all *F*'s are *G*. More plausibly, if less charitably, she may answer that Joe would believe both propositions. (Uncertainty about the answer explains the cautious "seem" in the previous paragraph.) Whatever the answer, there is no cause for localist concern.

The unrevisability worry about localism is a storm in a teacup. And if it were not it would be more of a worry about holism.

1.11. Levine's Response

Experience suggests that my critique will not allay the worries of many that molecular localism involves an unrevisability at odds with Quinean naturalistic epistemology. So I shall labor my point by considering an example of such a worrier.

Joseph Levine speaks of the "troubling epistemic consequences" (1993: 107) of an earlier version of my critique (1993b). What troubles Levine particularly is unrevisability: the alleged[30] consequence that it is not possible to cease believing an analytic sentence without changing its meaning.

Levine rightly takes me to be denying that molecular localism leads to "unacceptable *a priori* knowledge . . . knowledge based upon conceptual analysis and justifiable independently of experience" (p. 105). "A statement has this status if its truth is guaranteed by a meaning analysis to which the subject has *a priori* access" (p. 106n). So far, very good. However, a page later, he takes it to be partly definitive of a statement of belief being of this sort "that it cannot be given up without change of meaning" (p. 107). If he is right about this then clearly I am wrong.

Here is a reason for thinking that Levine is not right. If there is to be any a priori knowledge then, at least, there must be some way of justification other than the usual empirical way. *Any proposal that does not entail that there is such a nonempirical way of knowing is compatible with Quinean naturalism.* The traditional doctrine of a priori knowledge that Levine notes first − knowledge obtained by analysis of meanings to which we have privileged access − did indeed seem to propose a nonempirical way at odds with naturalism (although the proposal was incomplete because of its unexplained reliance on knowledge of logic). But Levine's partial definition − not revisable without meaning change − does not. First, that definition says nothing about *the way* of revision, hence nothing at odds with the empirical way. Second, as we shall see (2.2), an account of the empirical way will say nothing at all about the consequences of revision on meaning − indeed, nothing

30 I say "alleged" because although this unrevisability is a consequence of the "belief version" of localism, it is not, as I have pointed out, a consequence of the "inference version" that I prefer. I shall not fuss about this because I think it is important to see that there is nothing epistemologically troubling even about the belief version.

about meaning at all – and hence nothing at odds with the definition.

What, indeed, is the relevance of revisability to the issue of a priori knowledge? Only this: The naturalist thinks that any belief is open to disconfirmation and that the empirical way of disconfirming is the only way; the apriorist denies this. Meaning change has nothing to do with it.

Levine disagrees:

> If you can't revise a belief without change of meaning then you can't empirically disconfirm it. For suppose some empirical evidence ... convinced you to give up the relevant belief. Since ... to give it up entails changing its meaning, it isn't *that very belief* that you've given up. (pp. 107–8)

On the contrary, it is *that very token* in the belief box that has been dropped in the face of empirical evidence. *And the possibility of this is all that matters to naturalism.* It is true that in being dropped and moved to the disbelief box, it has changed meaning and hence become *a token of a different type,* but this is beside the point: It has still been empirically disconfirmed.[31] I suspect that the appeal of Levine's partial definition depends on the sort of equivocation between token and type exemplified in the preceding passage.

A token, *S*, in the belief box has indefinitely many relations to other tokens and to the external world. Some set of these relations presumably constitutes its meaning. Suppose that set *K* does. The naturalist claims that *S* can be dropped from the belief box because it has been empirically disconfirmed. If *S* were so disconfirmed and moved to the disbelief box, some of its relations would change. Perhaps it would no longer have *K,* and so its meaning would have changed. Yet this semantic fact would have *no privileged role* in the subject's decision whether to drop *S* and *no role at*

---

31 In a response to an earlier version of this discussion (1993b: 58–9), Fodor and Lepore claim that this sentence's being removed from your belief box does not count "as your ceasing to believe what the sentence says. . . . Rather . . . [it] counts as the sentence not saying what it used to" (1993b: 310). But these are not exclusive alternatives. It counts as *both.*

all unless the subject has access to the fact via the application of an empirical theory of meaning. So the decision procedure would remain entirely empirical.

Why does Levine insist on bringing meaning into his definition of a priori?

It is crucial that . . . revision doesn't amount to a change of meaning. Otherwise, Quine's argument amounts to no more than the trivial claim that we could always decide to use our words differently. (p. 105n)

This is off track. First, the arbitrariness of *linguistic* conventions could have no bearing on the primary issue, the revisability of *beliefs*. Second, there is no triviality problem. The claim that any *token,* whatever its meaning, can be dropped from the belief box *in response to empirical evidence* is not in the least trivial *as it stands.*

Suppose that this far from trivial claim is true. It is clearly consistent with the thesis that some beliefs fit Levine's partial definition and are unrevisable without meaning change. *So why should the naturalist care about the thesis?* There may, of course, be good *semantic* reasons for rejecting the thesis. But the challenge for Levine and company is to show the *epistemological* significance of the thesis.

Not only can a naturalist accept that some beliefs fit Levine's partial definition of the a priori, an apriorist might be able to accept that no beliefs fit it! Traditionally, of course, apriorists thought that some beliefs could not be revised without change of meaning but that may not be essential to their apriorism. Perhaps an apriorist could allow that all beliefs can be so revised while insisting that some can only be disconfirmed *non*empirically. In the absence of an account of the nonempirical way of knowing, how can this be ruled out?

1.12. The Unprincipled Distinctions

Quine is thought to have shown not only that analyticity has undesirable epistemic consequences but also that it involves unprincipled distinctions. Once again, Quine's argument does not undermine molecular localism.

(*a*) The inference version of localism involves no unprincipled distinction between "collateral information and the determinants of content" because it is not committed to *any* information being determinant of content. (*b*) Similarly, this localism does not involve any unprincipled distinction between "change of belief and change of meaning" because change of meaning is not a matter of changing belief but a matter of changing inferential practices. (*c*) Finally, this localism does not involve a *disturbing* distinction between encyclopedia entries and dictionary definitions. If the dictionary definitions are taken to use rather than mention words, then in *some* cases,[32] they may differ from encyclopedia entries in being weakly analytic. However, such definitions will still be informative.

The belief version of localism does involve a distinction between collateral information and the determinants of content. And it has the consequence that some changes of belief change meaning and some do not. But Quine's argument does not count against these consequences. The concern about a priori knowledge is irrelevant because the distinctions do not lead to a priori knowledge. And the revisability worry no more shows that these distinctions are unprincipled than it shows that the distinction between the properties that constitute being a capitalist and the properties that do not is unprincipled.

1.13. Conclusion

We have been considering the argument from the rejection of analyticity. If this argument against molecular localism and for the no-principled-basis consideration were good it would be even better against holism. But it is not good anyway. The Fregean localist (who accepts (1)) is committed only to weak analyticity.

---

32 But certainly not all: Many dictionary entries are obviously not candidates for analyticity.

Unless she also adopts some epistemological theses that are both unnecessary and mistaken, this analyticity has no disturbing epistemic consequences. It involves no commitment to knowledge not derived from experience. There need be no objectionable respect in which knowledge is unrevisable, to be held onto come what may in experience, even in the belief version of localism (which I do not recommend). The rejection of (2) is a semantic matter, not an epistemological one.

IV. THE ARGUMENT FROM PSYCHOLOGICAL EXPLANATION

1.14. Block's Ruritania Argument

The belief version of the first premise in our basic argument for holism is

(1*) Some of a token's associated beliefs constitute its meaning.

Why believe this? It seems to be common to believe it because of the role of tokens in psychological explanation. We must posit a difference in the meaning of two tokens in order to explain differences in behavior that result from them. It is thought that this difference in meaning can only be accounted for by a difference in associated beliefs. Some are tempted to go further:

(2*) If some of a token's associated beliefs constitute its meaning then they all do.

The holist conclusion follows.

I think that many arguments in the psychological literature come perilously close to this. Consider also the following:

Individuals with different theoretical assumptions are led thereby to accept different beliefs and to perform different actions. Why then insist that such individuals have the same causal-role concepts, when the tendencies to thought and action we want those concepts to inform us about are different? (Papineau 1987: 98)

38

Finally, Ned Block's adaptation (1991: 60–1) of Putnam's Ruritanian example (1983: 144–7) is an argument of this sort.

I shall bring out the flaws in this sort of argument by considering Block's version in some detail. The major flaw is the final move to (2★). This simply *assumes* what the holist is supposed to be arguing for, the no-principled-basis consideration. However, I think that this unargued move may seem plausible because of the reasoning for (1★): If that reasoning worked for some beliefs it may seem obvious that it would work for all. So I shall focus on showing that that reasoning is also flawed.

There are two stages to Block's argument: [33]

Stage one: Barry and Bruce are 10-year-old twins who were adopted at birth into different homes in North and South Ruritania, where they each observe adults drinking a liquid called 'grug' that causes the drinkers to act silly. Northern "grug" is Scotch whisky, southern "grug" is beer. Though there are many differences between Scotch and beer, none of these differences has *as a matter of fact* differentially impinged on Barry and Bruce. All that Barry and Bruce know about their respective "grugs" is that they are roughly earth-toned liquids that make the adults drunk. Now clearly their uses of 'grug' differ in reference and hence in "wide" meaning. However, since there are no relevant differences between Barry and Bruce "in the head," their uses of 'grug' are alike in "narrow" meaning. And narrow meaning is what we must advert to for the purposes of psychological explanation.

Stage two: Bruce and Barry reach adolescence and learn four ordinary but different facts about what they call 'grug'. For example, Bruce learns,

(B) It takes a lot of grug to make you drunk.

and Barry learns,

33 This is a modified and shortened version. I mean to capture the essence of his argument.

(W) It doesn't take much grug to make you drunk.

Now the behaviors of Bruce and Barry will clearly differ as a result of these changes. So the needs of psychological explanation require that we see their uses of 'grug' as now differing in narrow meaning. Yet the only changes from stage one are the acquisitions of these beliefs. So we must see these beliefs as constituting the respective meanings of 'grug'. But there is nothing special about any of these beliefs: Many other equally run-of-the-mill beliefs would have done as well. Every such change in belief must be seen as changing the meaning of 'grug'. Indeed, the narrow meaning of 'grug' continually changes with the acquisition of knowledge.

1.15. Rejecting Block's Argument

I think that there are three dubious steps in this argument: (i) the claim that the uses of 'grug' by Bruce and Barry at stage two have different narrow meanings; (ii) the claim that Bruce and Barry's different beliefs constitute that difference in meaning, supporting (1*); (iii) the claim that any difference in their beliefs would constitute a difference in narrow meaning, supporting (2*). I shall consider these in turn.

(i) The claim that the uses of 'grug' by Bruce and Barry at stage two differ in narrow meaning is an application of Block's quite general assumption that the narrow meaning of an ordinary term like 'beer' differs from that of 'whisky', 'tiger' from 'koala', and so on. I shall later make a critical examination of putative narrow meanings (5.10–5.12). This will show that the claim about 'grug' is open to argument.[34] Meanwhile, I shall merely note that the consideration that Block adduces in favor of the claim is insufficient.

It is indubitable that the expected difference between the behavior of Bruce toward beer and Barry toward whisky must be explained by a difference in the meanings of their tokens. But the

34 See note 42 in particular.

40

story itself supplies an obvious explanation: the *non*-'grug' difference between, for example, (B) and (W). The way in which a person who believes that it takes a lot of *x* to make one drunk behaves toward *x* will differ from the way in which a person who believes that it does not take much *y* to make one drunk behaves toward *y*, *whether their concepts of x and y are the same or different*. Where there is a difference in *conception* we have no need to hypothesize a difference in *concept* in order to explain behavioral difference.[35] We cannot establish, for example, that my 'tiger' concept is different from your 'koala' concept *simply* by pointing out that I run away when I think that a tiger is on the loose but you do not when you think that a koala is (cf. Block 1991: 60). For that difference is sufficiently explained by the fact that I think tigers are dangerous but you do not think koalas are. To assume that a difference in conception entails a difference in concept is to assume holism, not argue for it.

(ii) But suppose that after the acquisition of a few beliefs like (B) and (W) Bruce and Barry really do differ in their narrow 'grug' meanings. *Must* we say that this is attributable to those beliefs, thus accepting (1*)? Of course, if those beliefs really are the only changes that have taken place, then we must. But other changes are possible. I made the point earlier that extralinguistic links are important to meaning: direct links to the world or to proximal inputs and/or outputs (1.2, point 7). Consider the consequences of this for *narrow* meaning. One view of that meaning accepts the Fregean assumption and takes a word's narrow meaning to be a function that yields a wide meaning as a value given the external context as an argument. In this view, the narrow meanings of some words (at least) must be partly (at least) constituted by the fact that, given certain contexts, their wide meanings are partly (at least) constituted by certain direct links to

35   My conception of echidnas is a set of beliefs involving the concept **ECHIDNA.** So is yours. Unless holism has been established, we have no reason to reject the familiar view that these very different conceptions involve the same concept. Block himself notes the concept–conception distinction earlier (1991: 49) but ignores it in discussing Ruritania.

that context. The other view of narrow meaning, which Block favors, rejects the Fregean assumption. In this view, the narrow meanings of some words (at least) must be functional roles partly (at least) constituted by direct links to proximal inputs and/or outputs. In either view, the changes in the narrow meanings of 'grug' may be attributable to changes in the extralinguistic (which are not, note, extra-*head*) links – changes resulting perhaps from experiences of beer and whisky – not to the changes in beliefs. This issue cannot be settled by consulting our intuitions about the meager facts provided in examples like this. Settling it requires the application of a theory that accommodates the vast range of evidence relevant to a theory of meaning.

(iii) But suppose, finally, that some of these associated beliefs do indeed constitute the respective meanings. Where is the argument that they all must? Where is the argument for (2★)? On the Fregean assumption, for example, the beliefs that constitute meaning determine reference and so are in that respect "special." It does not follow that all beliefs determine reference and are special. Of course, it may be felt that there is no principled basis for distinguishing the ones that determine from the ones that do not. But, to repeat, *that is to assume holism not to argue for it.*

In general, the more plausible it is that a particular change, whether in beliefs or whatever, changes narrow meaning, the less plausible it is that just any such change will. For the theoretical considerations that lead to the view that the particular change is significant will show what is "special" about it and hence why others would not do as well.

In sum, psychological considerations of the sort adduced by Block do not show that the adolescent Bruce and Barry differ in their narrow 'grug' meanings. Even if they do so differ, that difference may not be attributable to differences in belief. Even if it is so attributable, no reason has been offered for thinking that all changes in belief change meanings. The argument does not establish holism; it begs the question.

V. THE ARGUMENT FROM FUNCTIONALISM

1.16. The Argument

Acceptance of (1) amounts to acceptance of a functional-role element to meaning. According to the Fregean assumption, this element determines reference. So it should be accommodated within a truth-referential semantics. This is the view I favor. However, many do not, claiming instead that a special functional-role semantics is required (1.5). The received view then seems to be that this semantics is essentially holistic. So we must accept (2). Thus Fodor claims that "functional-role semantics . . . is . . . inherently holistic" (1987: 83). Stich assumes without argument that the functional roles that constitute his "fat syntactic" properties are holistic (1991: 248–9). Ron McClamrock simply *identifies* an individualistic doctrine of the most alarmingly extreme sort (1.3) with functional-role semantics (1989: 260).

Why do people think that functional-role semantics must be holistic? They may of course be influenced by the arguments that we have considered so far. However, there is often no sign of this. I wonder whether a further argument is influential: *Functional-role semantics is functionalist, and functionalism is essentially holistic.* Functionalism may be thought to give no principled basis for distinguishing the functional roles that are constitutive from the ones that are not.

1.17. Rejecting the Argument

How holistic is functionalism? I shall answer using functionalist theories of the mind as examples.

According to David Lewis (1983: 99–107), what makes something the type *pain* is that its tokens typically have the causes and effects of pains captured by the platitudes of folk psychology; and then what makes something a token pain is that it is a token of that type. So this functionalist theory is, in some sense, holistic. I shall say that it is "type" holistic. We shall see that type holism is very mild.

We do not rest with folk psychology: We go scientific. As a result, we hope to come up with fresh generalizations. Do we then *have to* make these constitutive too and hence *have to* replace our old concept **PAIN** with a new one **PAIN★**? *Must* we take our new theory not to be telling us a lot that we did not know about pains but rather to be telling us about something different, but perhaps related, pains★? In brief, is functionalism *essentially* type holistic? The received answer to these questions seems to be, "Yes." Thus, Block, in a helpful account of functionalism, feels obliged to talk not of pain but of pain "relative to theory *T*"; every theory must have its own concept of "pain" (1980b: 174). When Fodor says that "psychofunctionalism type-individuates mental states by reference to the psychological generalizations that subsume them" (1987: 70), he means *all* the generalizations. William Lycan seems to think that *all* the relations of a mental state must go into characterizing it (1988: 49).

It is implicit in these discussions of type holism that it is only the *noticed* relations of mental states that constitute their natures: Platitudes and psychological generalizations are things we theorists believe. So any relations that pains or pains★ may have that we have not yet discovered are not constitutive of their natures as pains or pains★.

It is implicit also in these discussions that the relations that constitute mental states are ones that are realized in a population including at least all (normal) people: The platitudes and generalizations cover us all. So Nigel, Lawrence, and Anna can all have pains or pains★ even though what Nigel has makes him think of Eton, what Lawrence has turns him on, and what Anna has makes her angry. *There is nothing individualistic* about the type holism of functionalist mental properties (nor of functionalist economic properties, to take another example; see the discussion of **being a capitalist,** 1.9).

The extreme semantic holism that most alarms us differs strikingly from type holism in being individualistic: It is not a holism of *shared* properties; all the inferential relations of a token, whether shared or not, constitute its meaning (1.3). So, although the differences between Nigel, Lawrence, and Anna do not prevent them sharing pains, they do prevent them sharing meanings. This is the most implausible and the most damaging feature of extreme holism. It gets no support from functionalism.

The individualism comes from taking the basic argument for holism to concern expression *tokens*. I think there is good reason to think that this is what most holists intend (1.3). However, suppose we take the argument to concern types. Then its holistic conclusion is that all the inferential properties of an expression type – all the properties typical of tokens of that type – constitute its meaning. This is a move toward the type holism of Lewis's theory of the mind, but it still differs from that holism in an important aspect: It requires that all the *actual* inferential properties of an expression type constitute its meaning, whether we have noticed them in our theory or not. This aspect gets no support from functionalism.

Finally, if premise (2) of the basic argument – now taken to concern types – is to be supported by functionalism *alone,* then it needs to be established that functionalism is *essentially* type holistic. If it is simply an accidental matter of fact that some functionalist theories are holistic, we need further argument to show that functional-role semantics is one of those holist theories. The view that functionalism is essentially holistic seems to be common, but it is implausible and, so far as I know, unargued. I shall argue against it later (3.7).

Suppose, nevertheless, that functionalism were essentially holistic. Then functional-role semantics would be *type* holistic. The mildness of this "social" holism becomes apparent when we notice that only a few of a token's inferential properties *are* likely to be believed typical of tokens of its type. Thus, it may well be the case that the only inferential properties believed typical of tokens that mean **BACHELOR** are ones that relate those tokens to ones that mean **ADULT,** mean **UNMARRIED,** or mean **MALE.** Such properties are likely to be only a few of the inferential

45

properties of any given token that means **BACHELOR.** So type holism may be compatible with a moderate localism.

In sum, functionalism gives no support to extreme semantic holism. And it gives no support to any holism at all without an argument to show that it is essentially holistic. Even if this were shown, the resulting semantic holism would be very mild.

Some holists seem to find the no-principled-basis consideration *obvious,* too obvious to really need an argument. Functionalism should give these holists pause. If the consideration were obvious, why would it not be equally obvious that there was no principled basis for saying that Nigel, Lawrence, and Anna all have pains?

1.18. Conclusion

Semantic holism rests on (2) and the no-principled-basis consideration. I have examined four arguments for holism and found them all wanting. The argument from confirmation holism fails because it rests on verificationism. The argument from the rejection of analyticity is not really for holism, but it fails anyway because it saddles the localist with unacceptable epistemic assumptions. The argument from psychological explanation fails because it begs the question. Finally, the argument from functionalism could not establish an extreme holism and, in any case, is incomplete.[36]

36 I have not considered Stich's well-known discussion of Mrs. T (1983: 54– 8, 84–6). Yet Fodor claims that "the received view is that Mrs. T makes a case for the holism of belief content" (1987: 62). If this is the received view it ought not to be. I have noted that Stich assumes without argument that his "fat syntactic" properties are holistic (1.16). These are properties that he thinks *cognitive science ought to* (perhaps does) ascribe. His discussion of Mrs. T is part of one that is mostly concerned with the very different matter of what *the folk do* ascribe (1983: 73–110). When a person ascribes a belief, Stich argues, she ascribes something similar in certain respects to a certain belief of her own, the required similarity varying holistically with the context. He does seem to conflate this holism with the holism of content (pp. 54, 106), but *there is no clear argument for the latter,* i.e., for the view that the content that is appropriately similar in the context is constituted by a

To complete the case against semantic holism, we need to present the positive case for localism. That will be the task of Chapter 3. But, first, we need to tackle some general methodological questions: What are the semantic tasks? Why are they worthwhile? How should we go about accomplishing them? Answering these questions will help not only to rid us of holism but also to address other semantic issues.

large proportion of the belief's associations. Holistic ascription of content is one thing, holistic content ascribed is another. I discuss this matter further in section 3.9.

2

The methodology of naturalistic semantics

I. INTRODUCTION

2.1. The Problem

Semantics is a veritable Balkans of the intellectual world. Localists war with holists, truth conditionalists with verificationists, deflationists with substantivists, direct-reference theorists with Fregeans, one-factor theorists with two-factor theorists, and so on. An army of enthusiasts for narrow content have occupied the territory formerly held by the proponents of wide content. Finally, no settlement of these disputes seems to be in sight.

One sound stands out in these battles: the clash of semantic intuitions. Indeed, sometimes that is the only sound to be heard. Intuitions are almost always aired in "thought experiments."

This reliance on intuitions may be untroubling from some perspectives because it seems to exemplify the characteristic method of "armchair" philosophy. Yet it is surely troubling from the naturalistic perspective that I favor. According to naturalism, semantics is an empirical science like any other. Intuitions and thought experiments do not have this central role elsewhere in science. Why should they in semantics?

This question leads to the general ones that are the main concern of this chapter: How should we get to the truth in semantics? How should we go about settling semantic disputes? What is the right methodology for semantics?

A naturalistic approach to these questions can only hope for modest answers. We cannot expect to make more progress with the methodology of semantics than has been made with scientific methodologies in general. And we know how limited that progress is. It has turned out to be very difficult to say how we should get to the truth and settle disputes in science. My hope is only to bring semantic methodology close to other scientific methodologies.

In the next section, I shall say more about why the reliance on semantic intuitions is troubling. I move on to consider the question: What are the semantic tasks? To give a methodology for semantics, we need an answer to this question, and yet it is far from obvious what the answer is. I propose an answer and then a methodology. Finally, I make some predictions about the results of applying the methodology. Despite the modesty of the methodology, I think that it yields a speedy settlement of several, although certainly not all, semantic disputes. I shall attempt to show this in the rest of this book.

2.2. Intuitions, A Priori Knowledge, and Cartesianism

Clearly there could be no objection to the standard appeal to intuitions in semantics if the semantic task were simply the systematization or explanation of the intuitions. Some write as if they think that this is the task. Yet this task should be no more interesting or appropriate than that of systematizing or explaining our ordinary physical, biological, or psychological intuitions. The intuitions in each case are *about* the subject matter that should concern the science, they are not the subject matter themselves.

Reliance on semantic intuitions might also be appropriate if these intuitions were pieces of a priori knowledge. Many treat them as if they were. Yet, from the naturalistic perspective, we should deny that there is *any* a priori knowledge. I shall not attempt a detailed argument against this knowledge but will briefly outline my reasons. I have two: first, we no longer have a strong motivation for thinking that there is any a priori knowledge; second, the idea of such knowledge is deeply obscure.

Lack of motivation. It is overwhelmingly plausible that *some* knowledge is empirical, "justified by experience." The radical, yet attractive, naturalistic thesis is that *all* knowledge is; there is "only one way of knowing." This thesis faced an embarrassing problem that dogged empiricism: Some truths – most notably those of mathematics and logic – did not seem open to empirical confirmation or disconfirmation, but rather to be known by armchair reflection. It did not seem *possible* that such truths could be revised in the way that 'All swans are white' was by the sighting of black swans in Australia. Quine, following in the footsteps of Pierre Duhem, argued that we must break free of the naive picture of justification suggested by the swan example and view justification in a much more holistic way. We can then see how any sentence, even those of mathematics and logic, might be ultimately answerable to experience; the web of belief is seamless.

In claiming this I do not mean to suggest that the epistemological problem for mathematics is even close to solution. How *could* it be since the *metaphysical* problem of mathematics remains so intractable? The point is rather that we no longer have any reason to think that, if we solved the ontological problem, the epistemological problem would not be open to an empirical solution. The motivation to seek an a priori way of knowing is removed. This is so even though we do not have the rich details of the empirical way of knowing that we would like to have. For, what we do have is an intuitively clear and appealing general idea. It starts from the metaphysical assumption that it is the worldly fact that p that makes the belief that p true. The empiricist idea then is that experiences of the sort produced by that fact are essentially involved in the justification of the belief.

Obscurity. We are presented with a range of examples of what is claimed to be a priori knowledge. But what are we to make of this claim? What is the nature of a priori knowledge? We have the characterization: It is knowledge "*not* derived from experience" and so *not* justified in the empirical way. Doubtless we can expand this negative characterization in a satisfactory manner.[1] But what we need is a *positive* characterization. We need to

---

1 See Kitcher 1980, for example.

describe a process for justifying a belief that does not give experience the role indicated earlier and that we have some reason for thinking is actual. We need some idea of what a priori knowledge *is*, not just what it *is not*.[2]

The difficulty in meeting these demands is well-demonstrated by the failure of traditional attempts. Let the example of allegedly a priori knowledge be our belief that all bachelors are unmarried. Before considering the process of justifying this belief, we need some metaphysical information: What fact makes the belief true? According to the tradition, the fact was one about the relation between the meanings of the parts of the token involved in the belief: the relation between the meaning **BACHELOR** and the meaning **UNMARRIED.** This seemed promising for an account of a priori knowledge because it was thought that our linguistic-conceptual competence was partly a "tacit theory" that gave us privileged access to such facts. So the required nonempirical process of justification was thought to be one that used this access to inspect the relations between the meanings, a reflective process of "conceptual analysis." But, even if we grant this Cartesian view of the accessibility of facts about meaning, the account fails. The fact about meaning is only *part* of what makes the belief true: Its truth depends also on the fact that all unmarrieds are unmarried (1.6).[3]

---

2 In arguing against Georges Rey's attempt (1993) to provide a reliablist account of a priori knowledge, I wrongly insisted that Rey's "logical sub-system" would have had to have been produced by a reliable process for its output of logical truths to count as knowledge (1993b: 53–7; Kim Sterelny convinced me of my mistake). However, I stand by my main point: Rey has failed to show that the output is knowledge rather than, in the relevant sense, "a mere accident." It is not sufficient to say, as he does, that the sub-system is *un*affected by any sensory input. If the sub-system were like this it would follow that its output is *not* justified, in the usual empirical way, by the system's sensitivity to the world. It does nothing to show how the output *is* justified. There has to be a positive characterization of some sort, if not in terms of how the sub-system was produced, then in some other terms.

3 Laurence Bonjour emphasizes this in his "Rationalist Manifesto," arguing that attempts to explain apriority in terms of analyticity are "entirely bankrupt" (1992: 69). For him, "a priori justification occurs when the mind

This seems to be a worldly fact, for, if not, what? No satisfactory nonempirical account was ever given of how we could justify it.

In any case, we should not grant the Cartesian view that competence gives privileged access to meanings, despite its great popularity. I have already suggested a more modest alternative view of our competence that seems to fit the facts: Competence is an ability or skill, a piece of knowledge-how not knowledge-that (1.7–1.8). Why then should we believe the immodest Cartesian view, particularly because it is almost entirely unargued?[4]

directly or intuitively discerns or grasps or apprehends a necessary fact about the nature or structure of reality" (p. 56). He accepts that "the task of giving a really perspicuous account of such justification has hardly been begun" (p. 88).

4   For evidence of the popularity of semantic Cartesianism, consider:

It is an undeniable feature of the notion of meaning. that meaning is *transparent* in the sense that, if someone attaches a meaning to each of two words, he must know whether these meanings are the same. (Dummett 1978: 131)

The natural view is that one has *some kind of* privileged semantic self-knowledge. (Loar 1987: 97)

Since Descartes, it has seemed undeniable to most philosophers that each of us has a privileged way of knowing about his or her own mental states. . . . whenever we have a thought, belief, intention, or desire, we can in principle come to know *what* we think, believe, intend, or desire just by internal examination, without engaging in an empirical investigation of the external world. (McKinsey 1994: 308)

The discussion in Chapter 4 will reveal further evidence. Cartesianism seems to be an almost unquestioned part of the semantic traditions of Frege and Russell.

Consider, for example, the Cartesian assumption that our competence consists in propositional knowledge of *truth conditions*. Heidelberger (1980) has shown how widespread this assumption is with references to Wiggins, Strawson, Davidson, Frege, Wittgenstein, Quine, and Carnap. He points out that it seems to be regarded as "uncontroversial . . . harmless . . . perhaps unworthy of serious discussion" (p. 402). Evans says, "perhaps no one will deny it" (1982: 106). Yet, as Heidelberger notes, it is not "obviously true." He makes what so far as I know is the first attempt to argue for it. He does

The meaning of a person's token is presumably constituted by relational properties of some sort: "internal" ones involving inferential relations among tokens and "external" ones involving certain direct causal relations to the world. Take one of those relations. Why suppose that, simply in virtue of the fact that her token has that relation, reflection must lead her to *believe that* it does? Even if reflection does, why suppose that, simply in virtue of the fact that the relation partly constitutes the meaning of her token, reflection must lead her to *believe that* it does? Most important of all, even if reflection did lead to these beliefs, why suppose that, simply in virtue of her competence, this process of belief formation *justifies* the beliefs, or gives them any special epistemic authority, and thus turns them into *knowledge?* Suppositions of this sort seem to be gratuitous. We need a plausible explanation of these allegedly nonempirical processes of belief formation and justification and some reasons for believing in them.[5]

not claim success. I attempted to construct an argument based on hints in the literature (in, e.g., McGinn 1980, Wright 1976, and particularly Dummett 1978), but it turned into a travesty (1991b: 270–2). Apart from some brief and inconclusive remarks of Dummett (1981: 310–11), that seems to be all that has been said for the assumption. Yet, despite this unjustified popularity, the assumption has received surprisingly little criticism: Harman 1975: 286; Devitt 1981a: 95–110; 1983: 674–5 (on Heidelberger); 1991b: 270–5; Soames 1985a. Of course, given the link between truth and the equivalence, or disquotational, principle, someone who is *competent with 'true'* and with some sentence, say, 'water is wet', will know that 'water is wet' is true if and only if water is wet. But this does not imply that this trivial knowledge constitutes the person's competence with 'water is wet'; quite the contrary. If it is Cartesianism, it is an uninteresting sort (1991b: 34–5; cf. Lepore and Loewer 1986).

Semantic Cartesianism in general has only recently been identified as such and come in for criticism; see, for example, Owens 1989 and 1990, Wettstein 1989a and 1989b, and Rey 1993. (There is a similar Cartesianism in linguistics about access to syntactic facts. Interestingly, this Cartesianism has received more philosophical criticism. My own is in Devitt and Sterelny 1989.)

5 John Bigelow's account (1992) of a priori mathematical knowledge also suffers from Cartesianism. His view is that mathematics is the study of

In sum, the case against a priori knowledge is that history has shown that the notion is deeply obscure and that Quine has shown that we do not need it. And, even if there were some a priori knowledge, there clearly would not be enough of it to form an adequate evidential base for physics, biology, or economics. Why then would there be enough for semantics?

I shall assume that ordinary semantic intuitions are not a priori and that they have the same epistemic status as ordinary intuitions anywhere. They are parts of an empirical, fallible, and certainly inadequate set of folk opinions or, more pretentiously, "folk theory," the linguistic wisdom of the ages. What role then should they play in semantics? A major aim of this chapter is to answer this question.

Many assume that the armchair thought experiments characteristic of philosophy show that it has a special nonempirical way of knowing. A by-product of my discussion of the role of intuitions is a naturalistic account of this philosophical method (2.10).

II. SEMANTIC TASKS

2.3. What Is the Semantic Task?

If the semantic task is not to systematize or explain semantic intuitions, what is it? What is semantics trying to do?

There seems to be a simple answer: The "basic" semantic task is to say what meanings *are,* to explain their *natures.* It is thus analogous to such tasks as saying what genes, atoms, acids, echidnas, or pains *are* but not, we should note, to such tasks as saying what genes and so forth *do,* stating the laws that advert to them. (The difference is illustrated by the difference between molecular

patterns; that our representations of these patterns reflect the necessary connections in them; and finally, that we "can just *see*" (p. 160) these necessary connections in the representations. The Cartesianism is in the last step. We *have* representations with certain properties that enable us to think about the world. Why suppose that an inner eye gives us privileged access to those properties yielding *knowledge about* the representations? I suggest, rather, that any knowledge we have of representations is empirical semantic knowledge.

and Mendelian genetics.) However, we start the semantic task in rather worse shape than we do its analogues. With them, the subject matter of investigation is already identified relatively uncontroversially. This reflects the fact that we have clear and familiar theoretical or practical purposes *for which* we identify the subject matter. Semantics does not start out like that. It is far from clear what counts as a meaning that needs explaining. Indeed, the intractable nature of semantic disputes largely stems from differing opinions about what counts.[6] Lycan has brought out the problem wittily with his "Double Indexical Theory of Meaning":

MEANING = $_{def}$ Whatever aspect of linguistic activity happens to interest *me now*. (Lycan 1984: 272)

We start semantics in the unusual position of having to specify a subject matter. We should not insist on great precision about this in advance of theory, but we do need some explication of our vague talk of "meanings." And to avoid Lycan's mockery, we must specify a subject matter *worthy* of investigation; we need an explication that is *not ad hoc*. Finally, the semantic task of interest to philosophers should be not only worthwhile but *fundamental*. To meet these needs, I propose to address three questions. First, what might plausibly be seen as our ordinary way of ascribing meanings? Second, what do we ascribe them to? Or, putting this another way, what are the phenomena that concern semantics? Third, what is our semantic interest in these phenomena? Or, putting this another way, what purposes are we serving in ascribing meanings?

2.4. Ascriptions of Meaning; Semantic Phenomena

What might plausibly be seen as our ordinary way of ascribing meanings? Consider the following: "Ruth believes that Gorbachev has fallen" and "Adam said that Yeltsin has risen." Such

6 "The chief problem about semantics comes at the beginning. What is the theory of meaning a theory of?" (Higginbotham 1991: 271). "Meaning is notoriously vague" (Block 1986: 615).

"propositional-attitude ascriptions" mostly use no semantic words but nevertheless seem partly to ascribe meanings. My *working assumption,* for this section and the next, is that they do indeed partly ascribe meanings: We specify meanings by the 'that' clauses in attitude ascriptions (also by their 'to' clauses that follow 'want' etc. and by clauses that follow 'wonder whether'; briefly, by "t-clauses").

The meanings specified by t-clauses are complex. They are composed of simpler meanings like those specified by 'Gorbachev' and 'fallen'.[7]

I shall adopt a usage according to which meanings are *properties.* This usage sits well with one popular view of the "logical form" of attitude ascriptions, which I favor, but less so with another. (I shall argue for my view of the form later; 4.12.)

The usage sits well with the view that the t-clause in an attitude ascription functions like an *indefinite* singular term. So just as 'Ken loves an echidna' asserts a relation between Ken and some object that has the property specified by 'echidna', 'Ruth believes that Gorbachev has fallen' asserts one between Ruth and some object that has the property specified by 'that Gorbachev has fallen'.[8] In this view, the latter property is naturally called "a meaning" and the object that would have it if the ascription were true would be concrete: a token thought. And if the ascription were to an utterance then the object that would make it true would also be concrete, a token utterance.

The usage sits less well with the view that the t-clause in an ascription functions like a *definite* singular term; for example, like

7   This assumption is rejected, presumably, by those who think that t-clauses name structureless propositions, which are sets of "possible worlds." See Richard (1990: 9–37) for a nice critical discussion of this. Note that the assumption does not entail that the *vehicles* of meaning are complex, although I have already claimed that the ones that interest us are (1.2, point 2). I shall later claim that the mental vehicles are languagelike (4.4) – the language-of-thought hypothesis – but this view plays no role in this chapter.
8   This view goes back at least to Sellars 1963; see also, Davidson 1984: 93–108; Lycan 1988: 7–9.

a name. So just as 'Ken loves Gaelene' asserts a relation between Ken and the object designated by 'Gaelene', the belief ascription asserts one between Ruth and the object designated by 'that Gorbachev has fallen'. That latter object, "a proposition," is commonly called "a meaning."[9] In taking meanings to be properties, I depart from this usage. According to my usage, in this view of the logical form of ascriptions, the property of *having an attitude to* the proposition is called "a meaning." And the object that would have the property if the ascription were true would still be concrete.

My usage has two advantages. First, it avoids commitment to propositions. Second, whereas if the meaning of a token is an object then the token obviously has the property of being related to that object; it is not the case that if the meaning is a property then that property is obviously a relation to some object. My usage leaves the latter issue open.

We ascribe meanings to concrete thoughts and utterances. So, thoughts and utterances are the immediate phenomena of semantics. But thoughts, at least, are not so immediate to observation. What phenomena lead us to the view that an object has thoughts? Partly, the utterances of the object make us think this. Utterances are linguistic behavior. Clearly, the object's nonlinguistic behavior may also lead us to the view that it has thoughts.

2.5. Semantic Purposes

What is our semantic interest in these phenomena? What significant purposes − explanatory, practical, or whatever − are served by the ascription of meanings, which, according to our working assumption, is part of the ascription of thoughts and utterances like those to Ruth and Adam?[10] Doubtless there are several such purposes, but I shall focus on two: first, to explain and predict

---

9 For two recent examples of this view, see Richard 1990: 5; Schiffer 1992.
10 I have made several attempts to answer this question in the past, most recently in 1991b, Chap. 6. These answers all have similar elements, but I think that none of them has been right.

the behavior of the subject, which I shall abbreviate "to explain behavior"; and, second, to use the thoughts and utterances of others as guides to a reality largely external to the subject. I shall consider these in turn. Our interest in thoughts is primary, our interest in utterances, secondary. So I shall start with thoughts.

1. Consider this explanation of nonlinguistic behavior:

> Why did Granny board the bus? She wants to buy a bottle of scotch. She believes that she has her pension check in her pocket. She believes that the bus goes to her favorite liquor store.

Such "intentional" explanations of "intentional" behavior are familiar and central parts of ordinary life, of history, of economics, and of the social sciences in general. They all ascribe thoughts with meanings specified by t-clauses.

Consider this explanation of linguistic behavior next:

> Why did Granny produce the sound /I need a drink/? She believes that she needs a drink. She wants to express her belief to her audience. She participates in conventions according to which /I need a drink/ expresses that belief.

Again we ascribe thoughts with meanings to explain behavior. Such explanations are not that common because they are so obvious. They are implicit in our responses to communications.

2. Ascribing beliefs serves another remarkably valuable purpose. If a person believes that the world is such and such, and if the person is reliable, then we have good reason to believe that the world is such and such. Thus, attributing the property of meaning **IT IS RAINING** to Mark's belief not only helps to explain his rain-avoidance behavior but also gives us evidence about the weather. We can even learn from someone who is a reliable guide to the way some area of the world is *not*.

Turn now to the ascription of *utterances*. Granny's behavior leads us to remark, "Granny says that she needs a drink." If the English-speaking Mark produces /It is raining/, we may respond, "Mark says that it is raining." If we think that Granny's and

58

Mark's utterances are sincere expressions of beliefs, we will ascribe *the same* meanings to their beliefs as we do to their utterances. Utterances are indicative of thoughts. Indeed, it is *because of* our interest in thoughts that we are interested in utterances. Thus, it is because we want to use Granny's thoughts to explain her behavior that we are interested in her utterance. And it is because we want to use Mark's thoughts to explain his behavior and inform us about the weather that we are interested in his utterance.[11]

Return to our use of others as guides to reality. We have a wide range of interests in learning about the world. The direct way to serve these interests is to examine the world. The indirect way is to use reliable indicators. Sometimes these indicators are "natural" ones like tree rings. Sometimes they are artifacts like thermometers. Very often they are the beliefs of others. Some belief ascriptions serve our *theoretical* interest in explanation. Many, however, are like ascriptions of desires, hopes, and so on in serving interests that are not really theoretical at all. We have the most immediate *practical* interest in finding out quite humdrum facts about the world to satisfy our needs for food, shelter, a mate, and so on. So it helps to know what is on sale at the supermarket, where there is a hotel, who is available, and so on. Ascribing beliefs is a very good way of finding out about anything at all.

Humans gain most of their knowledge – what we learn at mother's knee, from teachers, and from books – by this process of attributing beliefs. The significance of this for the human species could hardly be exaggerated: We have a way, other than the slow and painful one through the genes, of passing on the discoveries of one generation to the next.

Or so it seems. But maybe we are all *wrong* in attempting to

11   The story is a bit more complicated because of the Gricean distinction between the speaker meaning of an utterance and its conventional meaning on the occasion. It seems that we ascribe the latter with the "says that" construction, yet we identify the former with the thought meaning in the normal situation. If we want to draw attention to a difference between the two meanings it seems that we use the construction "says that . . . but . . . means that."

learn from others in this way. Maybe we are also wrong in attempting to explain behavior in the earlier way. Perhaps we are totally mistaken and should become behaviorists or eliminativists of some other sort. Or perhaps we should be less radically revisionist, ascribing only "narrow" meanings or syntactic properties to serve our purposes. Still, my hypothesis is that, rightly or wrongly, we do ascribe meaningful thoughts and utterances to serve these purposes.

In identifying these two purposes – explaining behavior and guiding us to reality – as ones for which we ascribe meanings, I do not mean to suggest that there are not others. One other, for example, arises from our interest in a desirer: If we wish her well we may want to satisfy her desires; if we wish her ill we may want to frustrate them. My claim is only that the purposes identified are significant and that we expect our ascriptions of meanings to serve them, *at least*.

Doubtless these two purposes can be served in many ways. Our interest in meanings, together with the working assumption, have led us to two particular ways of serving them: directly, by ascribing to a token that is thought a property of the sort specified by t-clauses, and indirectly, by ascribing such a property to a token that is uttered. Let us say that in attempting to serve the purposes in *these* ways, our purposes are "semantic." And let us say that a property plays a "semantic" role if and only if it is a property of the sort specified by t-clauses, and, if it were the case that a token thought had the property, it would be in virtue of this fact that the token can explain the behavior of the thinker or be used as a guide to reality.[12]

2.6. Semantic Tasks

Earlier I stated the "basic" task as to explain the natures of meanings. This statement needed an explication that was not ad hoc;

---

12 Perhaps this should be broadened to allow tokens in, say, a visual module – hence not objects of *thought* – to have a semantic role, but I shall not attempt to do so.

we needed to specify a subject matter *worthy* of study. To meet these needs I adopted a working assumption: We specify meanings by the t-clauses of attitude ascriptions. Guided by this assumption I have described purposes and roles that I have called "semantic." Now, it is certainly worthwhile to study a property that plays a semantic role, that plays one or both of the roles just outlined in explaining behavior and informing us about reality. Furthermore, the study of such properties seems appropriately *fundamental*. So, I propose to add the following explication to the statement of the basic task: A property is a meaning if and only if it plays a semantic role. We can now drop our working assumption: What we specify by a t-clause will count as a meaning if and only if it does indeed have a semantic role. Any other property will count as a meaning if and only if it has such a role.

It might be objected that this explication is too liberal because not just *anything* that had a semantic role would be a meaning. Meanings are presumably constituted in some way from the "internal" and "external" relations of tokens (2.2). So it might be claimed that we should modify our explication so that only properties with this "appropriate" sort of constitution count as meanings.

Nothing in my argument hinges on my not adopting this modification, but I shall not adopt it. Note that my definition of "semantic role" slipped in the following constraint: A property has a semantic role only if it is "of the sort specified by t-clauses." So the "liberal" explication already places this constraint on meanings. In effect, the modification makes this somewhat vague constraint more precise by feeding in some of our *theory of* meanings. Yet *that* degree of precision seems undesirable in an initial attempt to specify the subject matter.[13]

This completes my explication of the basic task: **Being a meaning** is a property of certain properties, the ones that play a

---

13   It may be an advantage of the liberalism that it makes eliminativism about meaning harder: In general, the less that is essential to **being an *F*** the harder it is to show that there are not any *F*'s (5.1).

semantic role, and hence it serves our semantic purposes to ascribe. We have avoided the "ad hoc" charge.

This explication relates the basic task closely to another that I will call "the normative task." This is the task of explaining the natures of the properties we *ought to ascribe* for semantic purposes. Clearly, for an ascription to serve those purposes, the property ascribed must have one or both of the semantic roles. So, according to the explication, the property we ought to ascribe must be a meaning. On the other hand, prima facie, if something is a meaning then we ought to ascribe it for semantic purposes. Perhaps the reasons for thinking that a property plays a semantic role and hence for counting it a meaning are not always sufficient to make it something we should ascribe for semantic purposes. However, if the property is really not one we ought to ascribe, the question of whether or not to count it a meaning becomes uninteresting: *Interesting* meanings are ones we ought to ascribe. So, it will do no harm to adopt the prima facie view. We can assume that a property is a meaning if and only if it is one we ought to ascribe for semantic purposes.

In light of this, my *first methodological proposal is that we should tackle the basic task by tackling the normative one.*

We are already familiar with tasks of saying what we ought to ascribe for certain purposes. So one advantage of this methodological proposal is that it relates the basic task to these other ones. Another advantage is the obvious contrast between the normative task and what I will call "the descriptive task." This is the task of explaining the natures of the properties we *do ascribe* in attitude ascriptions for semantic purposes; it is the task of explaining the semantic status quo. It is what most people working in semantics – philosophers, linguists, and psychologists – are in effect doing. Yet it is very different from the normative and basic tasks. Note particularly that the properties it investigates are *meanings* only if ascribing them really does serve our semantic purposes, only if they really play semantic roles. Once the descriptive task is sharply distinguished from the others, the question of its bearing on them arises. I shall consider this bearing in section 2.9.

2.7. Other Views of Semantic Tasks

Semantics very often proceeds without *any* attempt to explicate the talk of "meaning" used, implicitly or explicitly, to define the task(s): The talk is simply taken for granted. Given the prima facie unclarity and vagueness of the talk, this practice is surely unacceptable: It leaves us both with no firm idea of what the issue is and with the likelihood of being at cross purposes. Once an explication is offered, there is little point in a verbal dispute about the appropriateness of using 'meaning' and hence 'semantics' in the way proposed. However, there is a lot of point in asking *why a task defined in terms of 'meaning' thus explicated is worthwhile*. We are, of course, free to study anything. But if semantics is a genuine science, as the naturalist thinks it must be, we should be able to say why it is interesting. A definition that does not say this will be ad hoc, an appropriate target of Lycan's mockery. Indeed, a definition of a semantic task in *any* terms that does not demonstrate the worth of the task is an appropriate target.[14]

My discussion of the semantic tasks is an attempt to meet these demands for explication and worth. How do other views of the task fare? This is not the place for a detailed answer, but some brief remarks are in order.

1. It is common to define the semantic task in terms of *truth* and *reference*. I think that truth and reference are indeed central to *accomplishing* the semantic task but have no place in the *definition* of it. If the definition is not to be ad hoc, we need to know *why* we should be interested in truth and reference. Implicitly, if not explicitly, the motivation is usually thought to come from the role of truth and reference in explaining meaning. But then the definition of the task ought to be in terms of meaning in the first place; truth and reference are not basic enough.

The point is illustrated by the range of apparently semantic

---

14 Similar remarks apply to psychological research into the nature of concepts, for this is, in effect, investigating the meanings of mental tokens: We need an explication of the talk of concepts together with a motivation for the research arising from the role of concepts thus explicated in psychology.

disputes that could be arbitrarily settled by a definition in terms of truth and reference:

(i) Some theorists think that truth and reference are deflationary and so think that they have nothing to do with explaining meaning.[15] In this view, to say that, in the specified circumstances, a sentence 'S' is true, is just to say that, in those circumstances, S. And to say that, in the specified circumstances, a name 'a' refers to x, is just to say that, in those circumstances, a is x. So views about truth condition and reference are really about extralinguistic reality and are irrelevant to semantics. Deflationists have in mind an explanation of meaning in other terms altogether, usually some sort of verificationist or "use" theory. Clearly, deflationism should be confronted with arguments, not ruled out by a definition.

(ii) Among those who agree that the properties of having certain truth conditions and of referring to certain objects constitute meanings, there is disagreement about whether such properties *exhaust* meanings. To adopt a definition of the semantic task that favors the view that these properties do exhaust meaning, as direct-reference theorists sometimes seem to, is to settle this dispute by fiat.

(iii) Finally, among those who think that the properties of having certain truth conditions and of referring to certain objects do not exhaust meanings, there is disagreement about what must be added. Fregeans think that we must add a *mode* of presenting a situation or object. Two-factor theorists think that we must add a nonrepresentational functional-role factor. To adopt a definition in terms of truth and reference that favors the Fregean view is to beg the question against the two-factor theorist.

To settle these disputes, we need to see what role truth and reference do play in the explanation of meaning.[16] And to do that

---

15 See particularly Brandom 1984, 1988; Horwich 1990. My 1991c, a critical notice of Horwich, explores the significance of deflationary truth.

16 So Lepore and Fodor are wrong in claiming that I think that it is "a truism that whatever determines reference is ipso facto meaning" (1993: 674). I think that it is a substantive truth, which I shall spend most of the rest of this book trying to establish.

64

we need an independent account of the task, if not the one I have given, then some other one.

2. Many think that the semantic task is to explain our *linguistic competence* or *understanding,* our *grasp of* meanings. This task is related to that of explaining meanings and can surely be shown to be worthwhile. So, provided it is not conflated with that of explaining meanings, which it usually seems to be,[17] I can have no objection to it. However, I would argue that the theory of the meanings we grasp is, in an important sense, prior to the theory of our grasp of them.

3. My tasks concern tokens. There are various tasks concerning types: for example, to describe the conventional meanings of sounds, inscriptions, and so on in a certain language, as dictionaries do; to describe and explain changes in such meanings, as some linguists do; to explain the nature of these conventional meanings in terms of, say, regularities in speaker meanings, as some philosophers do. All of these tasks are clearly worthwhile, but none of them is, I think, semantically fundamental.

4. Some linguists see the semantic task as that of explaining such matters as *synonymy, similarity of meaning, meaning redundancy, ambiguity,* and *entailment* (e.g., Katz 1972: 5–6). Why should we be interested in these matters? The implicit answer is that these are matters about which the speakers have semantic intuitions. But this is unsatisfactory for the reasons already indicated. A better answer would acknowledge that these explanations are contributions to the broader task of explaining *meaning* and so need supplementation by more basic explanations of meaning.[18] The answer would then need to go on to explicate this talk of meaning in a way that motivates our interest in it.

5. Insofar as "formal semantics" is concerned simply with the model-theoretic study of abstract formal languages its task is, of

---

17 E.g., "A theory of meaning is a theory of understanding" (Dummett 1975: 99); cf. Devitt 1981a: 92–5. Similarly, linguists seem to conflate explaining syntax with explaining syntactic competence; cf. Devitt and Sterelny 1989.

18 Without the supplementation the explanations rest on what David Lewis has nicely called "translations into Markerese" (1972: 18).

course, quite different from those I have described. Insofar as it is claimed to contribute to the task of explaining meanings in natural languages, it needs to be accompanied by an independent account of that task in order for us to assess the claim.[19]

6. Davidsonians take the semantic task to be that of saying how to construct a theory of "radical interpretation" for a language. From my perspective this task is worthwhile but not fundamental enough: It rests on semantic notions that need independent explanation. Davidsonians would disagree, for they think that there is no more to these notions than would be revealed by accomplishing their task. This reflects a very different view of the mind from mine. I favor a robust mentalism that takes thoughts to be objective states posited independently of language (2.4). Thoughts are in an important respect "prior" to the language that expresses them and can be used in the explanation of linguistic meaning (4.4). Davidsonians, influenced by Quine, start the explanation of language from a behaviorist assumption: "Meaning is entirely determined by observable behavior, even readily observable behavior" (Davidson 1990: 314; cf. Quine 1991: 272). This leads to the thesis of the indeterminacy of translation and to a generally

19 Jerry Katz (1984) thinks that the central issue in the philosophy of linguistics is the choice between three views of what linguistics is about: physical sounds – the "nominalism" of Bloomfield; psychological states – the "conceptualism" of Chomsky; or abstract objects – the "Platonism" that Katz himself now urges. This trichotomy does not sit well with the view of the task that I have presented. I take semantics to be about physical objects. Sometimes these are sounds, sometimes inscriptions, sometimes radio waves, and so on. But, importantly, sometimes they are thoughts and hence *also* psychological states. My view does not accept the theoretical constraints – antimentalism and antiabstractness – of Bloomfield's, yet it does not follow Chomsky in taking linguistics to be about psychological states of competence. It takes all the objects that linguistics is about to be concrete tokens, and so to that extent it is nominalistic. Where it stands ultimately on the nominalism issue depends, of course, on what we make of its ascription of meaning *properties* to those objects. However, it seems unlikely that the nominalist would have any *special* difficulty paraphrasing away this property talk.

antirealist view of meaning. Meanings are not for the most part objective properties with natures awaiting our discovery, and they do not play roles in explanatory theories of mind and language. The only independent reality captured by meaning talk is a set of verbal dispositions (Quine 1960, 1975). Beyond that, there is nothing but our *practice of interpreting* each other using principles of charity and rationality, a practice that should be seen more as *imposing* a semantic reality than as discovering one (Davidson 1984, 1990). This "interpretative perspective," reminiscent of the European *Verstehen* tradition,[20] has no place for the sort of tasks I have defined.[21]

The Davidsonians have given no argument for the behaviorism that underlies their perspective. From my perspective that behaviorism seems like just another dogma of empiricism.[22]

In conclusion, I emphasize that I am *not* claiming that the properties that I have called "meanings" are the *only real* meanings nor that the tasks I have called "semantic" are the *only proper* tasks for semantics. I doubt that there is any interesting matter of fact about such claims. I do claim that those properties are worth investigating and that those tasks are worth performing. I claim further that those tasks are appropriately fundamental. Perhaps all this is true of other tasks, but that always needs to be demonstrated.

This completes my discussion of the semantic tasks. One further matter must be discussed before making any further methodological proposals.

---

20 MacDonald and Pettit (1981) have derived a *Verstehen* view from an explicitly Davidsonian perspective. They have also claimed that this is the only good route to *Verstehen*.

21 It should be noted that some philosophers take over central ideas from Davidsonian semantics without adopting his interpretative perspective; e.g., Lycan 1984; Larson and Ludlow 1993.

22 On this, see Antony 1987, 1989; Rey 1993. I have discussed Davidsonian semantics elsewhere: 1981a: 115–18; 1991b: 186–99.

2.8. Does a Token Have More Than One Meaning?

Does a token have more than one meaning? Note that this question does not concern the familiar matter of ambiguity, which is a property of *types*.

Ordinary talk of "*the* meaning" of a word encourages the view that a token *does not* have, indeed *cannot* have, more than one meaning. This view is taken over in our semantic theories and disputes; for example, the dispute over semantic holism seems to be over whether the one and only meaning a token has is holistic or localistic. Yet the view seems to be nothing but a prejudice.[23]

I have been presuming that meanings are constituted by inferential relations among tokens and direct causal relations to the world. A token has many such relational properties and clearly different sets of them could constitute indefinitely many *candidates* to be meanings. To tell whether one of these really is a meaning we have to see whether it has one of the semantic roles. Prior to arguments one way or the other on this, we ought to take the property's candidacy seriously. And we ought to take the possibility of a token's having more than one meaning very seriously.

Given the situation in other areas, we should expect to find that a token does indeed have more than one meaning. Thus, a particular person may have a variety of economic properties: **being a capitalist, a landowner, a banker,** and so on. Each of these properties plays a role that economic properties are supposed to: for example, explaining economic behavior. We should expect that a particular token in thought or language will have a similar variety of semantic properties. Each of these will play a semantic

23 There is one respect in which some theories do not seem to follow the prejudice: Under the influence of Grice they allow that a token has both a speaker meaning and a literal or conventional meaning, although these meanings are usually the same. What theories do not contemplate is that a token might have more than one speaker meaning or more than one conventional meaning. That is the prejudice that concerns me here.

role: One might explain one bit of behavior; another, another; and a third might serve as a guide to external reality.[24]

If the early Quine is anywhere near correct in his view of ordinary attitude ascriptions, then the folk ascribe more than one property to a token for semantic purposes. Quine distinguishes between "transparent" ascriptions, where only the reference of a token is of interest, and "opaque" ascriptions, where some "finer-grained" meaning of the token is of interest.[25]

Consider also the popular two-factor theories of meaning. These theories often describe purposes for ascribing meanings that are similar to the two I have outlined. They then assign two relatively independent meaning factors to a token to serve those respective purposes, a functional-role factor to explain behavior and a truth-referential factor to serve as a guide to reality. They prefer to say that these factors jointly constitute *the* meaning of a token rather than that each severally constitutes *a* meaning of the token, but this preference seems to reflect only the prejudice that a token must have just one meaning.

In sum, I think that we should leave open the possibility that we ascribe more than one property to a token for semantic purposes (descriptive), that we ought to ascribe more than one (normative), and hence that a token has more than one meaning (basic).

24 The view that a token has more than one meaning seems to be an idea whose time has come. It has been independently suggested by Akeel Bilgrami (1992) and Eric Lormand (1995a, 1995b).

25 And I suspect that the folk would be prepared to call either of these properties "meanings." If not, this would be an example of the way that the ordinary use of 'meaning' was not perfectly suited to theoretical semantics. What we are considering here is the ordinary application of 'meaning' to *tokens*. It is probably more often applied to *types,* to what convention makes common to tokens, the sort of thing that is to be found in a dictionary. So, the meaning of a type that has tokens that do not conventionally have the same referent – for example, the type 'she' – is not thought to include a referent. In contrast, if the tokens do conventionally have the same referent – as, for example, tokens of 'echidna' do – ordinary usage may often treat that referent as the meaning of the type.

III. A SEMANTIC METHODOLOGY

2.9. The Methodology for the Normative/Basic Task

My first methodological proposal was that we should tackle the basic task by tackling the normative one. I turn now to the methodology of that task.

What should be the basis for our choosing to ascribe one rather than another of the many properties of a token that are candidates to be meanings? The answer is implicit in the task. We should ascribe the ones that play semantic roles and hence that it serves our purposes to ascribe: the ones that play the roles outlined in explaining behavior and informing us about reality.

We know from the history of science that it is not, in general, easy to tell which properties we should ascribe to serve our purposes. We know from the philosophy of science that it is not easy to say how to tell. The first sign of the modesty of my aims is that I shall attempt to say only a little on how we should tell what to ascribe in semantics.

However, I think that the little I shall say is important. It concerns the bearing on this normative task of the descriptive semantic task, the task of explaining the natures of the properties that we as a matter of fact do ascribe for semantic purposes. Perhaps the most unfortunate consequence of unclarity about the semantic tasks has been the lack of attention to the relations between the normative and the descriptive. On the one hand, semanticists seem to be concerned, most of the time, solely with the descriptive task. Yet, *meanings* should be our *primary* concern in semantics, and meanings are what we *ought to* ascribe for semantic purposes *not necessarily* what we *do* ascribe. So the descriptive task should proceed with at least an eye on the normative one. On the other hand, when normative questions are raised they are usually addressed without close attention to the descriptive facts. In this section I shall argue that these facts are very relevant to the normative task.

Suppose that our actual practice of ascribing certain properties serves our purposes in some area well. That is very good evidence that we ought to ascribe at least those properties to serve those purposes. The situation in semantics appears to be of this sort. For, consider how successful our ordinary attitude ascriptions seem to be at serving their purposes. Their apparent success in explaining behavior is certainly not limitless, but it is nonetheless impressive. Their apparent success in influencing our own thoughts about the world could hardly be exaggerated. So it is likely that, at least, we ought to ascribe to tokens that are thought and uttered the properties that we do ascribe and hence that those properties are meanings. Evidence for a descriptive theory will be evidence for a normative one and hence for a basic one.

We should go further: Given the apparent success of our current practices, it is unlikely that any normative proposal uninformed by a descriptive view will be plausible. Consider, for example, the epistemic problems faced by a revisionist proposal. How could we tell that nothing has the properties we currently ascribe to thoughts and utterances for semantic purposes without attention to the natures of those properties? How could we tell that those properties fail to play their semantic roles without a good deal of knowledge of what they do do? How could we assess the claim that some "new" properties do a better job than those "old" ones, including explaining the apparent success of the old, without having a clear picture of the old? In the absence of a detailed comparison with the semantic status quo, a revisionist proposal will have a credibility problem: It will always seem much more plausible that there is a flaw in the philosophical arguments offered in support of the proposal than that the apparently successful status quo is so radically mistaken.

In light of this discussion, I make my *second methodological proposal: We should look to the descriptive task for evidence for the normative/basic one.* Further, I suggest, although I shall not argue, that the main, if not the only, justification for the usual focus on the descriptive task is the bearing of that task on the normative one.

In the next section, I turn to the methodology of descriptive tasks *in general*. I shall consider this with an eye to its application to semantics. The application is in the following section.

2.10. The Methodology for Descriptive Tasks in General

In general, science is doubtless much more concerned with what things *do* – a matter of laws – than with what they *are* – a matter of natures. Still, from time to time the latter question does arise: What constitutes some property we ascribe, **being an F**? For example, presumably the question arises for **being a gene, an atom, an acid, an echidna,** and **a pain.** *How do we tell what the answer is?* Sometimes we already have a well-established theory; for example, thanks to molecular genetics, we have one for **being a gene.** But suppose that we do not have a theory and are starting pretty much from scratch, which is surely the supposition we should make for semantics. How then do we tell what is common and peculiar to *F*'s "in all possible worlds?" What is the "ultimate" method?

The answer breaks into two stages. First, we must identify some apparently uncontroversial examples of *F*'s and non-*F*'s. Second, we must examine the examples to determine the nature of **being an F.** My focus will be on the preliminary first stage, for it is here that there is a place for the sort of intuitions and thought experiments that are so prominent in semantics. But I start with the second stage.

This second stage is a straightforwardly scientific one. It is hard to accomplish this stage and, as is well-known, even harder to explain how we accomplish it. Modesty will again prevent my trying to say (including trying to identify what role, if any, intuition plays in accomplishing it). We should note, however, an important feature of this second stage: The examination can lead us to reject some of the results of the first stage; apparently uncontroversial examples can turn out to be controversial. Thus, we may conclude that some of the things identified as *F*'s are not; for example, whales are not fish. We may conclude that some things identified as non-F's are F's; for example, tomatoes are fruits. We may even conclude that *none* of the things identified as F's are F; for example, there are no witches. Usually, such revisions in our preliminary identifications take place only if our examination leads to a powerful theory.

Turn now to the preliminary first stage. How do we identify the examples that are to be examined in the second stage? Once again, sometimes we have a well-established theory to help with the job; for example, Mendelian genetics helps identify the genes that are to be examined by molecular genetics. But suppose that we do not have such a theory, which is, once again, surely the correct supposition in semantics. In the absence of reliable theory, we must consult the experts about F's and see what *they* identify as F's and non-F's. Often these experts will be scientists. Sometimes they will be engineers, tradespeople, and the like. And sometimes they may be just plain folk. But, whoever they are, our first stage consists in conducting "identification experiments" with them.

What we elicit in these experiments are the experts' most basic "intuitions" about **being an F**. We can elicit other intuitions by asking the experts not only to identify F's but also to tell us about them. These other intuitions are clearly richer and less basic than the identification ones: A person may be good at recognizing F's without having much reliable to say about them; this may be the situation of the folk with pains.

When we are starting from scratch, we need the identification intuitions, but we do not need the richer ones. This is not to say that we should not use them. They may well be a useful guide to what we will discover at the second stage.

The generalizations of these intuitions constitute a theory. There may be no reason to suppose that the experts consulted *represent* this theory, and so we should be careful about attributing the theory to them. Nevertheless, suppose, as is quite likely, that they would readily assent to the theory if it were presented to them. It is appropriate, then, to say that the theory is their "tacit" theory. If the experts are the folk, as they presumably are with pains for example, then the tacit theory is "folk theory."

So, we have found a place for intuitions. It is important not to exaggerate that place. At best the intuitions are likely to be seriously incomplete, reflecting only part of the theory we need. And they may be wrong: They are empirical responses to the phenomena. Our earlier brief consideration of the second stage shows that even the most basic intuitions, expressed in identification experiments, are subject to revision in the face of scientific examination. *Intuitions are often needed to identify the subject matter for the descriptive task, and may be otherwise helpful, but nothing ultimately rests on them.*

A worry may obtrude about identification experiments. "The identification of F's will consist in *calling* things *"F."* So you are assuming that if people who both understand 'F' and have the expertise to recognize things that have the property **being an F**, call something *"F,"* then it is likely to have that property (if anything has). This seems to be semantic. Yet you plan to apply conclusions drawn from this discussion to semantics." The "identification assumption" is indeed semantic, but it is so minimally so that it should be acceptable to semanticists of all persuasions. Its main interest is epistemological.

We have found a place for intuitions, but not yet for thought experiments. These experiments can have a role in identification. Instead of "real" experiments that confront the expert with phenomena and ask her whether they are F's, we confront her with *descriptions* of phenomena and ask her whether she *would say* that they were F's. These thought experiments provide valuable clues to what the expert would identify as an F or a non-F. They can do more: The descriptions that elicit the expert's response indicate the richer intuitions that, as we have already noted, can be a useful guide to the second stage. Some experiments may be difficult, perhaps impossible, to perform other than in thought.[26] Valuable

---

26 As David Chalmers pointed out to me.

and useful as thought experiments may be in practice, they are dispensible in principle: We can make do with real experiments. And the results of thought experiments have the same empirical status as the results of real experiments.

With an eye to our later discussion of language, we should note two special situations. The first arises if the F's we are investigating are the products of a human skill or competence; for example, if we are investigating the nature of a good tennis shot or a good chess move. Someone who has the relevant competence has ready access to a great deal of data that are to be identified as F's. She does not have to go out and look for data because her competence produces them. As a result, she is in a very good position to become an expert: She simply has to reflect upon her own performance. But this is not to say that she *will* become an expert. A person can be competent and yet reflect little on the output of that competence; knowledge-how is not knowledge-that. Even if she does become an expert, there is no reason to believe that her opinions carry special authority simply because she is competent; there is no reason to believe that competence gives her Cartesian access to *the truth*. She is privileged in *her ready access to data,* not in *the conclusions she draws from* the data. Her opinions are still subject to revision by the second-stage examination. Finally, to say that competence may lead to expertise is not to say that the incompetent cannot be experts, perhaps even better experts.

The second special situation arises if theorists count themselves among the identification experts. They then have the advantage of not having to consult other people to conduct real or thought experiments.

Thought experiments performed in this second situation are the characteristic "armchair" method of philosophy, a famous example of which is "the analysis of knowledge." So what I am proposing here amounts to a naturalistic account of that method. The naturalist does not deny "armchair" intuitions a role in philosophy but does deny that their role has to be seen as a priori:

The intuitions reflect an empirically based expertise in identification.[27]

In the last section, I argued that the descriptive task bears on the normative. Similarly, the normative bears on the descriptive, yielding another source of evidence. Suppose our current practice of ascribing certain properties is successful. Then it is likely that any properties that we ought to ascribe will include those ones. So any *independent* evidence we can get about the nature of the properties that we ought to ascribe – what ones it would serve our purposes to ascribe – is evidence about the nature of the properties that we do ascribe. (The evidence for the normative position must be independent, of course, to avoid a circle: It must not depend on the evidence for the descriptive position.)

One final methodological point. Some problems are not in the evidence but in reality: There may simply be no fact of the matter of whether or not certain objects are *F*. Consider, for example, a case where the various criteria of specieshood come into conflict; or consider the intermediate stages in the evolution of one species from another. The nature of **being an *F*** is to that extent indeterminate, or, given the semantic associations of that term, perhaps we should say, vague. This raises some interesting logical puzzles[28] but is otherwise an untroubling fact of life.

2.11. The Methodology for the Descriptive Task in Semantics

We now apply these findings to semantics. We must say how we should tell what constitutes the properties we ascribe for semantic purposes. These "*putative* meanings" will *be* meanings if they do indeed play semantic roles.

In the last section, I took a negative view about reliance on semantic theories. Philosophy and linguistics offer a variety of theories, or theory fragments, of meaning. However, these theo-

27 Cf. Bealer 1992.
28 See, e.g., Pelletier 1989.

ries are hardly ever well-enough established to settle the disputes that bedevil semantics. The theories themselves are as much in contention as anything is; they are part of the problem not the solution. So, I make my *third methodological proposal: We should use the "ultimate" method on putative meanings to accomplish the descriptive task*. And, in applying that method, we should not rely on those semantic theories to identify examples.

So little is established and settled in semantics that the need to use this "ultimate" method is pressing. Yet it is seldom explicitly applied to putative *meanings*. What we find in philosophy is that the "ultimate" method is, in effect, frequently applied to *truth conditions* and *reference*. And what we find in linguistics is that it is, in effect, frequently applied to *synonymy, similarity of meaning*, and the like. But these are not the right places to apply the method to settle some of the most burning issues in semantics: They are not basic enough (2.7).[29]

To apply the "ultimate" method to a putative meaning, we must first identify some apparently uncontroversial examples of tokens with that property and of tokens without it; and second

29 Apart from this, there are two reasons for being a little skeptical about folk identifications of cases of synonymy, similarity of meaning, and the like. First, we should wonder whether the "meanings" involved in these identifications are the same as the meanings we are investigating. Lycan's Double Indexical Theory of Meaning probably applies to the folk as much as to theorists. Second, these identifications involve terms, like 'synonymy', drawn from semantic theory and are rather distant from ordinary concerns. In contrast, identifications of tokens with a certain putative meaning need involve no such terms and are central to the folk's ubiquitous practice of ascribing thoughts and utterances. So we should expect the folk to be less expert at identifying synonymy and the like than they are at identifying putative meanings.

The second of these reasons for doubt applies also to folk identifications of *ungrammatical* tokens. 'Ungrammatical' is a term from syntactic theory, and folk identifications of what it applies to, unlike those of, say, "odd things for someone to say," are probably not common. The intuitions about grammaticality that play a key role in the study of syntax reflect a good deal of theory beyond folk theory.

we must examine the examples to determine the nature of the property. Who are the experts to be consulted in the first-stage identifications? The folk, in their frequent use of t-clauses in attitude ascriptions, are as expert as anyone. And the folk are in an advantageous position to become experts because they themselves are competent to produce token thoughts and utterances to which the properties are ascribed. Finally, theorists can count themselves among the expert folk. So, in the first stage, semantic theorists have two advantages: no need to consult others and ready access to data.

To identify examples in the preliminary first stage, we look to ordinary attitude ascriptions, to sentences that ascribe putative meanings to thoughts and utterances using t-clauses.[30] We bring these ascriptions to bear on the descriptive problem with the help of "the identification assumption": If people who both understand 'F' and have the expertise to recognize things that have the property **being an F**, call something "F," then it is likely to have that property (if anything has).

An illustration of the use of this assumption outside semantics will pave the way for its use in semantics. Consider the role that the assumption might once have played in the case for a theory of, say, echidnas. To discover what **being an echidna** amounts to we must first use experts to find some uncontroversial examples of echidnas and nonechidnas. Applying the assumption, we discover the examples: If people who both understand 'echidna' and have the expertise to recognize things that have the property

---

30   We can apply the "ultimate" method immediately to these putative meanings because the folk are experts at identifying them, as the folk's use of t-clauses reveals. We could not have applied the method earlier to discover the nature of the second-level property, **being a meaning,** precisely because nobody has the required expertise (2.3). When we start semantics we have access to apparently uncontroversial identifications of some "determinates" that are putative *particular* meanings but not of the "determinable" that these properties are candidates to share, **being a meaning.** It was this lack that led me to attempt to specify a subject matter worthy of semantic investigation (2.4–2.6). In semantics, we *really* start from scratch.

being an echidna, call something "echidna" then it is likely to have that property (if anything has).

We do the same in semantics for a theory of, say, the putative meaning **THIS IS AN ECHIDNA.** To discover what having that property amounts to, we must first use experts to find some uncontroversial examples of tokens with the property and of tokens without it. Applying the assumption, we discover the examples: If people who both understand 'that this is an echidna' and have the expertise to recognize tokens that have the property **THIS IS AN ECHIDNA,** call something "that this is an echidna," then it is likely to have that property (if anything has).[31]

This experiment elicits the experts' most basic intuitions about the property **THIS IS AN ECHIDNA,** reflections of their tacit theory. We could probe that theory further, revealing richer intuitions about the circumstances in which tokens with that putative meaning would be true, about what their parts refer to, about what would verify them, and so on. These richer intuitions are a guide to the second stage.

It is important to note that my application of the term 'tacit theory' here is quite compatible with my earlier rejection of its application to our conceptual competence (2.2). The present application is to generalizations of explicit intuitions about particular putative meanings, intuitions that deploy the concepts of the theory.[32] The basis for rejecting the earlier application was precisely that our conceptual competence – our capacity to think

---

31 We have to keep in mind that 'that this is an echidna' may be ambiguous, specifying more than one meaning (2.8).

32 "Simulation theory" (Gordon 1986; Goldman 1989) would reject this application. I have no quarrel with the theory's denial that these generalizations are *represented* in us. However, I take it that the theory goes further, denying that the generalizations are "psychologically real" at all – denying that we embody them without representing them in the same way that a simple calculator embodies the laws of addition without representing them; denying that they have become "hard-wired" into us. If simulation theory were right about this then my present talk of "tacit theory" would be inappropriate. But I follow Stich and Nichols (1992) in finding the theory poorly supported by the evidence. I think that the embodiment of these

certain thoughts – does *not* consist in intuitions deploying semantic concepts. The relation of competence to tacit theory is explored further in the next section.

Thought experiments can have a prominent role. We describe situations and ask whether we, and other folk experts, would apply the t-clause 'that this is an echidna' to them. These thought experiments provide valuable clues to what the expert would identify as tokens with the property **THIS IS AN ECHIDNA** and tokens without it and, via the descriptions that elicit the response, evidence of the expert's richer intuitions. Valuable and useful as these thought experiments may be, we could make do with real experiments.

With the results of the preliminary first stage in hand, we move to the second stage: We examine the alleged examples to determine the nature of the putative meaning, **THIS IS AN ECHIDNA.** This stage is hard both to do and to say how to do. However, we can say that, just as this stage led us to a theory powerful enough to overturn intuitions about what things are fish, fruit, witches, and so on, it might lead us to one that overturns intuitions about what tokens have the property **THIS IS AN ECHIDNA.** Even more, it might lead us to overturn the richer intuitions of folk semantics. And it will surely show these intuitions to be seriously incomplete. In some cases it may give no answer because there is no answer to be had: Meanings may be vague like the rest of reality.

Because of the dominant role played by intuitions in semantics, it is worth laboring the point. From the naturalistic perspective, semantic intuitions are like intuitions in any other science: open to revision in the face of empirical theory. We could be wrong about what has a putative meaning. We could be wrong in thinking that anything has it. Even if we are right that something has

generalizations provides the best explanation of our having the semantic intuitions. Should I be wrong, the talk could be dropped from my argument without cost.

it, we could be wrong in thinking that it plays a semantic role and so really is a meaning.

This point about intuitions does not need to be modified because of the special situation in semantics: The expert's intuitions may be partly the result of reflection on the product of her own competence. As a result of this competence, the expert herself produces tokens that may refer to x, be true in certain circumstances, be verified in such and such a way, and so on. So she is privileged in having *ready access to* such data. But there is no reason to believe that competence gives any privilege to *the conclusions that she draws from* the data; for example, that they *do* refer to x, *are* true in those circumstances, or *are* so verified. There is no reason to believe that competence gives her Cartesian access to *the truth* about the data. These conclusions of the competent, just like those of the incompetent, are empirical responses to the phenomena and open to question.[33]

This having been said, we should not expect our semantic intuitions to be overturned. I think that the considerations already adduced, and the one to come in the next section, give good reason for confidence in these intuitions, so far as they go.

Finally, any independent evidence that we can get on the normative issue of the meanings that we ought to ascribe is also evidence of the descriptive issue of what meanings we do ascribe. For, given the apparent success of our current ascriptions at serving our semantic purposes, it is likely that some of the meanings we ought to ascribe will be ones we do ascribe.

Before concluding, we need to look briefly at the meanings of attitude ascriptions themselves.

---

33 Similar remarks apply to linguistic intuitions. So I think that the small amount of sympathy I showed elsewhere (Devitt and Sterelny 1989: 523) to the Cartesian view that these intuitions are reflections of our underlying competence, "the voice of competence," was a mistake. I think that it is much more plausible that the intuitions are the result of central processor reflection upon tokens of the sort that are and are not the product of syntactic competence.

2.12. The Meanings of Attitude Ascriptions

There is undoubtedly something confusingly different about the use of the identification assumption in semantics because of the unusual way in which we ascribe putative meanings. To ascribe any sort of property we must, of course, use an expression for that property; thus, to ascribe **being a gene** we use 'gene' and for **being an atom** we use 'atom'. These words rarely *have* the property they are used to ascribe, and if they do, it is not in virtue of having the property that they ascribe it; thus 'gene' is not a gene and although 'short' is short it is not because the word is short that it ascribes shortness. Yet, in the case of meanings, the situation seems different. The expression 'that p', used to ascribe a putative meaning, seems to ascribe that property in virtue of the fact that its content sentence, 'p', has the property or one very like it. So there always seems to be "an intimate link" between the two properties.[34] However, in applying the "ultimate" method, we can abstract from this link, treating the t-clause 'that p' like any arbitrary expression for a property.

I have emphasized that *competence with* concepts and language is an ability that is logically distinct from any *expertise about* concepts and language. Yet the "intimate link" suggests an important causal relation between them. Perhaps expertise at applying 'that p' to the tokens of others is an essential part of the usual causal process of becoming competent with 'p'. So a human being in a normal

---

34 The link is assumed by all the following: Frege's view that expressions in a content sentence refer to their usual senses (1952: 66–8); Davidson's doctrine of "semantic innocence" according to which these expressions have their usual meaning and reference (1984: 108); and Kripke's "strengthened . . . disquotational principle": "A normal English speaker . . . will be disposed to sincere reflective assent to 'p' if and only if he believes that p" (1979b: 249). By trading on the intimate link, it is possible to mount a plausible defense of the view that if a person thinks "I am thinking that water is a liquid" then she is right; see Davidson 1987 and Burge 1988. This Cartesianism, if Cartesianism it is, is very different from the sort I am rejecting: It involves a privileged *identification* of the meaning of one's own thought but no privileged *knowledge of the nature* of that meaning.

situation would not acquire that competence without becoming an expert at identifying tokens with the property, **P**. Competence *is not* a tacit theory, but perhaps the theory *would normally accompany* the competence. This would add to the prima facie case for folk expertise in identification.[35]

I have said that the "ultimate" method is seldom explicitly applied to meanings. Yet, it may be objected, the close attention to attitude ascriptions recommended by this application is surely common. This attention is indeed common, but its focus is different. The method recommends a focus on the ascriptions as evidence of *the putative meanings ascribed,* "first-level" meanings. The common focus is on the ascriptions as evidence of *their own meanings,* "second-level" meanings.

This second-level investigation is almost always an application of the "ultimate" method to the *truth conditions* of ascriptions: We consult our intuitions about the situations that make a token ascription true. But, again, to assume that a truth condition is all there is to a sentence's meaning, or even that it has anything to do with it, is to beg a lot of semantic questions (2.7).

How then should the second-level investigation proceed? We can of course apply the "ultimate" method to putative meanings here too. This will require attention to ascriptions of attitudes *to attitudes*; for example, to "Ralph believes that Adam said that Yeltsin has risen." Furthermore, we can avoid the charge of question begging in applying the method to truth conditions if we can first establish the plausibility of truth-referential semantics at the first level. And we may hope to trade on the intimate link: Evidence of the meaning ascribed is also evidence of the ascription's meanings.

Finally, the second-level investigation is dominated by philosophers who talk of "propositions," Platonic objects that are separate from the concrete spatio-temporal world of meaningful tokens. This prompts my *fourth methodological proposal: that our investigations*

---

35 I am indebted to Carol Slater for criticism that prompted this paragraph. I explore this line of thought in my 1981a: 107–10.

in semantics should be guided by the slogan, "Put metaphysics first."[36] It is common, and surely correct, to think that many meanings involve relations to objects. When considering what objects might play that role, we should be guided by general metaphysical constraints. These should make us reluctant to posit objects in semantics that we do not have good independent reasons for believing in. I shall argue that we should not posit propositions (4.12).

2.13. Conclusions and Predictions

From a naturalistic perspective, contemporary semantics has some troubling features: the resort to intuitions and thought experiments; the inexplicit reliance on apparently ad hoc accounts of the semantic tasks; and broadly, the lack of a scientifically appealing method for settling the disputes that bedevil it. I have attempted to remedy this. I have defined the tasks by looking at the purposes we attempt to serve in ascribing meanings and have proposed a methodology for accomplishing the tasks. We should tackle the "basic" task of explaining the nature of meanings by tackling the "normative" one of explaining the properties that we ought to ascribe for semantic purposes ("first proposal"). Our ordinary attitude ascriptions ascribe certain properties for semantic purposes. These properties are *putative* meanings. Given the apparent success of the ascriptions, it is likely that these putative meanings are *real* ones. So we should look to the "descriptive" task of explaining putative meanings for evidence for the normative/basic one ("second proposal"). Because we approach the descriptive task pretty much from scratch, we should use the "ultimate" method ("third proposal"). The preliminary first stage of this method identifies examples for a straightforwardly scientific examination in the second stage. Intuitions and thought experiments of the sort that dominate semantics are important in the first stage. However, they are empirical responses to the phenomena and are open to

36   My 1991b is, in effect, an extended argument for this slogan.

revision at the second stage. Finally, in doing semantics, we should "put metaphysics first" ("fourth proposal").

I think that applying this methodology will help with all semantic issues. In the following chapters I shall use it in the hope of settling some, including some of the most notorious:[37]

1. We will discover that we do in fact ascribe more than one putative meaning to a token; indeed, I think that we ascribe as many as four to a pronoun such as 'I'. Not only do we ascribe more than one, we ought to, for our semantic purposes are served by so doing. So tokens have more than one meaning (Chap. 4).

2. The evidence against semantic holism as a descriptive doctrine will be decisive. Consider any putative meaning. We will find that the folk are prepared to ascribe it to tokens that differ enormously in their inferential properties. So, few if any inferential properties could constitute the ascribed property; it must be localistic. Given the success of folk ascriptions in serving our semantic purposes, we ought to ascribe such localistic properties. We will find independent support for this normative conclusion from the fact that only localistic properties have the sort of generality we are interested in. So holism is wrong not only about putative meanings but also about meanings (Chap. 3).

3. The direct-reference theory of proper names will turn out to be partly right and partly wrong. It is right in claiming that one of the properties we do, and should, ascribe to a name is simply its role of referring to its bearer. It is wrong in insisting, so determinedly, that this is *the* (one and only) meaning of a name. The evidence will show that we often ascribe a property constituted by a certain mode of referring to the bearer. And we ascribe this

---

37 The methodology also has consequences for the direction of psychological research on concepts. It suggests the strategy of testing when subjects *will ascribe* a particular meaning, truth value, reference, etc., to a thought or an utterance. Thus, rather than the present practice of testing reactions to birds or representations of birds, we test when subjects will ascribe the concept **BIRD** to a person in an attitude ascription (e.g., "*x* believes that . . . bird . . . ").

property as well because doing so serves our semantic purposes. Direct-reference theorists have no principled basis for denying this finer-grained meaning. Their position is theoretically ad hoc (4.8).

4. We shall find that there is indeed an intimate link: The meaning ascribed is always identical or closely related to one of the meanings of the content sentence in the t-clause (4.11). And it is in virtue of this link that the t-clause has *its* meanings, meanings that arise from its role of ascribing what it does (4.13).

5. I think that the evidence will show that the properties we ascribe for semantic purposes are all truth referential. So the evidence will count against any descriptive theory that claims otherwise; against, for example, two-factor, use, or verificationist theories (4.9, 4.10). Of course, such a theory might still be normatively correct and hence correct about meanings. But it is going to be hard to show this. Why do our ordinary ascriptions *seem* to serve our purposes so successfully if they do not really do so? What reason have we for thinking that the ascriptions recommended by the theory will better serve our purposes? The onus of answering these questions is heavy for any revisionist theory. I shall argue that the onus has not been discharged (Chap. 5).

Perhaps another naturalistic methodology reflecting a different view of the tasks would yield different predictions. But any such methodology needs to be set out and justified.

3

A case for semantic localism

I. A PRINCIPLED BASIS

3.1. Introduction

My concern in this chapter is to reject semantic holism and defend molecular semantic localism. The methodology described in the last chapter will play a central role.

I have pointed out (1.1) that holism is usually accompanied by a no-principled-basis consideration along the following lines:

> There is no principled basis for the molecular localist's distinction between the few inferential properties of a token alleged to constitute its meaning and all its other inferential properties. Only a token that shared all the inferential properties of the original token would really share a meaning with it.

Many who are not sympathetic to holism are impressed by the no-principled-basis consideration. Lepore and Fodor (1993) are striking examples. Quine has shown that an epistemic criterion like aprioricity cannot provide the principled basis. Lepore and Fodor think that the possibility of a nonepistemic criterion providing the basis is near enough empty:

there might, in principle, be something *non*epistemic that distinguishes meaning constitutive inferences from others; something that does not have to do with the conditions under which the inferences are accepted. Maybe it's their length; or whether they are tokened on Tuesday, etc. But it is, to put it mildly, hard to imagine what this distinguishing feature of inferences could be. (p. 674; see also 1.7, n. 25)

So, if we accept that some inferential properties constitute meanings, we have no principled basis for denying that they all do. Molecular localism is untenable. Fodor, at least, concludes that no inferential properties count, thus embracing an atomistic localism.

If the argument of Chapter 1 is correct, there is no *case against* molecular localism. It remains to give the *case for* it. This must start with a response to the no-principled-basis consideration. I shall argue that the demand for a principled basis is partly misconceived and that insofar as a basis is needed, we have one.

Given that semantic holism tends to be of the extremely individualistic sort (1.3), it is appropriate to take the no-principled-basis consideration to be concerned with *tokens* and thus intended to support:

All of the inferential properties of a token constitute its meaning.

However, suppose that we take the consideration as concerned with *types*. We could then see it as intended to support the following doctrine:

All of the inferential properties commonly believed to be typical of tokens of a type constitute its meaning.

I introduced this "social" doctrine in discussing the argument from functionalism. I called it "type" semantic holism and pointed out that it is so mild that the meanings it posits may be compatible with moderate localism (1.17). Doubtless the doctrine has some currency. For example, it is probably held by Thomas Kuhn (1962) about the language of a scientific community.

In defending localism, I shall be mainly concerned with versions of token holism (and "holism" and "holistic" should always be taken to concern tokens unless otherwise indicated). However, I shall look critically at type holism from time to time.

The ideal way to undermine semantic holism would be to present a localistic theory that had all the answers. Unfortunately, I am a long way from that. But then no holist is any closer to having all the answers either. So the argument is a programmatic one about which way the future lies. The received view is that the future must be holistic. In this chapter, I shall offer three independent arguments for the view that the future must be localistic. In later ones, I shall try to fill out some of the details of this localistic future.

From time to time in presenting the three arguments, I feel like I'm beating a dead horse. Any reader who feels the same should remember how alive and well holism is at present, even in the best circles.

3.2. The No-Principled-Basis Consideration

Two conclusions from the last chapter are important background to the discussion of the no-principled-basis consideration. First, I distinguished three semantic tasks (2.6). The "basic" task is to explain the natures of meanings. Something is a meaning if and only if it plays a semantic role. Assuming that if something is a meaning then we ought to ascribe it for semantic purposes, we can identify the basic task with the "normative" one of explaining the natures of the properties we ought to ascribe for semantic purposes. This task stands in nice contrast with the "descriptive" one of explaining the natures of the properties we do ascribe for semantic purposes. These latter properties will *be* meanings, of course, only if they really do serve those purposes. Second, I left open the possibility that we ascribe more than one property to a token for semantic purposes (descriptive), that we ought to ascribe more than one (normative), and hence that a token has more than one meaning (basic) (2.8).

In the light of these conclusions, what are we to make of the no-principled-basis consideration? I take it that the consideration is not making an *epistemological* point about *how we tell* what meanings are. Rather it is making a *metaphysical* point about how things are *in reality*. And the point seems to be a *basic* one about *what meaning a token has*. But perhaps the consideration is making a *descriptive* point about *what we take a token's meaning to be;* about the property we do, as a matter of fact, ascribe for semantic purposes; about its "putative meaning." I shall start with the less likely descriptive point.

Descriptive point. The point would be that there is no principled basis in reality for the distinction between the few inferential properties of a token alleged to constitute the property that we ascribe to the token for semantic purposes and all its other inferential properties. Only a token that shared all the inferential properties of the original token would really share the ascribed property with it.

From the naturalistic perspective, there is nothing special about semantics. If the semantic localist really has an onus to produce a basis for this distinction then localists in other areas ought to have similar ones. So, we can assess the no-principled-basis consideration in semantics by comparing it with analogous considerations elsewhere.

Take astronomy for example. We ascribe the property **being a planet** to Mars. A brief investigation will show that some of Mars' properties constitute its being a planet, but many do not (3.6). The distinction between these two sorts of property *needs no principled basis.* Nor do similar distinctions for the biological property **being an echidna,** the psychological property **being a pain,** the economic property **being a capitalist,** and the artifactual property **being a hammer.** We will see that these properties, like many others, are constituted localistically out of some properties and not out of others (3.6). That is the way the world is, and nothing more needs to be said. Venus does not share all of Mars' properties, and yet it still shares Mars' property of being a planet.

The same is true in semantics. We ascribe a putative meaning, **LM,** to a token for semantic purposes. An investigation might lead us to claim that some of the token's inferential properties constitute its having **LM,** but many do not. We would need no principled basis for this distinction. The world may simply be such that **LM** is constituted localistically in this way, and nothing more would need to be said. Another token that does not share all of the original token's inferential properties may still have **LM.**

If the no-principled-basis consideration is making a descriptive point, as it sometimes seems to be, it is misconceived.

Basic point. It is more likely that the no-principled-basis consideration is making a basic point. I have just dismissed the need for a basis for the distinction between the few inferential properties of a token alleged to constitute *what we take its meaning to be in our ascriptions* and all its other inferential properties. The basic point concerns the meaning the token *has:* There is no principled basis in reality for the distinction between the few inferential properties of a token alleged to constitute *the meaning of the token* and all its other inferential properties. Suppose, for example, that **LM,** the *putative* meaning we ascribe, is indeed constituted by only a few of the inferential properties of the token. The point is that there is no principled basis for distinguishing those few as *meaning* constituters because there is no basis for distinguishing **LM** from any other set of the token's inferential properties as *its meaning*. Although all of its inferential properties are not equally *LM* constituters, they are equally *meaning* constituters. So its meaning is really **HM,** the set of them all. Only a token that had **HM** would really share a meaning with the original token.

We do need a principled basis here, but it is not to distinguish one property as *the* meaning of the token: Perhaps the token has several meanings. We need a basis to distinguish *any* meanings it has from its other properties – to distinguish the properties that have the second-level property of **being a meaning** from those that do not. And, looking ahead to my disagreement with direct reference (4.8), molecular localism is not the only semantics that must satisfy this need: *Any* semantics, including a 'Fido'-Fido theory, must satisfy it. The framework developed in the last chapter provides the needed basis. A property is a meaning if and only if it plays a semantic role; that is, if and only if it is a property we ought to ascribe for semantic purposes. One inferential property may be distinguished from another in that the one but not the other constitutes a property that plays a semantic role and should be ascribed for semantic purposes; that is, that is a meaning.

91

Applying this basis, we shall discover that localistic properties like **LM,** constituted by only a few inferential properties, are meanings and that holistic properties like **HM,** constituted by many, are not. Tokens that share such localistic properties really do share meanings. *This is all the basis for localism we need.*

In sum, the roles played by properties and our purposes in ascribing them can provide a principled basis for ascribing localistic not holistic properties, hence, for there being localistic not holistic meanings. More importantly, those roles and purposes can provide a basis for ascribing *one* localistic property and *not another,* hence, for one localistic property and not another being a meaning. This is more important because, as we shall see, the idea that ascribing holistic rather than localistic properties would better serve our purposes plays little if any role in actual science. In contrast, the idea that ascribing one localistic property and not another would better serve our purposes is constantly before the scientific mind.

In the last chapter, I based an account of semantic roles on details of our semantic purposes (2.5). I claimed that our semantic purposes are to ascribe a property of the sort specified by a t–clause in order either to explain a subject's behavior or, using an assumption about the subject's reliability, to inform us about a reality largely external to the subject. It is important to note that providing a principled basis does not depend on those details.[1] If the task of explaining meanings is to be worthwhile there must be *some* purpose served by ascribing them (2.7). *Whatever the purpose,* it can provide a basis for counting a localistic property and not a holistic property, and one localistic and not another localistic property, as a meaning. So, those who object to my details can substitute their own. We can still have a principled basis for localism.

Drawing on the last chapter, I have dismissed the descriptive point and found an easy answer to the basic point. The no-

---

1 I am indebted to Ken Aizawa for this point. My 1994a overlooks it.

principled-basis consideration does, of course, leave us with an epistemic problem (although there is no reason to think that this was what prompted the consideration). The problem is that of *showing* that the application of our principled basis supports localism: that localistic properties and not holistic ones are meanings. This has become the problem of showing that our semantic purposes are served only by ascribing localistic properties. The rest of this chapter will be mainly concerned with this problem. And the chapter will conclude with a more theory-laden response to the no-principled-basis consideration (3.12).

3.3. Why Is the No-Principled-Basis Consideration Appealing?

If I am right, the no-principled-basis consideration that has caused so much concern in semantics turns out to be easily refuted. Why then is the consideration so appealing? The appeal is particularly striking in that it precedes any tackling of the epistemic problem.[2]

A theory in any area must show that its purposes are served by ascribing the properties that it does. I suggest that it would be surprising to discover that ascribing a holistic property *ever* served those purposes. It would certainly be surprising if there were some *general* reason why ascribing localistic properties *never* did so. If we could show that ascribing localistic properties did so in semantics, we would have shown that we have the only principled basis we need. Why then are so many philosophers convinced, in advance of investigation, that we cannot provide a principled basis?

Part of the answer must be the appeal of the arguments for holism considered in Chapter 1. Beyond that, I think that the answer is, at bottom, the sheer difficulty of semantics: This surely is an area in which we "do not know our way about." However, saying exactly where we are lost is difficult.

2   Consider Lepore and Fodor, for example. *Simply* on the strength of Quine having shown that an epistemic criterion will not supply the needed basis, they are totally convinced that nothing will (3.1).

My view of the no-principled-basis consideration reflects the framework set out in the last chapter. My best attempt at saying where we are lost must do so also. I think that the trouble starts with the failure to explicate talk of meanings in terms of semantic roles and purposes. As a result, the close relationship between the basic task of explaining what meanings are and the normative one of explaining what we should ascribe for semantic purposes is missed. The basic task is not then sharply distinguished from the descriptive task of explaining what we do ascribe for semantic purposes. And, finally, the basic no-principled-basis consideration, which the framework should be used to answer, is not sharply distinguished from the descriptive one, which should be dismissed.

I suspect that the failure to note that a token may have several meanings is important. It encourages confusion between the set of a token's meanings and one particular meaning of it; hence, between the properties that are candidates to be constituters of some meaning or other of a token and the actual constituters of a particular meaning of it; hence, between all of its inferential properties and a few of them.

Finally, I think that "an accident of history" may have contributed to the appeal. Historically, semantic theories have presupposed the Cartesian idea that meanings are things that competent speakers must *know about* (1.7–1.8). The combination of this idea with molecular localism's distinction between the inferential properties that are constitutive of a meaning and the ones that are not has been thought to yield a distinction between what is known a priori and what is known empirically. This epistemic distinction was then taken as the *criterion* for the localist's distinction. Quine has shown that there is no such epistemic distinction and hence no such criterion. So it was thought that we must find another criterion (see, e.g., Fodor and Lepore 1992). But there is nothing in this story to show that we *needed* a criterion for this purpose in the first place. And we do not need one, as the discussion of the descriptive no-principled-basis consideration showed: We do not need a principled basis for distinguishing what constitutes a particular property from what does not constitute it. The Cartesian

94

idea, which very likely has no place in semantics (2.2), presented us with a criterion that we did not need.

II. DEFINITIONS AND PLAN

3.4. Defining Semantic Holisms and Localisms

It is time to define the semantic localism that I wish to defend. In doing so it will help to describe the "logical space" of this holism-localism issue.

In Chapter 1 I characterized an extreme individualistic holism as follows:

> All of the inferential properties of a token constitute its meaning.

This stood opposed to an atomistic localism,

> No inferential properties of a token constitute its meaning,

and to a more moderate molecular localism,

> Few if any inferential properties of a token constitute its meaning.

These doctrines are about the meanings a token has and so are basic doctrines. In their use of "its meaning" they presuppose that a token has only one meaning. And the intended conclusion of the standard arguments for holism (Chap. 1) seems to be that a token has a holistic meaning and can have no other.

I shall start by defining some basic doctrines and by indicating how we might define and name others. I shall then do the same for normative and descriptive doctrines. My concern here is, as it is in Chapter 1, with the holism-localism issue having to do with *words,* which include the parts of thoughts.[3] Following the

---

3 I am thus assuming that the mental vehicle of a thought meaning has meaningful parts, but, despite the implication of my use of 'word', I am not assuming the language-of-thought hypothesis (1.2, point 2).

recommendation of the last Chapter, I shall not (mostly) presuppose that a token has only one meaning.

Some new usage will help these definitions. Call a putative meaning "Extreme-Holist" if it is a property of the sort referred to by the extreme doctrine: a meaning constituted by *all* the inferential properties of its token. Call a putative meaning "Holist" if it is constituted by *a large proportion* of the inferential properties of its tokens. Here are two holistic doctrines:

EXTREME SEMANTIC HOLISM: The only meaning any word token has is Extreme-Holist.

SEMANTIC HOLISM: The only meanings any word token has are Holist.

Three comments are necessary on the appropriateness of these definitions. First, contrary to the earlier recommendation, EXTREME SEMANTIC HOLISM does presuppose that a token has only one meaning because, if a token has an Extreme-Holist meaning, it *could* have only one. Second, in the light of what we shall say later about cluster theories, we should add that each inferential property that constitutes an Extreme-Holist or Holist meaning is *essential* to that meaning. Third, it should be noted that these doctrines are unlikely to appeal to two-factor theorists (1.5). These theorists often accept holism *so far as functional-role meanings are concerned* but are localistic about truth-referential meanings (because, for them, inferential properties have no role in constituting those meanings). Our definitions are suitable only for "one-factor" theorists who think, in effect, that all meanings are functional roles. The definition could be modified to cover both sorts of holist by talking only of *functional-role* meanings. I shall not modify the definitions because this subtlety adds irrelevant complications to the discussion. Rather, holistic talk of meanings should always be taken to be about functional-role meanings.

Holism can be more moderate than these two doctrines. For example, we could make doctrines partial in two ways. First, they might cover some but not necessarily all word tokens: Some tokens have only holistic meanings. Second, they might cover some but not necessarily all meanings of a token: At least one meaning of a token is holistic.

The popular "cluster" idea yields doctrines that are more interestingly moderate. The idea was first proposed by Wittgenstein (1953) and developed by John Searle (1958), Peter Strawson (1959), and N. L. Wilson (1959). According to a cluster theory of meaning, no single inferential property is essential to a token's meaning. Rather, the token has that meaning in virtue of having most − or a *weighted* most − of some set of inferential properties. A cluster meaning can be more or less holistic depending on how the relevant set of properties is constituted. Call a putative meaning "Extreme-Cluster-Holist" if *all* the inferential properties of its tokens go into the set, and "Cluster-Holist" if *a large proportion* go into the set. We could now define doctrines that are much more moderate; for example, one claiming that the only meanings a token has are Cluster-Holist. These cluster doctrines are more moderate because they lack the individualistic aspect: The tokens of many different people could, despite the differences in their inferential properties, share a meaning in virtue of each having a weighted most of the specified set of inferential properties.

By noting that a doctrine may be partial, and may concern holistic properties of many sorts − Extreme-Holist, Holist, Extreme-Cluster-Holist, or Cluster-Holist − we could define many semantic holisms.

Turn now to localistic doctrines. Call a putative meaning "Localist" if it is constituted by few if any of the inferential properties of its tokens. So a localist might claim that the only meanings any word token has are Localist. Call a putative meaning "Cluster-Localist" if it is constituted by the weighted most of a cluster and if only a few of the inferential properties of its tokens go into the cluster. So a localist might claim that the only meanings a token has are Cluster-Localist. By noting that a doctrine may be partial, and may concern Localist, or Cluster-Localist, properties, we could define many semantic localisms.

I shall be defending the following doctrine:

SEMANTIC LOCALISM: The only meanings any word token has are Localist or Cluster-Localist.

This is a *molecular* localism in *allowing* that a few inferential properties *may* constitute a meaning. However, the doctrine *does not require* that a few do – note the words "if any" in the definition of "Localist" – and so the doctrine is *consistent with* atomism. I think that it is important to leave open the possibility that inferential properties constitute a meaning (1.1), and I anticipate that it will often be the case that they do. I do not want to be committed to atomism but I shall not be arguing against it.

SEMANTIC LOCALISM is inconsistent with all the (token-) holistic doctrines just described. But let us now consider its relation to some other holistic doctrines.

SEMANTIC LOCALISM does not stand opposed to the earlier-mentioned mild type-holistic doctrine (3.1). Call a putative meaning "Type-Holist" if it is a property constituted by all the inferential properties commonly believed to be typical of tokens of a word type. Then that doctrine can be defined:

TYPE SEMANTIC HOLISM: The only meaning any word token has is Type-Holist.

Although this doctrine is consistent with LOCALISM, I shall argue against it in passing.

LOCALISM is also consistent with another sort of holism arising from a word's *indirect* links. The meaning of a word might be Localist or Cluster-Localist in that it is constituted by direct links to only a few other words and yet each of these others may be similarly constituted, and so on. Although these chains of dependence *could* lead to a holism of sorts, it is likely to be another very moderate one. First, it is like TYPE HOLISM in being at the level of types not tokens: It is a claim about the direct and indirect inferential links *shared by all tokens of a certain type,* for example, by the type meaning **BACHELOR.** So it is like TYPE HOLISM in being social, not individualistic. Second, we know that the chains of dependence cannot "go on for ever." I have emphasized that meaning must depend ultimately on direct causal links to reality. Some words may depend for their meanings on other words, but, in the end, we must reach words that (at least partly) do not (1.2, 4.5). In theory, the chain for a word could be long and could make the word dependent on very many others, but we have been given no reason to believe that this is so in fact. In any case, I shall not argue against this sort of holism.

LOCALISM *is* inconsistent with a holism suggested (in conversation) by Hilary Putnam. Consider a property that is just like a Localist or Cluster-Localist one in what *positively* constitutes it but differs in that there are things that "*negatively* constitute" it. It is a property that a token has in virtue of having a few of the token's inferential properties, or, a weighted most of a few, and *not having* a whole lot of other ones; and these other ones are not ones *already* excluded by the positive ones in the way that being inferentially linked to tokens meaning **UNMARRIED** might exclude being so related to ones meaning **MARRIED.** Call such a property "Negative-Holist." Someone inspired by the intuitive idea that a person's token cannot mean X if her associations with it are bizarre relative to the familiar X theory might urge:

NEGATIVE SEMANTIC HOLISM: The only meanings any word token has are Negative-Holist.

This is another moderate social holism at the level of types.

With each basic doctrine goes a normative doctrine that we can treat as equivalent. Thus, SEMANTIC LOCALISM is paired with:

NORMATIVE SEMANTIC LOCALISM: The only properties that we should ascribe to any word token for semantic purposes are Localist or Cluster-Localist.

Finally, we should consider some descriptive doctrines. In the last chapter I pointed out that these views of the status quo supply important evidence on the normative/basic issue (2.9). I think that the localism I want to defend is in accord with the status quo; so I shall also argue that the following doctrine is correct:

DESCRIPTIVE SEMANTIC LOCALISM: The only properties we ascribe to any word token for semantic purposes are Localist or Cluster-Localist.

Where might the normative holist stand on the descriptive issue? If he means to be conservative, taking his holism to be in accord with the status quo, he must adopt a descriptive holist doctrine like

DESCRIPTIVE SEMANTIC HOLISM: The only properties that we ascribe to any word token for semantic purposes are Holist.

If he means to be revisionist, he could even accept the preceding DESCRIPTIVE SEMANTIC *LOCALISM*. Holists do not give a great deal of explicit attention to these questions; there is not much interest in the distinction between describing and revising the semantic status quo. Nevertheless, I think it is clear that most holists mean to be revisionist. So they are implicitly committed to some form of descriptive localism while seeing all our ordinary attitude ascriptions either as false or as failing to serve our semantic purposes.

Just as the normative holist can be a descriptive localist, so also can the eliminativist. Where the holist wants to replace the ascription of localist meanings with the ascription of holist ones, the eliminativist wants to abandon the ascription of meanings altogether. I set aside discussion of eliminativism until Chapter 5.

3.5. Plan

My primary aim is to establish NORMATIVE SEMANTIC LOCALISM and hence the basic doctrine SEMANTIC LOCALISM. To establish this I must show that the properties we ought to ascribe for semantic purposes are localistic. I shall offer three arguments for this conclusion.

1. The argument from the success of our ascriptions: The methodology of the last chapter recommends that we argue for a normative/basic doctrine by looking at the descriptive issue (2.9). Given the apparent success of our current attitude ascriptions in serving our semantic purposes, evidence for a descriptive doctrine will be evidence for the related normative/basic one. Indeed, it is unlikely that any normative/basic doctrine uninformed by a descriptive one will be plausible. I will proceed in this way, arguing for DESCRIPTIVE SEMANTIC LOCALISM and inferring SEMANTIC LOCALISM from it. That will be the main concern of part III.

2. The argument from our interest in generality: A holism-localism issue can come up anywhere. So we can get analogues of these doctrines in biology, astronomy, and so on. Consideration in part II of a range of examples from various areas will show that, outside semantics, we ascribe properties that are localistic, not holistic. This descriptive view supports the normative one that we ought to ascribe localistic not holistic properties, for just as the descriptive supports the normative in semantics, so it does elsewhere. Normative localism has further support. I shall argue that our liking for the local is not surprising: Ascribing localistic properties meets our explanatory and practical purposes, particularly our interest in *generality*. These conclusions about the holism-localism issue elsewhere will be applied to semantics in part III, thereby providing an independent argument for the LOCALISM doctrines.

3. The argument from Representationalism: The last two arguments make, near enough, no appeal to any available theory in semantics. This is just as well because any such theory would be controversial in the current dispute. Nevertheless, I conclude with an argument for LOCALISM based on the popular overarching theory, "Representationalism": the view that meanings are entirely constituted by representational properties. If this theory is correct, then meanings cannot be holistic.

III. HOLISM AND LOCALISM ELSEWHERE

3.6. The Descriptive Issue

I turn now to the holism–localism issue outside semantics. In this section I shall consider the descriptive issue: To what extent are the properties we *actually* ascribe holistic or localistic? In the next section, I shall consider the normative issue: To what extent are the properties we *ought to* ascribe holistic or localistic. Before beginning the descriptive issue, some general remarks are appropriate about the ascription of properties.

In talking about the world we can ascribe or ignore properties at will. If we want to ascribe a property often, our interest in brevity makes it convenient to have a single word for that property, "a name," rather than have to make do with a lengthy description. We are free to choose which properties to name. Properties themselves vary from the most holistic to the most localistic. So, in ascribing and naming properties, we can be as localistic or as holistic as we would like.

What guides our choice of properties to ascribe or name? Clearly, our purposes. These purposes may be theoretical, practical, perhaps even frivolous. They led to our word 'echidna', referring to objects that must share the essential properties of echidnas but need not share the accidental ones. They have not led to a word for objects that share the property of straining the credulity of tourists from Peoria even though all echidnas, and many other things, have that property. However, we might want such a word – perhaps to help run a zoo – and are perfectly free to introduce one: say, 'peorincred'.

Metaphysical aside. Given the popularity of the view that we make the world with our language and minds, an aside is appropriate. The preceding remarks *have no metaphysical implications whatsoever*. I did not make echidnas peorincreds when I introduced the word. They always were peorincreds and would have been so even if nobody had ever introduced 'peorincred' or, indeed, any other word. Naming a property does not make an object have it;[4] ignoring the property does not prevent the object's having it. We are free to choose what properties to name. We are not free to choose what objects have properties whether named or unnamed. I have argued this at length elsewhere (1991b, particularly pp. 241–6).

How are we to "measure" the extent to which the properties we ascribe for our various purposes are localistic or holistic? We should follow the model of semantics. In that area, the measurement is in terms of the proportion of inferential properties that are constitutive. These inferential properties are natural *candidates* to be constitutive of meanings. So, in general, let us talk of analogous properties in an area as "candidate-constituters." (In the semantic case, we have taken the set of candidate-constituters to be large. We should also take it to be large in other areas, thus preserving the analogy with semantics.) We can then measure properties in general, just as we measured semantic properties, in terms of the proportion of candidate-constituters that are in fact constitutive. We can describe properties thus measured, just as we did semantic ones, as "Extreme-Holist," "Holist," "Localist," and so on. And we can name doctrines in terms of these descriptions. Thus, the biological analogue of DESCRIPTIVE EXTREME SEMANTIC HOLISM is

DESCRIPTIVE EXTREME BIOLOGICAL HOLISM: The only property that we ascribe to any object for biological purposes is Extreme-Holist.

It is immediately apparent that this individualistic doctrine is not true. We ascribe to Gaelene the biological property of **being an echidna.** Our best theory tells us that among the properties of Gaelene that are biological candidate-constituters are many that are not in fact essential to her being an echidna; for example, **being female** and **being brown** are not essential.

---

4 Cf. "The English language makes [objects] white just by applying the term 'white' to them" (Goodman 1979: 347).

Consider astronomy and our earlier example of Mars (3.2). We ascribe to Mars the astronomical property of **being a planet.** Our best theory tells us that among Mars' astronomical candidate-constituters are many that are not essential to its being a planet: for example, **revolving around the Sun, having a certain atmosphere, revolving on its axis at a certain rate,** and so on.

If DESCRIPTIVE EXTREME HOLISM were correct, all of an object's candidate-constituters would be essential to any biological or astronomical property we ascribe to the object. As a result, we could ascribe only one biological or astronomical property to an object, and the object would be unlikely to share that property with any other object. Clearly, our descriptions of Gaelene as an echidna and of Mars as a planet do not come close to according with this individualistic doctrine.

The doctrine fares no better in economics. Consider a particular capitalist, for example. Many of her candidate-constituters are not essential to her being a capitalist. She owns means of production. That is essential. She happens also to be a landowner, a usurer, and a Volvo owner. These are not essential.

In these cases, we have relied on well-established theories to tell us about the localistic natures of the properties we ascribe. We cannot always do this. We cannot do so with the property of **being a pain,** for example. In such cases we must use what I called the "ultimate" method (2.9). First, we must identify some apparently uncontroversial examples of pains and nonpains using the identification assumption: If people who both understand 'pain' and have the expertise to recognize things that have the property **being a pain** call something "pain," then it is likely to have that property (if anything has). Second, we must examine the examples to see what is common and what is peculiar to pains. If DESCRIPTIVE EXTREME PSYCHOLOGICAL HOLISM were correct, then all the functional roles of a particular pain would be essential to its being a pain, for those roles are the psychological candidate-constituters. Yet, applying the "ultimate" method, we discover, as we noted (1.17), that we ascribe pains to

Nigel, Lawrence, and Anna despite many functional differences between them.

Finally, consider what I shall call, for want of a better term, "artifactual"[5] properties: **being a chair, a boat, a hammer, a clutch, a wheel,** and so on. Artifactual candidate-constituters are functional properties – what things can be used for – and design properties – how things are designed to perform their function. A thing needs only a few such properties to instantiate an artifactual property. In particular, often *only one* functional property is essential. We can be confident about such a strong localism here because, to a large extent, *we give* the objects that have artifactual properties their nonholistic natures. In general, an object has an artifactual property in virtue of the fact that *we built it* a certain way to have a certain function or because it is a certain way and *we use it* for that function. Whatever other functions a thing may have – a chair can be a work of art, a hammer can be a weapon – whatever other design features a thing may have – a chair can have any number of legs (even none: a rocking chair), a hammer can be made of silver – are simply irrelevant to its having that property.

Sometimes, of course, it may be difficult to determine exactly what constitutes a property. To a degree, there may be no fact of the matter about this: The property may be vague (2.10). Nevertheless, the few examples we have considered are sufficient to dismiss DESCRIPTIVE EXTREME HOLISM. DESCRIPTIVE HOLISM does not fare much better: It is not the case in these examples that a large proportion of the candidate-constituters are essential to an object's having the property we ascribe.

What about cluster doctrines? These holisms have the great

5   The term is a bit misleading because the objects that have properties of the
    sort we have in mind need not be artifacts; stones found on the beach, and
    even cats, can be paperweights. And artifacts can have properties that are not
    of the sort we have in mind; *being plastic* is not of the sort. To simply call the
    properties "functional" would confuse them with biological properties like
    being a heart and/or psychological ones like being in pain.

105

advantage of not being individualistic: Though tokens differ from each other in their candidate-constituter properties it is likely that many will be alike in having (a weighted) most of those properties. These holisms also have the enormous advantage in the face of criticism of lacking sharpness, of being "fuzzy," and hence of being generally difficult to refute. However, the doctrine that has us ascribing only Extreme-Cluster-Holist properties is obviously false. For one thing, because all the candidate-constituters go into the cluster for a property in a given area, there can be more than one such property in the area only by an implausible variation of the weights given to all the candidate-constituters. The doctrine that has us ascribing Cluster-Holist properties is better and even seems to enjoy some measure of support in some biological theories about the identification of species. Nevertheless, I suggest that the doctrine is implausible. Given the extent to which token echidnas differ from each other in their candidate-constituters – similarly, token planets, capitalists, pains, and boats – it is plausible to think that many of these candidate-constituters are simply irrelevant to the natures of the properties in question. Thus Mars' properties of **revolving around the Sun** (in particular), **having a certain atmosphere,** and **revolving on its axis at a certain rate** are not only inessential to Mars' being a planet, they seem entirely incidental.

What about partial doctrines? The first sort is of no interest: That we only ascribe holistic properties is no more plausible if the ascriptions are to some objects than if they are to all objects. The examples have a less decisive impact on the second sort of partiality. They show that many properties we ascribe are not holistic, but this alone does not show that none are. Nevertheless, the discussion already makes it seem likely that none are.

Finally, what about NEGATIVE HOLISM? Is it essential for being an echidna and so forth that an object *not* have a whole lot of properties? We must remember that properties ruled out by what is *positively* essential do not count. Thus, it is probably essential to being a capitalist that an object not have the properties

106

of the normal echidna, planet, chair, and many other things. But these do not count because something with those properties could not play the economic role of a capitalist. Are there any other constraints? There seems to be no persuasive reason for thinking so. If something has the correct positive features for being an *X*, it seems that we would treat it as an *X* however bizarre it may otherwise be. Of course, if it is bizarre we may be reluctant to conclude that it is an *X*. But that is an epistemic matter.

In sum, outside semantics these examples count decisively against the most extreme descriptive holisms and cast considerable doubt on even the most moderate. We would need to examine these examples and others in more detail than is appropriate here to establish DESCRIPTIVE LOCALISM. What can be said is that the initial implication of these examples is that the status quo is rather localistic.[6]

3.7. The Normative/Basic Issue

We have seen that the properties we actually ascribe outside semantics tend toward the localistic. But perhaps we should ascribe other sorts. For example, perhaps NORMATIVE HOLISM is in general correct.

The preceding discussion supplies a good reason for supposing that it is not. In the last chapter I pointed out that if our actual practice of ascribing certain properties serves our purposes in some area well, then that is very good evidence that we ought to ascribe at least those properties to serve those purposes (2.9). It is surely the case that ascribing such localistic properties as **being an**

---

6   What about *confirmation* holism, which I have earlier endorsed (1.4)? The holism of confirmation is of a different sort, being at the level of realization not of constitution. The claim is not about the nature of the property, **being confirmed;** indeed, the property may even be atomistic. The claim is about the realization of the property in a sentence: Whether or not the sentence has the property depends on its relations to all other sentences in the web of belief, and on whether *they* have the property.

echidna, a planet, a capitalist, a wheel, and so on does serve our purposes well. So that is evidence that we ought to ascribe them.

We can do better. We shall see that our most pressing purposes motivate the ascription of localistic properties.

Our liking for the local is nicely illustrated by the artifactual property **being a wheel.** Wheels are to be found in an enormous variety of machines connected up in all sorts of ways to all sorts of other artifacts: to clutches, to brakes, in gears, in pullies, and so on. *Yet they are all wheels.* Any one of these connections is inessential to something being a wheel. It naturally suits us to have a word that names *what we design all wheels to have in common:* roughly, being a circular frame or disk that revolves on its axis. We are often interested in being a little more holistic about wheels, but we achieve this (always?) with a complex expression: 'steering wheel', 'fly wheel', 'bicycle wheel'. If we want an expression for a much more holistic property, we have to tell a long story: 'rear bicycle wheel that carries five gears, drives a dynamo,. . . ' . We do not have names for such properties because *we are seldom interested in being that holistic.* We probably *never ascribe,* let alone name, any Holist property of a wheel because we have no interest at all in such properties.

If we were to be confronted with a no-principled-basis consideration for artifactual properties analogous to the one for meanings (3.1), we would have an easy response. The principled basis for our localism is that it suits our purposes: practical purposes and perhaps theoretical purposes.

Economic and psychological properties are like semantic properties in being relational and in serving theoretical purposes. A more detailed consideration of these properties shows why those purposes lead to localism.

In economics we specify structures that are explanatory only insofar as the world realizes them. In naming the relational properties that make up these structures we are not compelled to name properties that are constituted by relations in some large explanatory structure; we are not compelled to name holistic properties. We are free to name properties that are constituted by relations in relatively simple structures; we are free to name localistic properties. And that is what we have typically done. The theoretical task is then to make use of these names to specify much more complicated structures that contain those simple ones and that the world realizes.

Suppose that all specifications of structures are "Ramsey sentences."[7] Then these points can be put as follows. We are not compelled to name properties that are specified by long "holistic-Ramsey" sentences, we can name ones specified by relatively short "localistic-Ramsey" sentences and have typically done so. The name, in effect, abbreviates the localistic-Ramsey sentence.

Economics illustrates the explanatory advantages of the localistic approach in the social sciences. (i) It is convenient to isolate disagreement about which complicated structures are realized from the hard core of agreement that is the basis of the science. This core is captured in the common use of words referring to localistic properties. The theories *disagree about* capitalists, money, and prices, but *they agree that there are* capitalists, money, and prices. (ii) It is convenient to have a language that reflects the cumulative progress of the science, that reveals what the present takes over from the past. Using language holistically would turn each progressive step into a language change that would conceal theoretical continuities. (iii) Most important of all, the science seeks explanatory generality. NORMATIVE EXTREME HOLISM would require the specification of a distinct set of properties for each time slice of the world economy and so would be totally futile. We want to specify properties that play roles *in many different complicated structures* realized by different aspects of reality. The names for these properties may be part of theories that are not in competition but are complementary. Thus, capitalists, money, and prices have roles in international trade, in some very

---

7   Along the lines of, say, Lewis 1983: 78–95.

different national economies, and in a great range of microeconomic activities. A social science needs to have names for localistic properties with a variety of roles.

Psychology, like economics, specifies a structure that is explanatory insofar as the world realizes it. The specification can be by a Ramsey sentence. Again we move far from NORMATIVE EXTREME HOLISM, choosing to name properties that can be specified by localistic-Ramsey sentences. In this way we achieve a generality that suits our purposes. We want to name properties that have an explanatory role in many different structures. The structures differ because people differ and because the one person differs from time to time. The structures may differ because there are *different types* of mind. Thus pains have a role in the very different psychological structures of humans, bats, echidnas, perhaps even of snakes, Martians, and the next generation of computers. The structures may differ because they are *different areas* of the one mind. Thus pains can have a role in the emotional, the cognitive, and the sensational areas.

This view of psychology is at odds with what seems to be the standard functionalist view discussed earlier (1.17). First, it seems that, in the standard view, in naming a mental property we have taken account of every generalization our theory makes about the property; we name properties specified by holistic-Ramsey sentences. The result is a holism of sorts, but it is TYPE HOLISM, a mild doctrine that is a long way from the token holisms that have been concerning us. We certainly *might have been* that holistic, but I rather doubt that we have been. Second, and more important, it seems that, in the standard view, *every* theoretical development redefines psychological terms; functionalist theories are *essentially* TYPE HOLISTIC. If this were so, we would be compelled to name Type-Holist properties in psychology. Yet, as we have seen, there can be no basis for this compulsion: We are free to name any properties we like. If we really are TYPE HOLISTIC, it is because we choose to be.

In sum, among the many properties any object has, ranging from the localistic to the holistic, the evidence suggests that science (and common sense) has, as a matter of fact, chosen to name ones that are localistic. So if we want to ascribe a holistic property, we have to use a complex expression. Why is our science like this? Because it suits our theoretical purposes. The holistic approach, especially that of NORMATIVE EXTREME HOLISM, is explanatorily futile. Probably, *any token of anything* differs in some (nontrivial) respect from anything else. We can make explanatory progress by abstracting from most of these differences until we reach properties that are shared by many tokens. We must be localistic to achieve the generality that the theoretical life is all about. Should our present theories prove wrong – should it turn out, for example, that nothing realizes pain – then our new theories will be just as localistic. Being localistic is as principled as could be.

This may seem a little hasty. Though it is clear that we could not achieve our purposes by ascribing Extreme-Holist, Holist, or Extreme-Cluster-Holist properties, perhaps we could by ascribing Cluster-Holist or Negative-Holist ones. Ascribing these properties would certainly suit our purposes much better than ascribing the others. However, in the case of the Cluster-Holist properties, it would not suit them well. The more candidate-constituters that go into a cluster the greater the likelihood of variation from theoretical group to group and from time to time in the cluster picked out by a name, hence in the property named. With differences in properties are likely to go differences in the objects that have them. We have no motivation to saddle ourselves with these problems. It is pointless to give a large proportion of an object's candidate-constituters some weight in naming a property for explanatory purposes. In the case of Negative-Holist properties, we simply have no motivation for choosing to name a property with any exclusions that go beyond those required by the positive features of properties. We have no reason for discontent with the simpler localistic properties.

One important point remains. The desire for generality, stemming from practical, theoretical, perhaps even frivolous, purposes, shows that we ought to ascribe localistic properties, but it does not show *which* localistic properties we ought to ascribe. We need to show that we have a basis for being localistic *in a particular way*. Showing this, however, has nothing to do with the holism-localism dispute: It is about choosing between localistic properties, not about choosing localistic properties over holistic ones.

Why do we ascribe **being an echidna, a wheel, a capitalist,** and so on rather than many other localistic properties that objects have? We could ascribe properties made up of many different small sets of candidate-constituters, each of which would be localistic and many of which might satisfy our desire for generality. How do we choose? The answer is to be found, once again, in our purposes: We think that **being an echidna** is explanatorily significant, that **being a wheel** is practically significant, and so on, but think that the unnamed and unascribed properties are not. That is why we do choose. And, because our reasons are good, it is why we should choose.

Whatever the philosophical interest of the no-principled-basis consideration, the idea that we need a basis for not ascribing holistic properties plays little if any role in actual science. In contrast, the idea that a theory should have a basis for ascribing the localistic properties that it does is important. If the theory cannot show that ascribing those properties serves our theoretical purposes, we have the very best reason for abandoning it.

In conclusion, in areas other than semantics, I have rejected a range of descriptive holisms from DESCRIPTIVE EXTREME HOLISM to the most plausible, a doctrine that has us ascribing Cluster-Holist properties. NORMATIVE LOCALISM is supported not only by this case for DESCRIPTIVE LOCALISM but also by a consideration of the theoretical and practical purposes that lead us to ascribe properties. These purposes provide the only principled basis we need for being localistic.

Finally, just as the descriptive supports the normative, so also does the normative, the descriptive (2.10). Given that our current practice of ascribing certain properties is successful, it is likely that any properties that we ought to ascribe will include those ones. So the independent evidence adduced that we ought to ascribe

112

only localistic properties – evidence that does not depend on the evidence that we do ascribe them – is evidence that we do ascribe only localistic properties.

IV. HOLISM AND LOCALISM IN SEMANTICS

3.8. The Descriptive Issue

We have seen that the properties we ascribe in various areas are localistic and that there is no good reason to change to more holistic ones. Because this is the way things are elsewhere, we should expect them to be like this in semantics. So we should expect DESCRIPTIVE and NORMATIVE SEMANTIC LOCALISM, and hence SEMANTIC LOCALISM, to be correct. However, we can do much better for SEMANTIC LOCALISM than this simple induction.

I shall now present three arguments for LOCALISM. This section and the next will be concerned with DESCRIPTIVE SEMANTIC LOCALISM. If this doctrine is correct then the properties we ascribe for semantic purposes, *putative meanings,* are localistic. Given the success of these ascriptions we have good evidence that these properties play semantic roles. So we have good evidence that the normative doctrine is correct too and hence that *meanings* are localistic. This is "the argument from the success of our ascriptions."

How do we tell about the natures of the properties we ascribe? In considering each holism-localism issue, we have looked first to theories in the appropriate science (3.6). There are theories available in semantics, but it would be rather tendentious to place much weight on any of these in the current dispute. To a considerable extent, these theories are precisely what is in contention. So we will have to rely on the "ultimate" method (2.11). Nevertheless, later, I will examine the consequences for the issue of one overarching theory (3.11).

The "ultimate" method has two stages. First, we must identify some apparently uncontroversial examples of tokens with the putative meaning P and of tokens without it. Second, we must examine the examples to see what is common and peculiar to the tokens with that property. In the first stage, we use the identification assumption: If people who both understand the t-clause 'that p' and have the expertise to recognize tokens that have the property P call something "that p," then it is likely to have that property (if anything has). We count the folk as experts and count ourselves among the folk. Thought experiments can have a role.

The advantages of this method are apparent here. It quickly yields results that are totally at odds with DESCRIPTIVE SEMANTIC HOLISM.

I am focusing on the properties of words. So, in the first stage, we consider what the folk call "that . . . F . . . " or "that . . . a . . . " in ordinary attitude ascriptions. We note that, whatever the 'F' or 'a', the folk apply these t-clauses to the tokens of many of their fellows: For any putative word meaning, the folk see many different people as having thoughts that include tokens with that property. Thus, the folk ascribe to almost everyone "wheel-beliefs" like that the wheel is an important invention, "atom-beliefs" like that atoms are small, and "Cicero-beliefs" like that Cicero was an orator. Moving to the second stage, even a cursory examination of tokens that are identified by the folk as sharing a meaning shows them to differ enormously in their inferential properties. Thus, the alleged believers vary from engineers to mechanical ignoramuses, from physicists to morons, from Cicero's acquaintances to those who read about him in *Word and Object*. As a result there will be great differences in the inferential properties of their tokens, all of which are thought to have the putative meanings **WHEEL, ATOM,** or **CICERO.** So, a set made up of a large proportion of the inferential properties of one person's token will include many that are not properties of another person's. So, contrary to HOLISM, it cannot be the case that the shared putative meaning is constituted by any such set: No such set is common and peculiar to the tokens to which the folk ascribe the one putative meaning.

The well-known "arguments from ignorance and error" by

114

Saul Kripke (1980), Keith Donnellan (1972), and Hilary Putnam (1975) against description theories of reference can be adapted to strengthen this case for localism. These arguments can be seen as showing that the folk ascribe the putative meaning **CATILINE** or **EINSTEIN** or **BEECH** to tokens that have very few inferential properties in common, far too few to distinguish them from tokens to which the meaning is not ascribed. Thus it may well be the case that the only inferential property common to tokens to which we ascribe **CATILINE** link it to tokens to which we ascribe **MAN;** similarly, **BEECH** to **TREE.** (Note that the argument from ignorance and error does not undermine the recent assumption of folk expertise. The folk are expert at identifying tokens that mean **BEECH** but rather poor at identifying beeches.)

This discussion supports a localism as strong as DESCRIPTIVE SEMANTIC LOCALISM: It is likely that few if any inferential properties constitute the properties ascribed in these cases. So the discussion goes against holisms that are much weaker than DESCRIPTIVE SEMANTIC HOLISM. Indeed, it even goes against TYPE HOLISM, a holism so mild that its meanings may be localistic: The number of inferential properties commonly believed to be typical of tokens with a certain putative meaning is simply too small in these cases to constitute the distinctive meaning of those tokens.

The discussion can hardly be said to count decisively against the very weak NEGATIVE HOLISM. According to this doctrine, we ascribe a certain meaning to a token only if it does not have a whole lot of associations that would be bizarre relative to the familiar theory involving that meaning and that go beyond those ruled out by what positively constitutes the meaning. Doubtless, if a token did have such bizarre associations, we would be reluctant to ascribe the meaning, but this seems best explained epistemically: It is unlikely that a token with these associations would have the positive features needed for the meaning. We did not find persuasive reasons for thinking that we ascribe Negative-Holist properties elsewhere. No more do we find them in semantics.

We have noted that there is something unusual and confusing about our ascriptions of putative meanings: There seems to be "an intimate link" between a property of the content sentence of a t-clause and the putative meaning the t-clause ascribes (2.12). Assume that the link is an identity, as it often seems to be. This gives further support to the case against HOLISM. Suppose that the putative meaning ascribed is constituted by inferential properties. The intimate link requires that the content sentence also has those properties. HOLISM requires that each such matching be of a large set of the inferential properties of the ascriber's token with a large set of the subject's. Reflection on the frequency of ignorance and error, and on the fact that experts ascribe beliefs to nonexperts and vice versa, shows that few of the vast number of folk ascriptions could meet the holistic requirement.

Finally, I make an unfashionable appeal to dictionaries as evidence of the localistic nature of the status quo. Dictionaries can be seen as embodying the results of a partial application of the "ultimate" method. Of course, dictionaries are little help with the causal links to reality that must partly constitute some meanings. But dictionaries are very helpful about inferential properties because they tell us of connections between words. They supply *candidates* for the essential inferential properties of the putative meanings we ascribe. It may take further research to discover if a candidate really is essential, but this need not worry us in our struggle with HOLISM because *there are so few candidates.*

It may, of course, be hard to tell many things about the natures of the properties we ascribe. Sometimes there may *be* no telling because these properties are vague like the rest of reality. Nevertheless, I claim, this brief discussion is sufficient to establish DESCRIPTIVE SEMANTIC LOCALISM. In the next section, I shall expand on this basic argument to take account of differing opinions about attitude ascriptions.

I conclude this section by returning to the no-principled-basis consideration. I claimed that, insofar as this consideration is making a descriptive rather than a normative point about localism, it should be dismissed (3.2). Just as we ascribe the property of **being a planet** to Mars, we ascribe a certain putative meaning to a token. Just as some of Mars' astronomical candidate-constituters are constitutive of its being a planet, but many are not, so also some of the token's semantic candidate-constituters – in particular, its inferential properties – may be constitutive of its having that putative meaning, but many may not be. In neither case do we need any principled basis for this distinction. Putative meanings, like planets and everything else, are the way they are and not some other way. That is the way the world is and nothing more needs to be said.

3.9. Opinions about Attitude Ascriptions

There are a range of opinions about attitude ascriptions that may seem to bear on the descriptive issue. I start with two points drawn from Quine's discussion and mentioned before (2.8). First, according to Quine, many attitude ascriptions are ambiguous: The truth of one construed "transparently" depends only on the reference of words in the utterance or thought in question; the truth of one construed "opaquely" depends on some finer-grained property. Second, the one token can have two putative meanings (in the sense I have explicated, of course; 2.6), one constituted by its property of referring to something and the other by something more fine grained. This second point is logically distinct from the first as we can see by considering the ascription 'This is a bank'. This ascription is ambiguous in that it can ascribe different properties, sometimes concerning financial institutions, at other times, rivers. Yet it does not follow that any object has both properties. Nevertheless, the second point does follow from Quine's discussion because it is rather obvious that the two properties ascribed are often had by the one token.

These points do not affect the basic argument. When the ascription is transparent, *no* inferential property of a word is constitutive of the property ascribed; only its reference is constitutive.

117

And when the ascription is opaque, the argument shows that the folk are not concerned with most of the inferential properties of thoughts and utterances.

I favor a Quinean view of attitude ascriptions, which I shall develop in Chapter 4. On this view, ascriptions have a mild context dependency (beyond any that arises from the presence in the t-clause of ordinary indexicals like 'she'): The context – in particular, the intentions of the speaker – often determine whether the ascription is transparent or opaque. Some philosophers think that these ascriptions are more radically context dependent with the result that, for example, 'echidna' in a t-clause ascribes various meanings as we vary the context.

These differences of opinion about ordinary attitude ascriptions are largely irrelevant to the holism issue. I shall later argue that, because of the "intimate link," only a fairly moderate context-dependency thesis has any plausibility (4.11). But we do not need to establish this to deal with holism. Even the most extreme context dependency of an ascription would not alone show that the property ascribed was holistic. To see this, consider the highly context-dependent expression 'this property'. By varying the context, this expression can be used to ascribe any property at all, from **being an echidna** to **being a wheel,** from the most holistic to the most localistic. In brief, *the context dependency of an ascription is one thing, the nature of the property ascribed in a context is another.*

This point needs emphasis. It is common to confuse ascriptions of beliefs with the beliefs ascribed: Thus, people talk, almost in one breath, of *de dicto* belief and of *de dicto* ascriptions (4.2, n. 5); a paper is written primarily about puzzling belief ascriptions (4.17) but called "A Puzzle about Belief" (Kripke 1979a).[8] Suppose that a person not only is in the grip of this confusion but also holds a sufficiently extreme version of the view that ascriptions are context dependent to make it seem appropriate to talk of that dependency as "holistic." Then he will conclude that the beliefs are

---

8 I discuss this confusion of ascriptions and thoughts further in my 1984, particularly pp. 388–94, 408.

holistic. I do not say that Stephen Stich has done this in his discussion of examples like Mrs. T, but it frequently seems as if he has.

The difficulty in interpreting Stich is instructive. The confusion of ascriptions with beliefs in the literature is often concealed by equivocal language. Stich seems to be an example:

The content we ascribe to a belief depends, more or less holistically, on the subject's entire network of related beliefs. (1983: 54)

Is it the content or our ascribing it that is dependent on the network? (Compare: "The food we eat depends on the weather." Is it the food or our eating it that is dependent on the weather?) In the next sentence, Stich describes his view as "holism in content ascription" and that is indeed the holism that he largely argues for. Yet the passage I just quoted, particularly in its context, seems to be a statement of content holism. Presumably this is how Fodor interprets it in claiming that "the received view is that Mrs. T makes a case for the holism of belief content" (1987: 62). My point is this: If the argument about Mrs. T and related examples were good, it would make a case for the holism of content ascriptions but *it would make no case at all for the holism of content.*[9]

9 I shall summarize my picture of Stich's argument. This summary brings out the way he interweaves claims about content with claims about ascriptions and shows why I find the argument elusive. Initially, Stich takes the examples to support his holistic "diagnosis" that *content* depends on a network of beliefs (1983: 54–60). Yet at most he has shown that content depends on *some* other beliefs. Later, he writes as if this initial argument was for the context dependency of *ascriptions* of belief (p. 67). Yet there was no sign of an argument for this very different conclusion (despite the talk of "the holism of content ascription"). The argument comes later still. Stich argues that the examples support his view that a person's belief *ascription* ascribes a similarity to a possible belief of her own (pp. 86, 93–5) and hence, because similarities are context dependent, support the context dependency of ascriptions. Independently, Stich argues that the examples show that beliefs are not really *content* identical but only content similar, supporting the view that our *ascriptions* are of similarity not identity (pp. 85–6). This argument is a "slippery slope" or "sorites" and should be no more persuasive than a similar one

Indeed, the examples that encourage the view that attitude ascriptions are context dependent count *against* the view that folk semantics is holistic. These examples suggest that, in some contexts, the set of inferential properties required for satisfying 'that p' will be *empty: All that is required is a certain reference*. So, relative to these contexts, the ascription functions like Quine's transparent one and ascribes a putative meaning as localistic as could be. The examples suggest further that, in many other contexts, the required set of inferential properties will be a *small* proportion of the inferential properties of the subject's token. So, once again, what is ascribed is localistic. Consider three of Stich's examples as illustrations: In certain contexts, Stich claims, we would be willing to attribute to a color-blind person who pulls a green lever the belief that it is red; and to an ignorant child the belief that $E = mc^2$ (1983: 86); and to Mrs. T the belief that McKinley was assassinated (p. 94). Very little is required of these subjects in these contexts. The properties ascribed are localistic.

If a context-dependency view of the sort that Stich seems to have in mind were right then its main consequence for meaning would be that the folk ascribe many different putative meanings to a token. The case for context dependency does not show that *any* of the properties ascribed are holistic, let alone that they all are. The evidence suggests that, once the context has been fixed, what property a person ascribes will always be localistic and will often be just the referent.

One further theory of attitude ascriptions must be considered. It is attractive to those who think that what a t-clause ascribes is very context dependent and who have the usual view that if a token has a meaning it has just one. It is the theory that t-clauses do not really ascribe meanings after all but rather *similarities in meaning*.[10] The simplest and most plausible version of the theory

claiming to show that nobody is really bald. Other considerations are also brought in favor of the conclusion that our *ascriptions* are of similarities (pp. 86–8, 92–3, 95–106).

10 For some suggestions along these lines, see Harman 1973: 109; P. M. Churchland 1979: 53–4, 76; Stich 1983: 85–92; Block 1986: 624.

takes an ascription to affirm that the subject's token is similar in meaning to the token content sentence (cf. the intimate link).

On this theory, the folk do not ascribe meanings at all; a fortiori they do not ascribe holistic ones. So, the theory *could* give no support to doctrines like DESCRIPTIVE SEMANTIC HOLISM. In any case, the theory is incoherent. Its idea that we ascribe similarities in meaning differs only verbally from the context-dependency view of ascriptions we have been discussing. So the idea is inconsistent with the theory's denial that we ascribe meanings.

If x is similar to y then it is similar in some respect: It is similar in virtue of sharing some property with y. Where x and y are similar in respect of meaning, then the shared property is precisely what the earlier view would call "a meaning" (provided that the property does indeed play a semantic role). So, to say that a t-clause ascribes to a token a similarity-in-respect-of-meaning to the content sentence, the respect being determined by the context, is much the same as saying that the clause ascribes to the token a meaning that is one of the meanings of the content sentence, the one determined by the context.[11]

Along the same lines, the claim that what we ordinarily call "that p" are really just tokens that are grouped together in a certain area of "similarity space" also implies that we are ascribing a putative meaning. For, ascribing something that is thus grouped in that area would be precisely what it was to ascribe that meaning.

In conclusion, application of the "ultimate" method to the descriptive issue has shown that tokens to which we ascribe the same property for semantic purposes – the same putative meanings – share few if any inferential properties: DESCRIPTIVE SEMANTIC LOCALISM is correct.

11   Fodor makes a related point (1987: 58–9), crediting R. McClamrock.

3.10. The Normative/Basic Issue

Whatever properties we *do* ascribe for semantic purposes, perhaps the ones we *ought to* ascribe are holistic; perhaps, NORMATIVE SEMANTIC HOLISM is correct. Assuming, as we are, that a property is a meaning if and only if it is one that we ought to ascribe for semantic purposes (2.6), SEMANTIC HOLISM would follow. And the localistic properties that we currently ascribe for semantic purposes – the putative meanings we have just been investigating – would turn out not to be ones we should ascribe and hence not to be meanings. The case for this sort of holism is no better in semantics than it is anywhere else.

The simplest argument against this holism is an application of the methodology of the last chapter (2.9): "the argument from the success of our ascriptions." Our current ascriptions of certain properties successfully serve semantic purposes: They are successful in explaining behavior and in guiding our opinions about reality. (I set aside revisionist doubts about this until Chapter 5.) This is very good evidence that we ought to ascribe those properties for semantic purposes and hence that they are meanings. Those properties are localistic, as we have just seen. So, at least, not all meanings are holistic and SEMANTIC HOLISM is false.

What about TYPE SEMANTIC HOLISM? There is no need for the localist to be very concerned about this doctrine because it is so mild that its meanings may be localistic: Only a few of the inferential properties of any token may be believed typical of tokens with a Type-Holist meaning (1.14). Nevertheless, it is worth noting that the argument from the success of our ascriptions even counts against this holism. We saw that it is often the case that the number of inferential properties commonly believed to be typical of tokens to which the folk ascribe a putative meaning is too small to constitute the distinctive meaning of those tokens (3.8). So the argument counts against the view that we ought to ascribe only Type-Holist properties. Furthermore, we found no support for TYPE HOLISM outside semantics (3.7).

The argument from the success of our ascriptions puts us well on the way to establishing SEMANTIC LOCALISM. We are not quite there, however, because LOCALISM claims that *all* meanings are localistic: Perhaps there are holistic meanings that we should ascribe *as well as* the localistic ones that we do ascribe. I note, first, the absence of any argument to show that this is indeed the case – to show that the ascription of "new" holistic properties would serve our semantic purposes. The LOCALIST can do better than this. Drawing on the discussion in part II, I shall offer an independent argument that we should *never* ascribe a holistic property for semantic purposes. This is "the argument from our interest in generality." Unlike the previous argument, it makes no assumption about the nature of our semantic purposes. I begin with two preliminary points.

First, in discussing the issue elsewhere, I emphasized our freedom of choice: We can name and ascribe any property we like, however holistic or localistic (3.6). So we can abstract from differences between planets, between echidnas, between capitalists, between pains, and between wheels, focusing on properties that are in common. I emphasized this because people write as if things were different in semantics, as if we were somehow *compelled* to take account of each difference in ascribing meanings. Elsewhere we can respond selectively to a complex reality, but with meanings we have no choice: It is all or nothing.[12]

Second, there is undoubtedly something confusingly different about our choices having to do with meanings. This arises from the apparent intimate link between the putative meaning ascribed and a property of the content sentence of the ascribing t-clause (2.12). Consider the implications of this at the level of words. Once we understand a word, we *already have a name* to ascribe a putative meaning to a token of the word (and to a token of any synonymous word) because we can use a token of it in a t-clause. So we do not, as a matter of fact, usually choose to name the putative meanings of word tokens the way we have, for example,

---

12 Stich's discussion of Helen Keller is particularly striking in this respect (1991: 248–9).

123

chosen to name the properties of planets. But, of course, we *could* choose to name putative meanings any way we like, for example, by assigning numerals to them. And, to the extent that a t-clause is context dependent, we can choose which putative meaning we want to ascribe with it.

Should we ever ascribe a holistic property for semantic purposes? Our discussion of choices showed that whether our purposes are explanatory, practical, or perhaps even frivolous, we tend to ascribe properties that are localistic because only localistic properties have the sort of generality we are interested in; localistic properties are likely to be shared by many objects (3.7). This yields the simplest, least theory-laden, argument against normative semantic holisms: *An interest in generality accompanies any semantic purpose we might have, and so we should always ascribe localistic properties.* This interest should lead us to properties that can be specified by localistic-Ramsey sentences (if by Ramsey sentences at all) just as it has led us in economics and psychology.[13]

It must be admitted that this argument from generality does not count decisively against ascribing Cluster-Holist properties and does not count at all against ascribing Negative-Holist properties. Yet, in semantics as elsewhere, we lack any motivation *for* choosing to ascribe these properties rather than the simpler localistic properties.

In contrast to this localistic recommendation, consider what NORMATIVE EXTREME SEMANTIC HOLISM recommends: that we should ascribe a property for semantic purposes that is likely to be unique to a time slice of an individual. This would be a pointless thing to do, *whatever our purposes.* In ascribing

---

13 This argument is related to one suggested by Dummett (1973: 599–600) and by Fodor and Lepore (1992: 8–9). Holistic meanings would be so difficult to learn, teach, and use. The problem is, briefly, that understanding a word with a holistic meaning would require grasping a lot of theory: The more holistic the meaning, the more the theory that would have to be grasped; the more the likely variation from person to person, time to time; and so on.

properties to words, we want properties that are instantiated in the one person at different times, in different cognitive areas of the one mind, in different minds, and perhaps even in different types of mind. This alone will push us toward ascribing properties constituted by few if any inferential properties. Thus it is that we ascribe to tokens of 'bachelor', we may plausibly suppose, sometimes a meaning constituted simply by its referent and sometimes a meaning constituted by inferential properties that are as a matter of fact among the very few shared by those tokens in our linguistic community.

Syntactic properties are like meanings in ways that help to make this point. Consider two formal systems that have minor differences in their axioms and rules. In discussing these systems, it suits us to say that they both have "names," "variables," "one-place predications," and so on. So it suits us to use the same terms to talk about syntactic properties in the two systems. Yet if we were guided by the individualistic approach of the EXTREME HOLIST, we should not do this. He points out that what we call "variables" in the one system have different inferential roles from what we call "variables" in the other. Therefore we should ascribe different syntactic properties to them.

This sort of holism is possible but totally pointless. It suits our purposes to have a name for what all variables have in common, just as it does for what all planets, capitalists, or wheels have in common. It is convenient to have terms with that amount of generality. And there is nothing to stop our having them.

It is interesting to note that holists themselves usually show awareness that we have *some* choices. They take the meaning of a word to be constituted by inferential properties. Yet most holists – although, sadly, not all – do not take its meaning to be constituted by mere associations of ideas, affective tone, and the like. Why not? Presumably, because they think that these properties are not ones that we are interested in for semantic purposes. Exactly.

The argument I have been presenting rests on very little because a desire for generality is a consequence of any plausible semantic purpose. So, relative to any such purpose, we should choose to ascribe localistic meanings. But we can strengthen the case by considering a particular semantic purpose.

I have claimed that we ascribe meanings *to explain behavior*. Our explanatory purposes in economics lead us to abstract from differences to find commonalities (3.7). We should do the same in semantics. We look for what is common in the inferential properties of tokens in many individuals because common properties will, other things being equal, lead to common behavior. Meanings constituted in this localist way are suitable to be adverted to in the explanatory generalizations of psychology. In contrast, holistic meanings are destructive of psychology.[14]

The desire for generality is alone sufficient for normative localism, but it does not show *which* localistic meanings we ought to ascribe. Justifying the choice of properties to ascribe is a general problem in science, but, as I pointed out (3.7), it has nothing to do with the holism-localism dispute. It concerns our choice of one localistic property rather than another, not the choice of localistic ones rather than holistic ones.

What is the basis for our choice among the many localistic properties of a token? We could ascribe properties constituted by many different small sets of inferential properties, each of which would be localistic and many of which might satisfy our desire for generality. How do we choose? To answer analogous questions about the properties of **being an echidna, a wheel, a capitalist,** and so on, we looked to our purposes. And so we must here. We ascribe those localistic properties that we think serve our semantic purposes in explaining behavior and teaching us about the world. Our ascriptions are remarkably successful, good evidence that we are right in thinking this. So we have shown that we should choose to ascribe the particular localistic properties that we do ascribe.

The natures of these properties that we should ascribe is the main concern of section 3.12 and of the next chapter.

14 Fodor is particularly horrified by this consequence of holism (1987: 56–7).

I have presented two independent arguments for SEMANTIC LOCALISM. The argument from the success of our ascriptions began by establishing DESCRIPTIVE SEMANTIC LOCALISM: We ascribe only localistic properties for semantic purposes. Given the success of those ascriptions, we ought to ascribe at least those properties. So they are meanings. This is sufficient to reject SEMANTIC HOLISM, but it leaves us a little short of SEMANTIC LOCALISM: Perhaps there are *also* holistic meanings. The argument from our interest in generality concludes that there are not. Given this interest, it never suits our semantic purposes to ascribe holistic properties. These purposes provide the only principled basis we need for being localistic.

The two arguments are independent, but the second gives further support to the descriptive premise of the first. For, the second argues for normative localism without depending on the argument for descriptive localism. Given the success of our current practices of ascribing certain properties for semantic purposes, it is likely that the properties that we ought to ascribe will include those ones. So the evidence of the second argument that we should ascribe only localistic properties is further evidence that we do ascribe only those properties.

Finally, what about the mild TYPE SEMANTIC HOLISM? We began this section by noting that the argument from the success of our ascriptions counts against the doctrine. But the argument does not show that we never ascribe *any* Type-Holist meanings, nor that we ought not to; perhaps the meaning **BACHELOR** is such a meaning. And the argument from our interest in generality does not show that we should not either. However, any such meaning *may* also be localistic, and according to the latter argument *will* be localistic.

3.11. The Argument from Representationalism

My two arguments against semantic holism make, near enough, no appeal to any available theory in semantics. This is just as well because any such theory would be controversial in the current dispute. However, in this section, I will offer a third, more theory-laden, argument by considering the consequences of one overarching semantic theory. (I shall ignore NEGATIVE HOLISM here.)

I have called the theory "Representationalism." It is the view that meanings are entirely constituted by representational properties. The "representational properties" of a token include any property that plays a role in determining what it represents. So the meaning of *a sentence* is exhausted by the properties that determine its *truth conditions*.[15] And the meaning of *a word* is exhausted by properties that determine its *reference*. The 'Fido'-Fido theory – recently embraced for some words by the "direct-reference" movement – is an extreme version: The meaning simply is the property of referring to its referent. Representationalism need not be so extreme, counting a word's *mode* of reference as a referential property and hence a candidate for meaning. Thus, it allows meanings to be constituted by inferential properties provided those properties are also referential; that is, provided the Fregean assumption (1.5) holds. It also allows one view of narrow meanings, the view that these meanings are functions that, given an external context as argument, yield a wide truth-referential meaning as value. (Narrow meanings will be discussed in Chapter 5.) Representationalism excludes from word meaning only those properties that are not part of reference determination.

Representationalism is a basic theory about what meanings *are*. So it is also a normative theory about what properties we ought to ascribe for semantic purposes. And, assuming that the properties we do ascribe for those purposes are indeed meanings, it is also a descriptive theory.

Representationalism is catastrophic for all the holistic semantic doctrines we have characterized because *no word meaning fully constituted by referential properties is holistic*. Yet, Representationalism

15 Not quite. A sentence represents some situation that would make it true, complied with, or whatever, but it also asserts that the situation obtains, requests that the situation be brought about, or whatever; a sentence has "a force." I shall overlook these forces.

is a venerable theory that still enjoys considerable theoretical support, despite the popularity of holism. In my view, Representationalism is correct. Arguing for it will be a central concern of the next two chapters.[16]

The conflict between Representationalism and holism is obvious where the reference of a word is not determined by *any* of its inferential properties. If no such property determines the word's reference then none constitutes its meaning. So, a fortiori, no significant proportion does, and any kind of holism must be false for that word. It is likely that many words will be of this sort given that not every word can depend for its reference on links to other words (1.2, 4.5). The 'Fido'-Fido theory is one that fits this sort of a word: The word's meaning simply is its role of referring to something. I seem to be almost alone in taking seriously the possibility of another theory that fits: The meaning of a word is its mode of referring even though that mode is not constituted by the word's inferential properties; the mode is constituted by the word's direct causal relations to its referent. I shall consider the difference between these two theories in relation to proper names later (4.5–4.8).

The conflict is less obvious if the constitutive referential properties include inferential properties: The inferential properties that determine the reference of a word constitute the meaning in question (cf. the Fregean assumption). This is the typical view of those who give a "description theory" of reference for the word (although one *might* give a description theory of reference that

16 Representationalism in semantics should not be confused with the related "representational theory of the mind." The latter is usually taken to be the view that a thought is an attitude toward a mental representation. I subscribe to this view too. Indeed, given my semantic Representationalism, the view is implicit in my discussion of thoughts (2.4–2.5). However, the representational theory of the mind does not entail semantic Representationalism. It entails that a thought involves a representation and hence that representational properties are *part of* meaning, but it does not entail that those properties *exhaust* meaning. Thus, a two-factor theorist (1.5; to be discussed further in 4.9) subscribes to the representational theory of the mind but not to semantic Representationalism.

129

was not a theory of meaning). The conflict emerges in two distinct ways.

1. Set aside cluster holisms for a moment. The first problem that the description theory poses for holism is, in effect, set out earlier in the discussion of the Fregean assumption (1.5): If a large proportion of each word's inferential properties determined its reference, then any significant error in a person's theory would be likely to lead to the reference failure of all her words. And with loss of reference would go loss of the world. Holism can be saved in the face of this only at the cost of a bizarre metaphysics: The theory is not really in error, and reference does not really fail because the theory is true "for its world," a world of its own construction. Such antirealism should not be contemplated. So, reference is not determined by a large proportion of a word's inferential properties. So meaning is not constituted by a large proportion.

The earlier-mentioned "arguments from ignorance and error" against description theories of reference push us further from holism (3.8). These arguments demonstrate the extent of human ignorance and error, thus raising a difficulty not just for the description theories of names and natural-kind terms against which they are primarily aimed, but for description theories in general. They push us away from holism because the more holistic a description theory is, the greater the difficulty. For, the more holistic it is, the greater the number of descriptions involved in determining reference, hence the more likely that ignorance and error would lead to reference failure or the wrong referent. In sum, reference is determined by at most a few inferential properties. So meaning is constituted by at most a few.

In the face of these considerations, the only holistic description theory with any plausibility would be a cluster theory, for such a theory can allow fairly extensive error without reference failure. However, it is no help with ignorance. And error is so extensive that even a cluster theory would have trouble with it.

2. In part II, I have argued that the worldly properties we

ascribe are localistic. This has consequences for referential theories of meaning, including description theories. Briefly, *if a worldly property is localistic then the meaning that represents that property must be localistic also.* Consider the meaning **WHEEL,** for example. In accepting that referential properties constitute this meaning we accept that, necessarily, a token that has the meaning refers to x if and only if x has the property **being a wheel** (because that is part of what it *is* to have the meaning **WHEEL**). Suppose that **being a wheel** is indeed **being a circular frame or disk that revolves on its axis.** Then anything that has the meaning **WHEEL** must refer to objects that have the property **being a circular frame or disk that revolves on its axis** and to nothing else "in each possible world." So, on the description theory, inferential properties that serve to pick out an object in virtue of its being a circular frame or disk that revolves on its axis could be constitutive of meaning **WHEEL** *but not any other inferential properties*; any other properties would give a token with that meaning *the wrong referent.* As a result, it is likely that the constitutive inferential properties will include, at most, those of being inferentially related to tokens with the meaning **CIRCULAR,** the meaning **FRAME,** and so on. So the localistic nature of **being a wheel** implies the localistic nature of the meaning **WHEEL.**

In sum, the problems of ignorance and error and the localistic nature of the worldly properties that interest us show that a Representationalist theory cannot be holistic. So, if there is to be any theoretical support for holism, it must come from theories that are to some degree not representational, theories according to which word meanings are not *only* referential; the Fregean assumption must be abandoned. Three theoretical alternatives seem possible. First, a theory might hold that word meanings are not fully referential; they are partly constituted by referential properties and partly by inferential properties that do not determine reference. It might be possible then to be holistic about the meanings in virtue of being holistic about their nonreferential parts. Second, a theory might hold that some meanings are referential and some are not. It might be possible then to be holistic about the latter. Two-factor theories (1.5) can be seen as exemplifying one or other of these first two "semi-Representationalist" alternatives. Third, a theory might hold that meanings are entirely nonreferential, "anti-Representationalism." It might be possible then to be holistic about those meanings. Verificationist and "use" theories tend to exemplify this alternative.

In the rest of this book, I shall be presenting a case for Representationalism and against these three alternatives.

3.12. Representationalism and the Principled Basis

It is thought that the no-principled-basis consideration makes molecular semantic localism untenable. My response to this has been as follows (3.2). If this consideration is concerned with the descriptive issue, it should be dismissed: We need no basis. If it is concerned with the normative/basic issue then it is mistaken: We have a basis. The basis is that localistic but not holistic properties play semantic roles and are ones we should ascribe for semantic purposes. How do we know this? First, because our current practice of ascribing localistic properties for semantic purposes is a success. Second, because our interest in generality, whatever the area, is served by ascribing localistic properties.

This response is sufficient for the problem that has impressed so many: What is the principled basis for molecular localism? But this problem is accompanied by another: What is the principled basis for ascribing some but not other localistic properties to a token? What makes some but not other localistic properties *meanings?* My response to this has been similar. The basis is that ascribing some but not other localistic properties serves our semantic purposes. How do we know this? Our answer cannot appeal to an interest in generality because ascribing any localistic property would be likely to serve that interest. However, we can appeal again to the success of our current practices. Ascribing the localistic properties that we do *works:* It explains behavior and helps inform us about the world. So we have good reason to think that ascribing those properties serves our purposes. We have no reason as yet for thinking that ascribing other localistic properties would serve our purposes.

We could leave it at that, but it is interesting to pursue the matter further. What is it about the localistic properties that we ascribe that *makes* them serve our semantic purposes and hence *makes* them meanings? What do all the sets of inferential properties that constitute those meanings have in common? Let K be some set that we do *not* ascribe. What would make it the sort of property we *should* ascribe for semantic purposes? To answer these questions, we need more theory. We need the beginnings, at least, of a theory of what meanings *are*.

Representationalism is such a theory. According to it, the localistic properties we ascribe are meanings because they determine reference. K would be the sort of property we should ascribe if its inferential properties determined reference (cf. the Fregean assumption).

So Representationalism yields a further, more theory-laden, criterion for distinguishing the inferential properties that constitute meanings from the others.[17] This criterion does not come "out of the blue": It is essential to Representationalism. I have emphasized that all meanings cannot be constituted solely by inferential properties: Some place must be found for direct causal links to reality. Consider a meaning constituted by such links. Why should we ascribe *that* property to a word rather than one constituted by any of the many other direct causal links the word has to reality? This is analogous to the question that we are addressing: Why should we ascribe a property constituted by one set of inferential properties rather than one constituted by others?

17 Note that contrary to what Lepore and Fodor claim in replying to my 1993a the criterion does not "assume that inferential role determines reference" (1993: 674). Rather, it assumes that *if* an inferential role determines reference, *then* it constitutes a meaning. In other words, it meets their challenge to molecularism to provide a criterion.

A strength of Representationalism is that it gives the one good answer to both questions: We should ascribe only properties constituted by properties that determine reference.[18]

Fodor takes word meaning to be constituted entirely by direct causal links to reality, giving inferential properties no place. His main reason for this is the earlier-mentioned pessimism about finding a criterion for distinguishing those constitutive inferential properties from the others (3.1). Ironically, a criterion that would do the only job that needs doing is already at work in his theory distinguishing the constitutive causal links to reality that are of interest to us from the others.[19]

The Representationalist can explain why our semantic purposes are served by ascribing some localistic properties and not others. Those with a different view of meaning – for example, a two-factor view – must give a different explanation. The difficulty in finding such an explanation is a symptom of the implausibility of non-Representationalist theories. Once we set aside the determination of a word's reference, there is no reason for thinking that our semantic purposes will be served by ascribing properties constituted one way rather than another out of the word's inferen-

18 Lepore and Fodor claim that this is not one answer but "just a sort of pun." Their reason for thinking this describes the molecularist as "a sense theorist . . . making what he takes to be a conceptual point" (1993: 674). I do not recognize the molecularism I am defending in this description. The sense of "determine" is exactly the same in answering each question.

Responding to my 1993b, Levine also raises problems about my use of "determine" (1993: 113–17). I mean by it just what it ordinarily means: an object's having x determines that it has y if and only if it is in virtue of having x that it has y.

19 There is a deeper irony. Fodor is committed to direct reference (to be discussed later; 4.8). In this view, the meaning of, say, 'Cicero', is simply its property of referring to Cicero: That it has a certain (noninferential) *mode of referring,* one that distinguishes it from 'Tully', is irrelevant to its meaning. The deeper irony is that, although Fodor insists that the molecular localist provide a principled basis for her discrimination against some inferential properties, he does not seem to recognize any need to provide a principled basis for his own discrimination against modes.

tial properties; we lack the criterion we need. (This may partly explain the appeal of the no-principled-basis consideration; 3.3.) I return to this in section 5.11.

In the previous section I used Representationalism to refute semantic holism. But we do not need Representationalism to achieve this: The two arguments that have taken up most of this chapter – the argument from the success of our ascriptions and the argument from our interest in generality – will do the job. In this section I have used Representationalism to provide a principled basis for distinguishing the localistic properties of a token that are its meanings from its other localistic properties. But, once again, we do not need Representationalism to achieve this: The argument from our semantic purposes will do the job (3.2).[20]

A vast amount remains to be done in semantics. I have presented three independent arguments that it should be done localistically. The evidence for any one localistic semantic theory is decidedly underwhelming, but the evidence for localism in general, in particular for SEMANTIC LOCALISM, is overwhelming.

20 Cf. my 1993a, which fails to offer the argument from our semantic purposes and relies solely on Representationalism for a principled basis.

4

Meanings and their ascription

I. A REPRESENTATIONALIST PROGRAM

4.1. Representationalism

In the last chapter I have argued against the holistic threat to semantic localism. I have claimed that we ascribe localistic properties to our words for semantic purposes (descriptive), that we ought to do so (normative), and hence that these properties are meanings (basic). This raises the question: *Which* localistic properties do we and ought we to ascribe for semantic purposes? That question will be my main concern in this chapter. Certain well-known arguments for eliminativism and revisionism will be set aside until the next chapter. My aim is to present a localistic program rather than a detailed theory.

The program I shall be presenting will be Representationalist. Representationalism is the view that meanings are entirely constituted by "representational" properties (3.11). So the meaning of *a sentence* is exhausted by the properties that determine its *truth conditions.*[1] And the meaning of *a word* is exhausted by properties that determine its *reference*. Representationalism made an appearance in Chapter 1 in the guise of the Fregean assumption, but it played only a minor role in the critique of the case for holism. In Chapter 3, I argued that Representationalism counted decisively against holism, but I did not rest my case for localism on it. In the rest of this book, with holism rejected, I shall be arguing for Representationalism.

---

1   I am overlooking "forces"; see 3.11, n. 15.

I start by noting just how plausible Representationalism is, as the history of semantics demonstrates. Indeed, has Representationalism ever been doubted before this century? Its appeal is reflected in the very words we use to pick out the objects that have meanings: We call them "symbols" or "representations." There are other considerations that add to its initial plausibility.

The properties we ascribe with t-clauses seem to serve our semantic purposes and hence be meanings. In the last Chapter, without argument, I proposed that these properties serve the purposes because they are representational (3.12). Here is a little argument. One purpose is to use the thoughts and utterances of others as a guide to the world. If thoughts and utterances represent the world, and are reliable enough, then it is not surprising that ascribing their representational properties serves our purpose. Another purpose is to explain behavior. If people represent the world in their thoughts and utterances, then the way that they represent it will affect their behavior, for their behavior is *directed toward* the world as they represent it. So it will serve the purpose to ascribe the way that they represent it. This argument is only little, of course, because it may also serve those purposes to ascribe other properties of thoughts and utterances.

We can go further by considering the following questions: What does having meaningful thoughts and utterances do for an organism? What are meanings *for*? These questions should not be confused with the earlier one about our semantic purposes: In effect, this was the question, "Why do we ascribe meanings?" (2.5). The contrast is like that between "What are hammers for?" and "Why do we ascribe *being a hammer?*," between "What are hearts for?" and "Why do we ascribe *being a heart?*," and between "What are planets for?" and "Why do we ascribe *being a planet?*" The ascription question in each pair is always appropriate. The other question is appropriate only about things that can reasonably be thought to have a *function* of some sort. So it is clearly appropriate about hammers, arguably appropriate about hearts, and clearly inappropriate about planets. I think that it is appropriate about meanings and that the plausible answer to the question is a representational one: The function of meanings is to represent aspects of the world of interest to the organism. (I shall not venture an opinion on how this talk of function is to be explained.)

An organism has a range of basic needs. Representing its environment leads to responses that help it to satisfy those needs. Humans have a capacity for highly complex interrelated representations, manipulated in a variety of subtle ways in thinking and leading to remarkably flexible responses to the environment. This capacity has been largely responsible for the success of the species so far.

The representational properties of primitive organisms must be constituted in some way from involuntary actual or potential causal relations between the organism and what is represented. At bottom, this must also be true for humans. However, as our discussion of the naming of properties illustrates (3.6), we have the power to build on this involuntary basis by bestowing meanings. Stipulative definitions like mine of 'peorincred' provide uncontroversial examples of this bestowal. More interestingly, we put ourselves in the way of causal interactions with the world by traveling, probing, experimenting, building, and so on and with each other by communicating, all partly with the intention of creating representations of the world. For this creative process is an essential part of our deliberate attempt to discover what the world is like and to manipulate it.

This initial case for Representationalism is of course far from decisive. Perhaps ascribing nonrepresentational properties could serve our semantic purposes. Perhaps meanings can be seen as having some other function or none at all. I shall be attempting to throw doubt on both these possibilities in the argument to follow.

I shall continue to argue for my Representationalist program in the rest of this part of the chapter. In part II, I shall defend the program by criticizing its rivals: first, the more extreme Representationalism of direct reference, which urges a 'Fido'-Fido, or Millian, theory for names (4.7–4.8); second, the "semi-Representationalism" of two-factor theories (4.9); third, the "anti-Representationalism" of verificationalist and "use" theories (4.10). In part III, I shall consider "second-level" meanings, meanings of the attitude ascriptions that ascribe the "first-level" meanings that have, until then, been the subject of discussion. In part IV, I shall develop the program by considering various puzzles, including those due to Mark Richard, Hector-Neri Castañeda, and Saul Kripke.

A sentence represents the situation that would make it true. So in seeking a Representationalist semantics, we seek one in the spirit of the slogan "The meaning of a sentence is its truth condition": We seek a truth-conditional semantics. Many semantics of this sort have been proposed. I have proposed one myself (1981a). The semantic program that I shall be offering in this part of the chapter differs from all these. One notable difference is its claim that tokens have more than one meaning (4.2–4.3). With this claim goes a partial acceptance and partial rejection of two influential views of singular terms: first, the 'Fido'-Fido view that a (simple) token's only meaning is its property of referring to its bearer; second, the Fregean view that a token's only meaning is its "mode of presenting" its bearer. I shall argue that all singular tokens, simple *and complex,* have both meanings. I shall agree with Frege that the meaning that is a mode *may* be descriptive, involving inferential links to other terms; thus, I shall be arguing for a molecular rather than an atomistic localism. I shall disagree with Frege, and just about everybody else, in arguing that some meanings are nondescriptive causal modes of reference (4.5–4.6). However, I shall be rather fashionable in accepting the language-of-thought hypothesis (4.4).

A version of truth-conditional semantics has been made popular by Davidson (1984), but his approach is very different from the ones I shall be considering. From his "interpretative" perspective, the semantic task is to *say how to construct theories of interpretation* (2.7). From the "factual" perspective that I favor, the task is to *explain meanings.* Each sentence's property of being true if and only if a certain situation obtains – its property of having certain truth conditions – is central to that explanation. This property itself must then be explained in terms of the structural properties of the sentence and the referential properties of its words. These properties must then be explained in turn. In particular, we need theories of reference. The interpretative perspective makes no such explanatory demands.

My concern here is not with the details of these explanations. So there will be only a little, for example, on the explanation of reference. My concern is the more programmatic one of arguing for the broad outlines of a Representationalist theory with the features just mentioned. In arguing this I shall of course follow the four methodological proposals of Chapter 2: that we should tackle the basic task of explaining the natures of meanings by tackling the normative one of explaining the natures of the properties we ought to ascribe for semantic purposes; that we should look to the descriptive task of explaining the natures of the properties we do ascribe for semantic purposes for evidence for the normative/basic one; that we should use the "ultimate" method on meanings to accomplish the descriptive task; that we should "put metaphysics first." I shall start by using the "ultimate" method on the descriptive task.

My main examples of meaningful sentence tokens will be beliefs, but I take the discussion to generalize to other thoughts and to utterances. My focus will be on the part of the meaning of a sentence that is ascribed to it by a singular term in a t-clause. On a few occasions, I shall briefly confront the fact that this term might be empty, but I shall mostly not clutter my discussion with qualifications to take account of this fact. Also, I shall mostly, but not always, ignore "tacit" beliefs (ones held but not entertained) and thoughts that cannot be expressed in a public language.

4.2. The Descriptive Issue

The "ultimate" method has two stages (2.11). First, we must identify some apparently uncontroversial examples of tokens with, and of tokens without, the putative meaning, P, a property we ascribe for semantic purposes using 'that p'. Second, we must examine the examples to see what is common and peculiar to the tokens with that property. We count the folk as experts at identification and count ourselves among the folk. Thought experiments have a role.

I shall draw on Quine's earlier-mentioned (2.8, 3.9) classic discussion of attitude ascriptions.[2] The discussion concerns the roles of definite and indefinite singular terms, and some subtle issues about "quantifying in."[3] I shall draw only on the part that concerns definite singular terms. The discussion is a series of thought experiments about the truth conditions of attitude ascriptions. It is naturally taken to bear on the theory of the meanings of *those ascriptions,* a topic that we will take up later (part III). But, using the "ultimate" method, we shall see that it also bears on a theory of *the meanings ascribed;* in particular, on a theory of the part of P ascribed by singular terms.

According to Quine, most attitude ascriptions are mildly context dependent. That is the basis of the view I shall urge in the next few sections. Others have claimed that these ascriptions are much more radically context dependent. I shall argue against these views later (4.11).

Suppose that Ralph's suspicions have been raised by a certain man in a brown hat whom Ralph has glimpsed several times under questionable circumstances. As a result, Ralph says, "The man in the brown hat is a spy." The man is, in fact, Ortcutt. However, Ralph does not know this and would not assent to "Ortcutt is a spy." Now consider,

(1) Ralph believes that Ortcutt is a spy.

Quine noted that there seemed to be two ways of interpreting (1). On the first, in the situation described, the sentence is false. On the second, it is true. On the first, which he called "opaque," 'Ortcutt' is not "used as a means simply of specifying its object"

---

2 Quine 1953: 139–59; 1960: 141–51, 166–9; 1966: 183–94.
3 See Kaplan 1986 for an elegant and learned discussion of these subtleties.

and is not subject to "the law of substitutivity of identity." On the second, which he called "transparent," the opposite is the case.

How can we learn about the putative meanings ascribed from this discussion? To judge that '*x* believes that *p*' would be true (false) in certain circumstances is to judge that we would (would not) in those circumstances call a certain mental token "that *p*." Thus the judgment provides evidence of what is common and peculiar to tokens with the property *P*, the evidence sought by the "ultimate" method. And the property ascribed for semantic purposes is a meaning provided that, contra revisionism, it does indeed play a semantic role.

What then *do* we learn from the discussion? The ambiguity of (1) seems to demonstrate nicely the truth and falsity in both a 'Fido'-Fido theory and a Fregean theory. Construed opaquely, the things that utterers of (1) call "that Ortcutt is a spy" seem to have in common not merely the property of referring to Ortcutt but a certain *mode* of referring to him, the mode exemplified by the name 'Ortcutt' in (1) itself. A sentence in Ralph's "belief box" that would make (1) true would contain 'Ortcutt', a token with a property of referring to Ortcutt by that mode. A Fregean theory posits such "fine-grained" meanings (ignoring, as I mostly shall, that its meanings tended to be objects rather than properties; secs. 2.4, 4.12). On the other hand, it seems that (1) can be understood in a transparent way with substitutivity applying to it. On this construal, the things that utterers of (1) call "that Ortcutt is a spy" seem to have in common only the property of referring to Ortcutt. A sentence in Ralph's belief box that would make (1) true might contain any term with a putative meaning constituted by that property, perhaps the name 'Ortcutt', but perhaps some other term. A 'Fido'-Fido theory posits such "coarse-grained" meanings (ignoring, again, that its meanings tended to be objects rather than properties). 'Ortcutt' is a name, but if we test any definite singular term in the content sentence we seem to get the same result: Sometimes the ascription ascribes a coarse-grained meaning and sometimes a fine-grained. (If the term in the content sentence is a demonstrative or pronoun, the fine-grained meaning ascribed involves the "demonstrative" mode that such terms share but not necessarily the mode of that particular demonstrative or pronoun; see section 4.14.) And just as 'Ortcutt' or any other name in the belief box seems to have a property of both sorts so also does any other definite singular term, simple or complex. So, assuming that the properties ascribed do indeed play semantic roles, the Fregean theory and the 'Fido'-Fido theory are each right in claiming that a term has a meaning of the sort the theory posits but wrong in thinking that the term has only that sort of meaning.

So the discussion provides evidence that we ascribe more than one meaning to definite singular terms, as I have mentioned before (2.8, 3.9). It also provides evidence that all these meanings are referential, as Representationalism requires. However, caution is appropriate: Perhaps this appearance can be explained away by giving a deflationary interpretation of the talk of reference. I set this aside until section 4.10.

Quine made two further suggestions: (a) that the transparently construed (1) could be paraphrased along the lines of the explicitly transparent:

(2) Ortcutt is such that Ralph believes him to be a spy;

(b) that the "exportation" of a singular term involved in the move from the opaquely construed (1) to (2) was generally "implicative." But these suggestions seem to be mistaken.[4]

Consider (a). If we construe (1) in our straightforwardly transparent way, it would be true if Ralph had a belief he would express, "*x* is a spy," where the place of '*x*' was filled by *any singular term at all* that referred to Ortcutt. So it would be true if, for example, Ralph had a rather trivial belief that he would express, "the shortest spy is a spy" and Ortcutt should happen, unbeknownst to Ralph, to be that spy. Yet (2) seems to require more. There are various ways of trying to capture this extra requirement: Ralph must have "Ortcutt in particular in mind" in

---

4   The following argument is based on Sleigh 1967: 28; Kaplan 1968: 220.

expressing his belief; he must be "en rapport with" Ortcutt; his thought must have "a special sort of aboutness"; the thought must be "referential" and not merely "attributive." The property that (2) ascribes to Ralph's belief is different from the property that the straightforwardly transparent (1) ascribes, contrary to Quine's suggestion.

Consider (b). Suppose that Ralph had the above trivial belief. It would be true to say, opaquely,

(3) Ralph believes that the shortest spy is a spy.

Unrestricted exportation would allow us to infer

(4) The shortest spy is such that Ralph believes him to be a spy.

Yet (4) does not seem to follow from (3): (4), like (2), requires rapport with Ortcutt, whereas (3) does not. Some restriction on exportation seems to be required.[5]

Let us call the transparent (2), "rapport-transparent," and the straightforwardly transparent construal of (1), "simply-transparent" (often shortened to simply "transparent"). The difference between them lies in the scope of 'Ortcutt'. In the rapport-transparent (2), this scope includes 'believes' and so the scope is wide. In the simply-transparent (1), the scope does not include 'believes' and

---

5 In discussing these matters it is usual to talk of *"de dicto"* and *"de re."* I have argued that this talk is confusing, often confused, and unnecessary (1981c: 214–5; 1984: 388–90, 392–4). It is confusing because *'de dicto'* and *'de re'* are usually unexplained, seem to have several uses, and have misleading associations from their uses in talk about modalities. It is often confused, first, because the terms are applied indiscriminatively to ascriptions of thoughts and to the thoughts themselves. Second, because the application of *'de re'* to ascriptions conflates two very different ideas: that of being a transparent ascription and that of ascribing en rapport reference, something that can be done by *opaque* ascriptions; e.g., by the opaque (1). One pair of terms cannot capture the two distinctions that have emerged in this area: the distinction between the transparent and the opaque, which is about ascriptions of thoughts, and that between en rapport and attributive reference, which is primarily about the thoughts. The talk is unnecessary because we have other, relatively clear, terminology to mark the distinctions, as this discussion shows.

144

so the scope is narrow.[6] This discussion suggests that this scope difference makes a difference in the property ascribed.

Where does this discussion leave us? Many examples in the literature support Quine's view that all ascriptions like (1) and (3) have an opaque construal. Despite this, some direct-reference theorists have denied the view. I set this denial aside until section 4.8. So I take it that (1) and (3) can be construed as ascribing a property involving the mode of reference of the singular term in the content clause. I think that there is room for disagreement over (2) and (4), but, for the sake of argument, I shall also go along with the view that they ascribe a property involving rapport with Ortcutt and hence are appropriately called "rapport-transparent," and that there must be some restriction on exportation. The discussion suggests that there is a third sort of ascription in question, the simply-transparent construal of (1) and (3), and hence a third sort of putative meaning. Is there really? If not, then we have no evidence yet of the sort of meaning posited by the 'Fido'-Fido theory. And, if so, we have evidence that such meanings are more widespread than 'Fido'-Fido theories usually suppose: One of the meanings of a *complex* singular term – for example, 'the shortest spy' – is its property of referring to a certain object.

An example due to Stephen Schiffer[7] shows that there is indeed a simply-transparent construal of (1). Smith is found dead. Ralph, the famous sleuth, suspects murder. Furthermore, the manner of the slaying makes him think that whoever is responsible is insane. A newspaper reports this:

6 Where the scope of 'Ortcutt' is wide, the scope of 'believes' is narrow, and vice versa. The focus in my 1984 on the scope of 'believes' led me to call the rapport-transparent "narrow-scope" and the simply-transparent "wide-scope."

7 (1979: 67). Sosa (1970: 890) has an example like Schiffer's. See also Pastin (1974). In effect, I am here defending what we might call, following Chisholm (1976: 9–10), a "latitudinarian" ascription of belief about an object. I have discussed Schiffer's example before with somewhat different results: 1981a: 273–4; 1981c: 220; 1984: 401–3.

(5) Ralph believes that Smith's murderer is insane.

The murder was in fact committed by a well-known mobster:

(6) Big Felix is Smith's murderer.

Big Felix's moll knows this. She reads the newspaper and remarks to one of the mob:

(7) Ralph believes that Big Felix is insane.

This seems clearly true. Yet, construed opaquely, it is not true because Ralph would not express his belief using 'Big Felix'. It is not true construed like (2), as rapport-transparent, because Ralph does not have anyone in particular in mind as the murderer. The truth of (7) seems to require the simply-transparent construal that allows Ralph to have his insanity belief of Big Felix under any mode of referring to him at all.

Extending the example confirms this. The moll says to Big Felix:

(8) Ralph believes that you are insane.

Big Felix says to a mobster:

(9) Ralph believes that I am insane.

The moll is talking to people who are fascinated by mobsters without knowing any. She rightly thinks that Big Felix is more successful than any other mobster and so thinks it appropriate to say:

(10) Ralph believes that the most successful mobster is insane.

Big Felix frequents a certain bar, as do Mary and Fiona. One evening, Mary overhears Big Felix's conversation and concludes that he murdered Smith. She reads the newspaper report of the murder and says to Fiona:

(11) Ralph believes that the man seen at the bar is insane.

There seems to be a way of understanding each of these so that Ralph's belief makes them true. Yet, for the same reasons as before, they cannot be true if they are opaque or rapport-transparent. The evidence suggests that *any term at all* that refers to the murderer can be substituted for the singular term in these t-clauses to yield a truth even though Ralph does not have a suspect in mind, that is, that there really is a simply-transparent construal. And, the particular mode under which Ralph represents Big Felix is irrelevant to the truth of ascriptions construed in this way. So an extreme 'Fido'-Fido theory, covering simple and complex singular terms, is correct about one of the meanings we ascribe (provided that what we ascribe really is a meaning).

I have argued that sentences like (1) have a simply-transparent construal as well as an opaque construal.[8] Do they also have a rapport-transparent construal, making them equivalent to sentences like (2), as Quine originally suggested? Are they three-way or only two-way ambiguous?

It will be difficult to find persuasive evidence of the rapport-transparent construal of sentences like (1). This construal would entail the simply-transparent: If Ralph has Ortcutt in mind in referring to him, then he is referring to him. So evidence of a nonopaque reading of (1) could be just evidence of the simply-

8 Richard is dubious: "To my knowledge, no one has ever given a very good reason for supposing that there is such an ambiguity" (1990: 131). I see the Big Felix example as strong evidence for the transparent reading. As noted, the literature is full of evidence for the opaque reading. Further developments of this case for the ambiguity are to be found later, particularly in section 4.3. The case is not undermined by Richard's criticism of Quine's worries about quantifying in (pp. 129–30) because it is not based on those worries. Nor is it undermined by Stich's earlier criticism focused on *indefinite* singular terms (1983: 111–23; 1986). Following Chastain (1975) and Wilson (1978), Stich thinks that these terms are ambiguous, functioning sometimes in the Russellian way as quantifiers and sometimes "referentially." He argues that the appearance of ambiguity in attitude ascriptions arises from this. I agree that these terms are ambiguous (Devitt and Sterelny 1987: 85), but my case for the ambiguity of ascriptions does not involve them; it involves *definite* singular terms. Moreover, I would argue that the same ambiguity can be found in ascriptions involving indefinite ones: Replace 'Ortcutt' in (1) with a 'a man in a brown hat', *construed referentially,* and the resulting ascription has both a transparent and an opaque reading.

147

transparent. To establish that there is also a rapport-transparent construal we need cases where the sentence is true on a transparent construal yet it seems false *and that falsity cannot be explained by an opaque construal.* We must look for cases where the subject's mode is the same as the ascriber's so that the falsity cannot be blamed on opacity. This mode cannot involve rapport for if it does the ascription will not be false on a rapport-transparent construal. It does not seem obvious that a sentence meeting these constraints comes out false on any construal. Consider the earlier sentence, for example:

(5) Ralph believes that Smith's murderer is insane.

It is not obvious that there is any way of understanding this so that it is false in the circumstances.

Whether or not sentences like (1) and (5) have a rapport-transparent construal, we are going along with the idea that sentences like (2) and (4) do. So, little seems to hang on this issue. I shall assume that the sentences like (1) and (5) do not have this construal and so are only two-way ambiguous.

I conclude that the examples we have discussed provide persuasive evidence that the folk ascribe at least three different sorts of putative meaning to a definite singular term: the property of (purportedly) referring to a specified object under a specified mode (opaque ascription); the property of referring to a specified object (simply-transparent ascription); the property of referring en rapport to a specified object (rapport-transparent ascription). So, strictly, if these putative meanings really are meanings then we should talk not of "the meaning" of a token but of its "meaning set"; and to understand a token is to associate the right set with it. But mostly I shall not be so strict.[9]

9   What does all this show about the so-called relational sense of belief that relates a believer to an object? In my view, believing is a relation between a person and a sentence token. Ascriptions of belief say *which type* of token the person is related to. So, *primarily*, (1) does not affirm a relation between Ralph and Ortcutt. However, *derivatively*, it may. For, the type in question is a meaning. It may be a consequence of being related to a sentence with a

Aside from this it is apparent that a sentence like

(12) Ralph believes that someone is insane

ascribes a different sort of putative meaning to a singular term. It is a property that *in*definite singular terms like 'someone' have: the property of referring to some person or other. The question arises whether this is also a further putative meaning of *definite* singular terms. It does seem that the fact that Ralph has 'Smith's murderer is insane' in his belief box is sufficient to make (12) true; it seems that we would also call this sentence, "that someone is insane." We could go along with this but there is a good reason for not doing so. It arises from a fact that I said I would mostly ignore: that most of a person's beliefs are "tacit" in being ones that she never entertains. She believes her *core* beliefs and any others she is disposed to infer readily from those core ones (Dennett 1978; Field 1978). So, the sentence 'Smith's murderer is insane' in Ralph's belief box makes (12) true not in virtue of 'Smith's murderer' sharing a putative meaning with 'someone' but in virtue of Ralph's disposition to infer 'someone is insane' from the sentence.

The evidence of attitude ascriptions produced in this section suggests that the putative meanings of singular terms are all referential. This confirms Representationalism as a descriptive doctrine. I predict that we would get further confirmation of this if we looked to attitude ascriptions for evidence about general terms, mass terms, and so on. In so doing we would make use of the distinction between "extensional" and "intensional" contexts, the more general distinction of which the transparent-opaque distinction is an instance. This examination would show that the folk

certain meaning that one is related to Ortcutt. Indeed that is straightforwardly the case with the meaning specified by the simply-transparent construal of (1). On that construal, (1) can then be taken as affirming a relation between Ralph, Ortcutt, and a certain type of predicate token. The rapport-transparent (2), in contrast, is only open to a complicated relational construal. And the opaquely construed (1) is not open to a relational construal at all because it may be true even though its singular term is empty.

ascribe to a token sometimes the property of having a certain extension[10] and sometimes the property of having a certain mode of (purportedly) referring to an extension. And I think that an examination would very likely yield a similar result about structure: evidence that the folk ascribe to a sentence sometimes the property of having a certain truth condition and sometimes the property of having a certain syntactic mode of presenting a truth condition; on occasion it may matter that the subject is disposed to assent to "If not q then not p" and not merely to "If p then q."

If I am right about all this, it presents a strong case that Representationalism is descriptively correct. I have postponed until section 4.10 considering whether this case can be explained away by a deflationist.

4.3. The Normative/Basic Issue

We have found evidence for the descriptive thesis that we ascribe three sorts of properties to definite singular terms for semantic purposes. These putative meanings are *really* meanings if they play semantic roles and so are properties that we *ought to* ascribe for semantic purposes. On its face, this normative thesis is acceptable because our ascriptions of these properties seem to be successful: They explain and predict behavior or serve as guides to reality (2.9). So, on its face, the basic thesis that these properties are meanings is acceptable. In the next chapter, I will defend this

---

10 The Big Felix case exemplifies a general strategy for creating examples of extensional belief ascriptions. Thus, for an extensional construal of the context of 'F' in 'Ralph believes that x is an F', we imagine a situation where (i) Ralph has a belief he would express "x is a G"; (ii) 'G' is coextensive with 'F'; (iii) 'G' "means nothing" to the audience but 'F' does. It is worth noting, however, that even an extensionally ascribed meaning has some fineness of grain. So, very likely, Fred's readiness to assert "x has a liver" does not make 'Fred believes that x has a kidney' true; the ascribed meaning involves the extension of 'kidney' not simply the extension of 'has a kidney'. (Thanks to Frank Jackson.)

thesis against various revisionist and eliminativist considerations. Meanwhile, in this section, I shall attempt to add to the case for the thesis by looking further into how ascribing these putative meanings serves our purposes. This examination will also add to the evidence of the last section for the descriptive thesis: Given the success of our current ascriptions it is likely that any properties that we ought to ascribe will include the ones we do ascribe (2.10).

Set aside for a moment properties identified by rapport-transparent ascriptions. Our semantic purposes give us an immediate interest in properties identified by the opaque and the simply-transparent ascriptions.

Opaque ascriptions serve our purposes of explaining and predicting behavior:

when we articulate the generalizations in virtue of which behavior is contingent upon mental states, it is typically an opaque construal of the mental state attributions that does the work. (Fodor 1980a: 66)

For example, in his investigation of the murder, Ralph is careful to avoid, opaquely, anyone he suspects. He does this because he represents that person to himself as Smith's murderer; under another mode Ralph may be happy to keep the person company. So, in the generalization that covers this, the contexts that describe both the behavior and the belief must be opaque. Take the generalization to be: Ralph (indeed, anyone) tends to avoid *a* if he believes that *a* is insane. This generalization, together with

(5) Ralph believes that Smith's murderer is insane,

both construed opaquely, explain Ralph's behavior.

The opaquely described behaviors that meanings are supposed to explain are *intentional* behaviors (2.5); they are *actions*. We need opaquely ascribed properties to explain them. Later it will be necessary to say more about actions and their relation to thoughts (4.17).

Transparent ascriptions help us to learn about the world. If a

151

person has a belief about a certain object, and is reliable, then we can learn about that object from that belief, whatever the person's mode of representing the object. Thus, the moll's utterance,

(7) Ralph believes that Big Felix is insane,

can provide the mobster addressed with vital information about his world.

If transparent ascriptions serve our purpose of learning about reality, then opaque ones must be able to do so also, because opaque ones convey *additional* information: They tell us not only which object Ralph has his belief about but also under which mode he has the belief. Although this extra information is irrelevant to what most concerns us, *the truth condition* of the belief, it is relevant to *our assessment of the likelihood of the belief's being true* and hence of the object being as Ralph believes it to be. Ralph may be unreliable about Big Felix's insanity under one mode ('the man seen at the bar') but reliable under another ('Smith's murderer'). So the opaque form enables us to kill two birds with one stone.

Have we then shown that there is, after all, no need for transparent ascriptions, thus undermining our recent motivation? The vital information that the mobster gets from (7) shows that we have not. If the mobster knows that Big Felix murdered Smith then he would indeed have done a little better had the moll uttered the opaquely construed (5). But if he knows nothing of the murder of Smith, he would get no vital information from (5). "What," he is likely to think, "is Smith's murderer to me?" What matters most to the mobster is that he should identify the person who is the object of Ralph's insanity belief with someone playing an important role in the mobster's life. And, we may assume, the moll is trying to help with that identification. So, whatever the term for Big Felix that features in Ralph's belief, her first concern is to find a term for Big Felix that is familiar to the mobster. The transparent (7) serves the purpose of guiding the mobster to reality where the opaque (5) would fail. Similarly, the transparent

(11) Ralph believes that the man seen at the bar is insane

152

guides Fiona where (5) would not. The opaque form provides bonus information about Ralph's mode of representing Big Felix, but that bonus is useless if the main message does not get through. The transparent form gets it through.

Note that the fact that the moll needs to use a term that is familiar to the mobster for her message to be effective casts no doubt on the transparency of her utterance: She would need to do this also in choosing between such paradigms of transparency as "Big Felix is insane" and "Smith's murderer is insane" in order to express *her own* opinion.

Transparent ascriptions are needed to guide us to reality, although opaque ascriptions also serve this purpose. Opaque ascriptions are needed to explain and predict behavior. Do transparent ascriptions serve this purpose also? Surprisingly perhaps, it seems so. Suppose that Ralph comes to suspect a certain person that he comes across in his murder investigation and so starts avoiding him. Unbeknownst to Ralph, the person is Big Felix. A mobster observes Ralph's behavior and asks the moll, "Why is Ralph avoiding Big Felix?" The moll responds with the transparent (7). This seems to be an adequate explanation. Yet how can it be if we are right in claiming that the explanation of behavior requires opacity? The answer is that the explanatory *generalizations,* and the explanations that follow immediately from them, do indeed require opacity. However, (nonempty) opaque ascriptions, together with appropriate identities, imply transparent ones. The transparent ones serve as explanations *on the presupposition that they follow from good opaque ones.* Thus the transparent (7) explains the transparently described behavior, avoiding Big Felix, on the presupposition that there is some term, *'a',* such that $a =$ Big Felix, and, opaquely, Ralph is avoiding a and Ralph believes that a is insane. And, once again, the transparent ascription will serve the purpose where the mobster is unaware that Big Felix is Smith's murderer.

Finally we must consider ascriptions like (2) and (4). The evidence that these ascribe a distinct sort of putative meaning, en rapport reference, and hence are appropriately called "rapport-

153

transparent," is persuasive (although I think less so than for the other meanings). Why would we need to ascribe such meanings? I think that the answer must come from the epistemic significance of having a particular object in mind. I shall later describe a theory according to which to have an object in mind is to stand in a certain sort of causal relation to it. If a belief about an object is partly based on this sort of relation to the object then that fact seems relevant to our assessment of the likely truth value of the belief. So, when the purpose of an ascription is to guide us to reality, and an opaque ascription of an en rapport belief is not suitable, the rapport-transparent ascription is more informative than the simply transparent.

In sum, if the audience knows all the relevant identities, opaque ascriptions would best serve the purposes of explaining behavior and guiding us to reality, but where the audience does not, simply- or rapport-transparent ascriptions are essential.

In the last section, a consideration of ordinary ascriptions provided evidence that we ascribe three different sorts of referential properties to singular terms for semantic purposes (descriptive). The success of these ascriptions suggests that we ought to ascribe these properties (normative) and that they are meanings (basic). In this section, we have confirmed this suggestion by exploring the ways in which these ascriptions serve our purposes. I predict that we would get similar results about the referential meanings of general terms, mass terms, and so on. Perhaps there are other meanings that we do and ought to ascribe to all these terms. I shall begin to address this question in part IV. The rest of the present part will be concerned mainly with the task of explaining the natures of the referential meanings I have posited.

4.4. The Structure of Thoughts and Utterances; Griceanism

Before considering the explanation of these referential meanings it is appropriate to consider briefly the explanation of the *structures* of thoughts and utterances. These structures, together with the referential meanings of the words they contain, explain the meanings of the thoughts and utterances.

I have assumed that the meanings of thoughts and utterances are complex (1.2, 2.4). This is relatively uncontroversial. And an examination of attitude ascriptions would confirm it; thus the meanings **ORTCUTT** and **SPY** are parts of the meaning **ORTCUTT IS A SPY** ascribed to Ralph's thought by

(1) Ralph believes that Ortcutt is a spy.

I went further, assuming that the token thoughts and (normal) token utterances that have these complex meanings are themselves complex: They have their meanings in virtue of their parts having meanings. This is clearly a further step because simple things can have complex properties. Consider a nonsemantic example: The property **being a bachelor** may well be complex, consisting partly of **being unmarried,** but it is not the case that part of a bachelor is unmarried. And, in semantics, a simple thing like a flag can have a complex meaning; for example, the meaning **THIS SHIP HAS YELLOW FEVER.**[11]

This further step does not quite take us to the language-of-thought hypothesis, as we shall see, but the familiar arguments offered by Fodor for that hypothesis count in favor of the step. The first of these arguments is a "methodological" one, inferring the complexity of the thought that causes a behavior from the complexity of the behavior (1987: 141–3). The second argument claims that we need to see thoughts as complex in order to explain *thinking,* the process of inferring one thought from another (pp. 143–7). The third is the classical argument from productivity, based on the potential infinity of a person's thoughts, and its more persuasive recent variant, the argument from systematicity: A per-

11 For those who prefer to think of meanings as propositions (2.4), the point can be put like this: The complexity of a proposition is one thing, whereas the complexity of the tokens that express it is another. See also Fodor (1987: 136–9) on the distinction between the complexity of an intentional object and the complexity of the mental state that has it. I discuss the positing of propositions in section 4.12.

son's capacity to think one thought is systematically related to her capacity to think many others (pp. 147–53). Set aside for a moment whether these arguments establish that thought tokens have *linguistic* complexity and hence establish the language-of-thought hypothesis. The arguments do seem to make it overwhelmingly plausible that the tokens have at least the complexity that I have been assuming: that their complex meanings arise from the meanings of their parts.

This assumption falls short of the language-of-thought hypothesis in that *non*linguistic tokens – for example, maps – can have this sort of complexity. The language-of-thought hypothesis requires that the simplest meaningful parts of a thought token be like *words* and that the meanings of the token are determined by those words and the *syntactic* structure that contains them, just as the meanings of a sentence are determined by its words and its syntactic structure.

In my discussion I have called thought tokens "sentences" and their parts "words" through lack of any better terminology. However, my argument against holism does not depend on the language-of-thought hypothesis. Should we accept the hypothesis now that we are setting out a localistic program? I think so. Perhaps the view that a thought token has some nonlinguistic complexity – for example, the complexity of a map – could meet the requirement of Fodor's first methodological argument and could account for the systematicity that is the concern of his third argument, but it is difficult to see how it could account for the mental processes that are the concern of his second argument. Formal logic and computer science have given us a very good idea of how thinking proceeds if thought tokens are languagelike. We have very little idea how it might proceed if they are not, if they are maplike, for example.

The task of *explaining* the meanings of thought tokens provides further support for the language-of-thought hypothesis. I take it as established that the thought that Yeltsin has risen, like the utterance "Yeltsin has risen," has a part that means **YELTSIN.** How are we to explain the contribution that parts like this make to the meanings of wholes? When we are concerned with utterances, we look to linguists, particularly the movement started by Chomsky (1957, 1965, 1980), for information about syntactic structures. And we look largely to logicians (e.g., Tarski 1956; see Field 1972) for information about how truth conditions depend on structure. We are a long way from having all the details, of course, but the approach seems quite promising. If the language-of-thought hypothesis is correct then the same approach is just as promising for thoughts. And, once again, we have very little idea of any alternative explanation. Consider maps, for example. We see clearly how a map represents spatial relations and so can see, perhaps, how it could represent other relations and hence relational properties. But we wonder how it could represent intrinsic properties and quantification.

I think that this point about explanation is strengthened a little by some assumptions that Representationalism should make about *the relation between* thought meanings and utterance meanings. We ascribe the same meanings to the thought that Yeltsin has risen and the utterance "Yeltsin has risen." How do we account for this? I have claimed already that *our interest* in thought meanings is prior to that in utterance meanings (2.5). I have argued elsewhere (1981a: 80–6; Devitt and Sterelny 1987: 119–28) that we should give a certain *explanatory* priority to thought meanings. Briefly, (i) the "speaker meaning" of an utterance – what the speaker means by it – is the meaning of the thought that produces it, that it "expresses." (ii) The "conventional meaning" of an utterance in a language – what it conventionally means given the context – is explained in terms of regularities in speaker meanings: Speakers of the language regularly use one physical form to express one word meaning, another, another; they regularly use one physical arrangement of grammatical categories to express one syntactic structure, another, another. So far, I follow Grice (1989). We are left with the problem of explaining thought meanings. Here I depart from Grice. For, (iii) conventional meanings play a role in this explanation even though, ultimately, thought meanings are explained in other terms. So there is no circle in the explanation;

rather, a spiral.[12] In light of these assumptions, consider the syntactic structure that goes into determining the speaker meaning of an utterance. In virtue of what does the utterance have that syntactic structure? The assumptions imply that the utterance has that structure in virtue of having been produced by a thought that has that structure. Indeed, it is unclear how a thought with a different sort of structure – say, a maplike structure – would yield an utterance with that syntactic structure. So the assumptions strengthen the case for the language of thought.[13]

In sum, once the complexity of a thought token is granted, the further move to the language-of-thought hypothesis is supported by two inferences to the best explanation: The first involves an explanation of thinking; the second, an explanation of thought meanings.[14]

4.5. Referential Meanings

I turn now to the explanation of the referential meanings I have posited. This explanation demands theories of reference. I suggest

12 Stephen Schiffer misses the possibility of (iii) in his taxonomy of positions to be criticized (1987; e.g., pp. 14–15).

13 To what extent is the language of thought the same as the public language of the thinker? To answer this we need to consider what is required for something to be a sentence of, say, English: It must consist of English words in an English structure. But what is required to be an English word and an English structure? The answer is not too clear. However, in light of (i) to (iii), and of what I shall be suggesting about the involvement of the physical forms of a public language in the finest-grain meanings we ascribe to most mental words, I think that we should conclude that most of the language of thought of normal adult humans is very closely related, if not identical, to their public language (or, if the individual is multilingual, to one or the other of her public languages). The thoughts of human babies and nonhuman animals are briefly discussed later (4.11).

14 David Lewis is dubious of the language-of-thought hypothesis (1994: 421–3). He may be right in insisting that the hypothesis is not part of folk psychology, but he does not address these two inferences to the best explanation.

that three sorts of theory of reference are possible and that very likely each sort has some application.

"Description" theories are one sort. According to these theories, the reference of a word is fixed by certain of the descriptions that speakers associate with the word; it refers to whatever those descriptions, or a weighted most of them, apply to. In the terminology of our discussion of holism, the word's reference is determined by certain of its inferential properties. Description theories were once popular for proper names and natural-kind words, but they foundered because of the already noted problems of ignorance and error (3.8, 3.11): Speakers who seem perfectly able to use a word to refer are too ignorant to provide the appropriate descriptions of the referent; worse, speakers are often so wrong about the referent that the descriptions they would provide apply not to the referent but to other entities or to nothing at all.

Description theories of reference have a deeper failing: They are *essentially incomplete*. A description theory explains the reference of a word by appealing to the application of descriptions associated with the word. So the theory explains the reference of the word by appealing to the reference of other words. How then is the reference of those other words to be explained? Perhaps we can use description theories to explain their reference too. This process cannot, however, go on forever: There must be some words whose referential properties are not parasitic on those of others. Otherwise, language as a whole is cut loose from the world. Description theories pass the referential buck. But the buck must stop somewhere.

This deep failing of description theories is brought out by Hilary Putnam's slogan (which he supported with his famous Twin-Earth fantasy): " 'Meanings' just ain't in the *head*" (1975: 227).[15] The association of descriptions with a word is an inner state of the speaker. No such inner state can make the word refer to a particular referent. For that we must look for some relation

---

15 Burge (1979) argues a similar line. Searle (1983) rejects Putnam's slogan; my 1990a is a response.

that language and mind have to things outside themselves – we must look for an external relation.

If we are to be naturalistic, it seems that the external relation that we seek must be a causal one. Thus, a naturalistic explanation of reference requires a "causal" theory. This is the argument for my frequent earlier claims (e.g., in 1.2) that noninferential causal links to reality must directly or indirectly constitute all meanings.

To emphasize the importance of these causal links is not to endorse the extreme localist view, atomism, according to which the explanation of reference requires only causal theories. Although description theories seem to fail for names and natural-kind words, perhaps they work for some other words: 'bachelor' and 'pediatrician' are likely candidates; 'paperweight' and 'sloop' are not unlikely ones. If description theories do work for some words, then they pass the referential buck, but that does not matter provided that the buck finally stops with some words that are explained by a causal theory. The localistic program I am arguing for is molecular in allowing that a description theory may be true for some words.[16]

So, we have identified two sorts of theory: description theories and causal theories. A third sort is possible: "descriptive-causal" theories, which explain the reference of a word partly in terms of its direct causal links to reality and partly in terms of its inferential properties. (Taking account of this possibility in the following

16 Traditional description theorists embraced Cartesianism (1.7, 1.8). Consider their theory of names, for example: The reference of '*a*' is determined by its association with 'the *F*'. Description theorists claimed that the competent speaker must not only associate 'the *F*' with '*a*' and hence believe truly that *a* is the *F*, she must *know* that *a* is the *F*; so she must *know* a fact about *a* sufficient to identify it. Why did the theorists make this move from belief to knowledge? Because they assumed that if 'the *F*' determines the reference of '*a*', the competent speaker's privileged access to meanings enables her to *tell* that it does; she must tacitly know that it does. From this knowledge, she can infer that *a* is the *F*. However, Cartesianism is in no way essential to description theories as described in the text and thus need not be part of any such theory that finds a place in my localist program.

discussion would add complications but, so far as I can see, make no difference in the end. So I shall mostly ignore it.)

Naturalistic attempts to explain the direct noninferential links to reality that determine the reference of a token have appealed to one or more of three causal relations between representations and reality: (i) the *historical* cause of that particular token (the idea for this arises from Kripke 1980, Donnellan 1972, and Putnam 1975); (ii) the *reliable* cause of tokens of that type (the idea for this was first suggested in Stampe 1979 and Dretske 1981);[17] and (iii) the *purpose* of tokens of that type, or of the mechanism that produces them, where the purpose is explained causally along Darwinian lines – the *teleological* cause (the idea for this was first suggested in Papineau 1984 and 1987 and Millikan 1984).

All known theories adverting to these three relations seem to face difficulties, and I doubt that any of them gives a *generally* satisfactory explanation of the ultimate referential link. Nevertheless, I think that we should assume that a satisfactory theory or theories along these lines can be found.

Theories of reference of these three sorts will straightforwardly explain one of the referential meanings of a singular term: the transparently ascribed property of referring to an object. What about another, the opaquely ascribed property of referring to the object in a certain way? Thanks to Frege, we are already familiar with meanings of this sort (not quite, though, because Frege's "senses" are objects rather than properties, but we can mostly ignore this difference). The modes that he had in mind seemed all to be descriptive, consisting of inferential links to other terms; they seemed to be like the mode of 'Smith's murderer' in (5). But, as we have noted, all modes cannot be like that: Some must be causal. It is plausible to suppose that the mode of a name like 'Ortcutt' in (1) is causal.

17 Strictly speaking, perhaps, a reliablist theory need not be causal. It may be "logically possible" that the reliable connection that determines reference is not sustained by causality. However, as a matter of fact, any such connection would be so sustained. (Thanks to Eric Lormand.)

The idea that a meaning might be a property of referring by a certain causal mode (or, taking meanings to be objects rather than properties, the idea that a meaning might *be* a causal mode of referring) is so alien to the semantic tradition – as our discussion in the next few sections will dramatically demonstrate – that more needs to be said in its favor.

First, note that we have no alternative but to accept the idea, if my argument so far is correct. For, it *follows from* these two conclusions:

A term token's mode of referring to its extension is one of its meanings.

All modes of referring cannot be descriptive; some must be causal.

Why resist these conclusions? One might resist, of course, because of doubts that the causal modes can be adequately explained. But, in the naturalistic picture, *all* reference rests ultimately on these causal modes: Even a token with a descriptive mode depends for its reference on others that have a causal mode. So, this doubt amounts to the doubt that *reference* can be explained.[18] So, if the causal modes really cannot be explained, the naturalist should abandon (nondeflationary) reference and hence truth-referential semantics altogether. But if they can be explained then there is no reason for not identifying them with meanings.

Second, it is important to avoid a simple misunderstanding. The idea that a meaning is a property of referring by a certain causal mode does not imply that some description of that mode

18 One of Schiffer's reasons for doubting that there are any modes of presentation (1990b) rests on his skepticism about naturalistic explanations of reference (1987). Note that Schiffer uses 'mode of presentation' widely so that it could apply to things like stereotypes that do not determine reference (see also Adams, Stecker, and Fuller 1993). I follow Frege in using it only of things that do determine reference. (Note that this usage still leaves open whether non-reference-determining things are *meanings*. However, I shall later *argue* that they are not; 4.9–4.10.)

expresses that meaning and so is synonymous with the term.[19] Indeed, the idea that a meaning is a property of referring by a certain *descriptive* mode of reference does not imply that some description is synonymous with the term. Thus, suppose that the reference of 'bachelor' were explained by its inferential links to 'adult unmarried male'. It would not follow that 'bachelor' and 'adult unmarried male' shared all their meanings. It may well serve our semantic purposes to distinguish the ways in which these two expressions refer to bachelors (4.18). Whether the theory is causal or descriptive, its aim is to *explain* meanings not express them.

Third, in the next section, I shall attempt to undermine resistance to the idea of meanings as causal modes by outlining a theory *to illustrate* how this might work. The theory is one I proposed in earlier works (1974, 1981a, 1989b, Devitt and Sterelny 1987). It also offers an explanation of the third meaning, en rapport reference to an object, and a solution to the problem of exportation. And I shall use the theory as an example from time to time.

4.6. An Illustrative Theory of Referential Meanings

The illustrative theory, which I shall call "IT," is a historical-causal one, placing the ideas of Donnellan (1966, 1972) and Kripke (1980) in a naturalistic framework and developing them in two ways.

First, IT draws a distinction at token level, based on Donnellan's distinction at type level, between referential and attributive descriptions, and then applies this new distinction across the board, covering names, demonstratives, and pronouns, as well

---

19 But it does not imply either that this meaning is "strictly inexpressible," as Adams, Stecker, and Fuller think (1992: 380): You can express the meaning of a term with a causal mode by using the term! They would not find this satisfactory because they presuppose that an expression of meaning must be descriptive. A consequence of my argument is that this presupposition is false.

as definite descriptions. I preferred the term 'designational' to 'referential'. So my distinction was between designational and attributive singular-term tokens.

Signs of this distinction are to be found in folk semantics: We distinguish using a singular term "with a particular object in mind" from using it to refer to whatever is the such and such. Donnellan argued for this intuitive distinction with a number of examples of confusion and mistake. I argued for it by focusing on the relation between "incomplete" descriptions like 'the man' and demonstratives. It is implausible to see these descriptions as like Russellian descriptions.[20]

Second, IT gives a historical-causal account of reference for all the designational tokens.[21] These tokens depend for identifying reference on a certain sort of causal chain, a "d(esignating)-chain." Such a chain starts with a person's face-to-face perception of an object, a "grounding," and may run through many people by the device of "reference borrowing" in communication. There are usually several d-chains involving the one object and word, all linked together to form a network. A designational token refers to the object, if any, in which the causal network underlying the token is grounded. I called this mode of identifying reference, "designation." An attributive token, in contrast, refers to the object, if any, to which the appropriately related description

20 See also Wettstein 1981 and Wilson 1991. Kripke thinks that Donnellan's distinction does not have semantic significance (1979a). My 1981b is a response to Kripke. Neale 1990 is a detailed defense of Russell's theory of descriptions from criticisms inspired by Donnellan. In my view, this defense fails mainly because it does not address the crucial argument: (i) The description 'the F' in its designational use is just like the deictic demonstrative 'that F'. (ii) The plausible theory of these demonstratives is not a Russellian description theory but a historical-causal theory.

21 Donnellan did not offer a theory of reference for his referential descriptions. In particular, he did not extend his causal theory of names to cover those descriptions (although he remarks in a footnote that such a description is a "close relative" of a proper name; 1972: 378n). Kripke and Donnellan did not offer their causal theories of names in a naturalistic setting, but it is appropriate to propose them in that setting; see Field 1972.

(sometimes the token itself) uniquely applies. I called this mode of identifying reference, "denotation."

Applying IT to names, I claimed, in effect,[22] that Frege was right in thinking that a name had a meaning or "sense" but wrong in thinking that this meaning was descriptive (except for a few attributive names like 'Jack the Ripper'). I identified the meaning of a name with the property of referring by a certain type of d-chain, each name by a different type.[23] Similar remarks can be made about the meanings of demonstratives, pronouns, and descriptions.[24] So IT provides the illustration we seek of a meaning identified with a property of referring by a certain causal mode.

22   The qualification is necessary because of my caution with the *word* 'sense'. Initially, I was anxious to emphasize the difference between the causal theory and the description theory. This led me to use 'sense' as if it applied only to *Fregean* descriptive senses and hence to deny that names had senses (1974). Later I allowed, tentatively, that we might think of the property of referring by a certain causal mode as a non-Fregean sense (1981a: 236). Had I anticipated the rise of direct reference, I would have emphasized the difference between the causal theory and the 'Fido'-Fido theory by not being at all tentative about this. I have not been tentative recently (Devitt and Sterelny 1987: 56–8).

Some seemed to think that my talk of senses was inappropriate because what I called a sense is very different from a Fregean sense (see, e.g., Taylor 1990). This is surely an uninteresting verbal issue. The only substantive issue is whether what I called "a sense" does the explanatory work that I claimed it does. In this work, that sense is *one of* a name's meanings.

23   1974: 203–4; 1981a: 153–7. I was rather careless about the difference between taking a meaning to be a property and taking it to be an object (2.4, 4.12) and so sometimes described the view briefly as identifying the meaning with the type of d-chain itself.

Ackerman is sympathetic to the historical-causal theory and ascribes "a non-descriptive connotation" to a name, but she does not identify this connotation with the property of referring by a certain causal mode. This is largely explained by her view that the semantic task is a priori conceptual analysis (1979a, 1979b, 1980, 1989).

24   Similar, but also importantly different about most of these terms because, strictly speaking, the theory of them was *descriptive*-causal (Devitt and Sterelny 1987: 84–5); examples of such terms are pronouns like 'he', complex demonstratives like 'this book', and definite descriptions.

Before saying more about these types of d–chain, I note two problems that IT can solve. (i) It can give an account of the third meaning ascribed to singular terms: en rapport reference to an object. For example,

(2) Ortcutt is such that Ralph believes him to be a spy

requires that Ralph have Ortcutt in particular in mind as the spy. According to IT, Ralph has an object in mind if his mode of reference is *designational*; he has it in mind in virtue of his term being related to it by a d–chain. So for (2) to be true, Ralph must have a belief involving a term that *designates* Ortcutt.

(ii) IT solves the problem of exportation. An exportation is valid *only when the exported term is (nonempty and) designational*. Thus the inference from the opaque (1) to (2) is valid, as Quine supposed: Because 'Ortcutt' is designational, if the opaque (1) is true then Ralph has Ortcutt in mind and so (2) is true. On the other hand, the inference from (3) to (4) is not valid: Because 'the shortest spy' is attributive, (3) could be true without Ralph having anyone in mind as a spy; yet (4) requires that he has.

According to IT, the causal mode of referring involved in the meaning of a name is a certain type of d–chain. In virtue of what are d–chains of this type? Clearly, they must be d–chains of the sort that underlie names (rather than, for example, demonstratives) and be grounded in the referent (if any). But this is not sufficient, because our opaque ascriptions distinguish between coreferential names. We have to capture the intuitive idea that d–chains are of the relevant type only if they underlie "the same name."[25]

25 This idea is closely related to the view that opaque attitude ascriptions ascribe the property of referring to the name's bearer *by means of that very name;* for examples, see Richard (1990: 136–7) and the theory that these ascriptions express a relation to an "interpreted logical form" partly constituted by "linguistic forms" (Larson and Ludlow 1993). Such theories need to be supplemented by an account of the respect in which the names and other linguistic forms must be the same. Richard favors a view like IT (pp. 183–5).

The d-chains for a name are formed in groundings[26] and reference borrowings, all of which involve tokens of certain "physical" types. These types are the conventional forms of the name: certain sounds in speech, shapes in writing, and so on through other media. So, let us add that the d-chains must involve tokens of an appropriate physical type. The following unusual case suggests that this is still not sufficient.

Imagine a person who is leading a double life – say, one as a burglar, the other as a wealthy aristocrat – with such success that everyone wrongly thinks that there are two people. Now suppose that in both lives, by chance, he is known as "George." So the d-chains underlying the "two uses" of 'George' would be of the same type according to our account so far. Yet it seems likely that our opaque ascriptions would distinguish these two uses. Given our semantic purposes, particularly that of explaining behavior, we *should* distinguish them as much as we *do* distinguish two names of one person – for example, 'Samuel Clemens' and 'Mark Twain' – and two uses of one name for different people – an ambiguous name. Something needs to be added to our account. IT's talk of d-chains "linked together to form a network" indicates what. D-chains are of the type that interests us only if they are causally linked by the mental processing of the speech community into the one network of groundings and reference borrowings.

Consider an example of this processing. Suppose that Charles already has the ability to use the sound type /Gail/, the inscription type 'Gail', and perhaps other conventional forms of the name, to designate a certain object, Gail. So he has a "file" consisting of a set of thoughts that include tokens that dispose him to say /Gail/, 'Gail', and so on and that have underlying them d-chains that are grounded in Gail. Suppose now that Charles is in the position to borrow reference from Kate's uses of, for example, /Gail/. These sounds, as a matter of fact, have underlying them d-chains

---

26 It is important to the plausibility of the historical-causal theory of names that the theory allows a name to be *multiply* grounded in its referent, not simply grounded in an initial dubbing (1974: 198–9; 1981a: 56–7).

grounded in Gail. If he is to take advantage of Kate's utterances, amending his Gail file, he must process Kate's tokens of /Gail/ so that they are brought to bear on that file. He must process the input as if he had formed the identity belief "Gail (the subject of this conversation) = Gail (the subject of these thoughts)."[27] This processing task may not be easy because he may know several people named 'Gail'. Similarly, if he is to amend his file in a grounding situation as a result of experiencing Gail herself, he must process the input as if he had formed the identity belief "That person = Gail." Thus d-chains including these causal links to Gail and Kate's /Gail/ are made part of the network underlying Charles's thoughts about Gail that dispose him to use /Gail/, 'Gail', and so on.

Now that we have required that d-chains are of the relevant type only if they are linked by this sort of mental processing, can we drop the requirement that they involve tokens of an appropriate physical type? We cannot, because d-chains of the relevant type will be similarly linked to others involving different physical types. Thus if Charles has another name for Gail, and has the appropriate identity belief, he will process tokens of the conventional forms of it to the same file and, similarly, any demonstratives, pronouns and definite descriptions that he takes to designate her. We cannot exclude d-chains involving tokens of these other physical types simply by the talk of processing.[28]

Let us define the identity conditions of "a network" for a name: It is constituted by d-chains involving tokens of certain physical types linked together by the preceding sort of mental processing in the speech community. Then we can sum up the discussion by saying that the opaquely ascribed meaning of a name is a property of referring by means of d-chains in a certain network, the network specified by the ascribing t-clause. That partic-

---

27 In my 1981a (pp. 134–6) I required that the subject actually form the identity belief. This is an overintellectualized account of the processing.

28 My view of the typing of d-chains in earlier works (particularly, 1989b: 227–8) was mistaken in this respect. (That earlier view is badly misdescribed in Adams, Stecker, and Fuller 1992.)

ular network is specified because underlying the name in the t-clause are d-chains in that very network. Consideration of several puzzles later will lead us to developments in this view (4.16–4.17).

Different name networks normally arise from groundings in different objects. Where they do not, they will almost always involve tokens of different sound types, inscription types, and so on and different circumstances of use; the case of 'Samuel Clemens' and 'Mark Twain' is an example. Very rarely, different networks may arise from the same object and involve the same sound types, inscription types, and so on because of different circumstances of use; the case of 'George' is an example.

I do not pretend that IT's historical-causal theory of reference is fully adequate or that I know how to make it so. I think it has a deep problem, "the *qua*-problem" (Devitt and Sterelny 1987: 63–5, 72–5), which I doubt that it has the resources to solve. However, I do think that the theory is plausible as far as it goes: It is plausible that a historical-causal relation along roughly the lines of a d-chain is a central part of the explanation of reference of names and of some other singular terms. The theory illustrates how a meaning could be a property of referring by a causal mode.

In presenting IT, I claimed that this property was the one and only meaning of a name. From my present perspective, this was a mistake. However, the view that this property could be a meaning *at all* has turned out to be more radical than I expected. The received view is that the historical-causal theory of names is committed to the 'Fido'-Fido, or Millian, theory that there is no more to the meaning of a name than its property of referring to its bearer.[29] And the 'Fido'-Fido theory for names, and any other terms that are similarly "nondescriptive" and "rigid" ('cat' and

29 To see just how received this view is, consider the support it gets from the following: Loar 1976 (cf. my 1980); Ackerman 1979a: 58; 1979b: 6; Schiffer 1979 (cf. my 1981c); Marcus 1981: 502; McGinn 1982: 244; Baker 1982: 227; Almog 1984: 482; Lycan 1985; Block 1986: 660, 665; Lepore and Loewer 1986: 60; Wagner 1986: 452; Wettstein 1986: 187; Katz 1990: 31–4.

'water' perhaps), is a central plank in the popular platform of direct reference,[30] which is usually associated with the causal theory. Yet, the causal theory is a theory of *reference,* whereas the 'Fido'-Fido theory is a theory of *meaning,* so they seem logically distinct. The non-'Fido'-Fido theory that I proposed on the basis of the causal theory, IT, demonstrates this distinctness. What then are we to make of the received view? And why has 'Fido'-Fido become so popular given the apparently overwhelming problems for it that have been familiar since Frege and the early Russell?

30 By "direct reference" I have in mind particularly the movement arising from David Kaplan's "Demonstratives" (1989a). For evidence of the move-ment's commitment to the 'Fido'-Fido, or Millian, theory of names (some-times also called, inappropriately, the "new" theory), see Salmon 1981: 11; 1986; Barwise and Perry 1983: 165; Almog 1984: 482; 1985: 615–6n; Wettstein 1986: 185, 192–4; Crimmins and Perry 1989: 686; Braun 1991: 302. I take the theory to be implicit in Soames 1985b, 1987, 1988. Interest-ingly, Kaplan's own commitment to the theory is somewhat tentative in "Demonstratives" (1989a: 562), and, in a final footnote, he raises the possibility of a view like IT (p. 563n). In his "Afterthoughts" he sometimes seems close to adopting such a view (1989b: 574–6, 599). Credit for direct reference's 'Fido'-Fido theory of names is usually given to Saul Kripke and Keith Donnellan, as well as Kaplan. In assessing this attribution we need to distinguish 'Fido'-Fido from other planks in the direct-reference platform for which Kripke and Donnellan do bear responsibility: the thesis that names are nondescriptive, the thesis that names are rigid designators. and the causal theory; see my 1989b: 209–12. Kripke does not subscribe to 'Fido'-Fido (1980: 20–21) but Donnellan does (1989: 275–6). Although direct-reference philosophers typically associate their views with the causal theory, their *interest* in this theory, or in any other attempts to give *ultimate* explanations of reference, seems to be small.

Lycan sees himself as a direct-reference theorist and subscribes to 'Fido'-Fido (1985; see Devitt 1990b and Lycan 1990a for a discussion). Fodor proposes a "denotational theory" that is, in effect, a direct-reference theory, though he does not mention any of the direct-reference literature in his discussion (1987: 72–95; 1990: 161–76).

Although IT rejects 'Fido'-Fido, it accepts the other planks of the direct-reference platform for names. IT is also consistent with much of the direct-reference approach to demonstratives and indexicals, the main focus of Kaplan's discussion. IT differs from that approach, however, in insisting that a demonstrative's historical-causal link to its referent is semantically crucial.

I shall begin the next part of the chapter by describing these problems for 'Fido'-Fido. I shall then answer the questions. In the rest of the part I shall consider other rival programs.

II. RIVAL PROGRAMS

4.7. 'Fido'-Fido and the Identity Problem

Both a 'Fido'-Fido theory and a theory that follows Frege in taking the meaning of a term to be its property of referring by a certain mode make the mistake of assigning only one meaning to a name. But the Fregean mistake is much less serious because, although the theory does not call the property of referring to a certain object "a meaning," it gives the property a central place in *the theory of* meaning, in semantics. In contrast, the 'Fido'-Fido theory, as direct-reference theorists emphasize, has no place for a name's mode of referring in semantics.

The four traditional problems that drove people away from the 'Fido'-Fido theory are as follows: the differing meanings of '$a = a$' and '$a = b$', "the Identity Problem"; the nontriviality of true positive existence statements and the meaningfulness of true negative ones, "the Existence Problem"; the meaningfulness of empty names, "the Emptiness Problem"; and the failure of substitutivity of identicals in attitude ascriptions, "the Opacity Problem." [31]

The most popular of these problems is the Identity Problem, yet the case for it has not been well argued. The difference in meanings it adverts to is intuitively clear: I have never met a beginning student who denied it. Yet philosophers have rightly felt that more needs to be said. What they have said, however, has not been satisfactory, and this has encouraged direct-reference

---

31 The discussion in this section and the next draws on a more detailed discussion in my 1989b (pp. 219–29). However, my present view differs in some respects. Most importantly, I now draw some consequences from my anti-Cartesianism that had previously escaped me, particularly in handling the Identity Problem. In this respect I have moved closer to direct reference.

philosophers not to take the Identity Problem as seriously as they should. The rest of this section will be mainly devoted to presenting a case for the Problem.

Philosophers have often found evidence for the difference in meaning between '$a = a$' and '$a = b$' in the alleged fact that the former sentence, unlike the latter, is "necessary," "known a priori," or "analytic." Yet Kripke has shown that both sentences are necessary (if true) (1980); no naturalist should accept that either is a priori (2.2); and I would argue that they are both "weakly analytic" (1.8). So there is no evidence for the meaning difference here.

Under the influence of Frege (1952: 56–7) it is common to generate the Identity Problem by applying an epistemic principle along the following lines:

'$S1$' and '$S2$' mean the same only if they are alike in informativeness and cognitive significance to all competent speakers.

So, '$a = a$' and '$a = b$' must differ in meaning because the latter is informative whereas the former is not. William Taschek points out that principles of this sort, assuming that "cognitive significance must mirror objective semantic differences" (1987: 162), are "the received view in the philosophy of language" (p. 161). But, why should we believe them? What have *epistemic* issues about informativeness got to do with *semantic* issues about meaning?

The general acceptance of epistemic principles provides dramatic evidence of the pervasiveness of Cartesianism in semantics. For, what do the principles rest on? Assumptions like the following:

(A) '$S1$' and '$S2$' mean the same only if all competent speakers know that they do.[32]

32 Remember, for example, this previously quoted passage (2.2, n. 4): "It is an undeniable feature of the notion of meaning . . . that meaning is *transparent* in the sense that, if someone attaches a meaning to each of two words, he must know whether these meanings are the same" (Dummett 1978: 131).

(B) A competent speaker knows that '*S1*' and '*S2*' mean the same only if they are alike in informativeness and cognitive significance to the speaker.[33]

The Cartesianism of (A) is blatant. There is no good reason to suppose that a person who is competent with a sentence – who has the ability to use it with a certain meaning – must thereby have any propositional knowledge about what constitutes its meaning (2.2). Hence there is no good reason to suppose that she must know whether another sentence she understands is similarly constituted. What is synonymous need not be "synonymous-for-her." Indeed, given that much of meaning "just ain't in the head" (4.5), much of what determines synonymy is not open to the gaze even of a Cartesian inner eye.[34]

Consider IT's picture of competence with a name, for example. Briefly, a person has this competence if she is appropriately linked into the causal network for the name and is disposed to assign inputs of the name to the network and to produce outputs of the name that are causally based in the network. The competence does not involve any knowledge about these matters (1981a: 30–1, 106–7).

The Identity Problem is best generated by a straightforward application of the earlier methodology. When we look at what is common and peculiar to the tokens that the folk ordinarily call "that $a = b$" the evidence is overwhelming that '$a = a$' and '$a = b$' differ in putative meaning. The folk are normally prepared to assert "Flora believes that $a = b$" on the basis that Flora has a

---

33 These assumptions bring the Cartesian chickens of conceptual analysis home to roost in "the paradox of analysis." If an analysis is an articulation of propositional knowledge of meanings and concepts arising from our competence – and what else could it be if it is not to collapse into the articulation of empirical folk opinion about the world? – then there is a problem showing how it can be informative.

34 For attempts to reconcile the "externalism" of Putnam's slogan with mild Cartesianism, see Lepore and Loewer 1986 (cf. 2.2, n. 4), Davidson 1987, and Burge 1988 (cf. 2.12, n. 34).

belief she would express using '$a = b$', but not simply on the basis that she has a belief she would express using '$a = a$' (even if the folk know that $a = b$). The latter belief does not have what is common and peculiar to beliefs that the folk would call "that $a = b$." One way of putting this is that the folk normally construe ascriptions of identity beliefs opaquely.[35]

So, if the putative meanings are meanings, the two identity sentences differ in meaning. Yet, according to the 'Fido'–Fido view, they cannot do so, for the two names in them have the same meanings, the property of referring to a certain object.

Consideration of identity sentences not only goes against 'Fido'–Fido, it supports a theory that takes meanings to be modes of reference. We will normally assert 'Flora believes that $a = b$', only if we think that Flora has an identity belief involving two modes of representing the object, one associated with 'a', the other associated with 'b'. Modes matter to the meaning ascribed.

Not only do we normally ascribe different properties to '$a = a$' and '$a = b$' for semantic purposes, but the success of our ascriptions suggests that we ought to. We can add to this case by examining our purposes. One purpose is to explain and predict intentional behavior. This purpose clearly gives us an interest in distinguishing a person who is ready to assert '$a = b$' from one who is merely ready to assert '$a = a$'. For example, Ralph comes to the point where he would assert 'Big Felix murdered Smith'. He would not assert 'Jones murdered Smith' because he does not know that 'Big Felix' is just an alias for Jones, an apparently

35 Contempory philosophers often attempt to capture the Fregean epistemic principle with one along the following lines:

> '$S1$' and '$S2$' mean the same only if to believe that $S1$ is to believe that $S2$.

This can then be used to show that the two identity sentences differ in meaning. But why should we accept the principle? Interestingly enough, its justification need make no appeal to Cartesianism, showing that the principle is very different from the earlier epistemic one. The justification can appeal to considerations like those in this paragraph.

respectable citizen well known to Ralph. Of course, Ralph would assent to 'Jones = Jones'. Yet, on the strength of our knowledge of all this, and of

(5) Ralph believes that Smith's murderer is insane,

we have no reason to predict that Ralph will avoid (opaquely) meeting Jones. On the other hand, that is just what we predict when Ralph comes to learn of the alias and says, "Jones = Big Felix." So, our interest in this prediction gives us a very good reason for distinguishing the meanings of the two identity sentences and corresponding beliefs.

It may not be so obvious that we have a good reason for distinguishing these meanings when we are concerned not with behavior but with using the belief as an indicator of reality, but nevertheless I think that we do. We think that a exists and that b exists. We are interested in knowing whether this commits us to two entities or just one. Part of the reason for this interest is that we want to unify our knowledge and avoid inconsistency: If a and b are the same then we should "merge" our information about each. Distinguishing the meaning of '$a = b$' from that of '$a = a$' serves this interest.

We see then that our semantic purposes are served by distinguishing these meanings. So we ought to distinguish them. So we are not surprised to discover that the folk do in fact distinguish them. 'Fido'-Fido is neither descriptively nor normatively correct.

Consider also the Opacity Problem: that substitutivity often does not hold for names in attitude ascriptions. I have drawn on Quine's argument, and alluded to the ample evidence elsewhere, that substitutivity may indeed fail for sentences like,

(1) Ralph believes that Ortcutt is a spy.

It is easy to see from that discussion that the Opacity Problem is closely related to the Identity Problem: The discussion showed that we ascribe different putative meanings to 'a is F' and 'b is F', even though $a = b$. And our discussion of the Identity Problem yields particularly clear examples of the failure of substitutivity.

175

We have seen that whereas a person's utterance, "Flora believes that $a = a$," is certainly true, his utterance, "Flora believes that $a = b$," may well be false. Yet, according to the 'Fido'-Fido theory, 'a' and 'b' have the same meaning, and so the two ascriptions should have the same truth value.

I have talked of the meanings we "normally" ascribe to '$a = a$' and '$a = b$' because we can doubtless imagine circumstances in which we would ascribe the same meaning to these identities. These would be circumstances in which 'Flora believes that $a = b$' is *transparent*. A source of hope for direct-reference theorists as they struggle with the Identity Problem and the Opacity Problem is that a transparent construal of a belief ascription is often natural and appropriate. Transparently ascribed meanings fit the 'Fido'-Fido theory, as we have seen. What makes an identity ascription like 'Flora believes that $a = b$' particularly difficult for direct reference is that it is hardly ever open to a transparent construal; any normal purpose we might have for uttering it suggests an opaque construal.

In sum, evidence for the Identity Problem should not be sought in alleged differences in the necessity, apriority, or analyticity of '$a = a$' and '$a = b$', nor in the results of applying epistemic principles about informativeness. It should be sought in the direct application of the methodology: The folk ascribe different properties to the two identities for semantic purposes, and they are right to do so; so the identities differ in meaning.

This having been said, a later consideration of various puzzles will reveal a non-Cartesian truth underlying Fregean epistemic principles: The cognitive difference between names reflected in a competent person's failure to accept an identity is sufficient for a difference of meaning. The difference need not be in the conventional meanings of the names; it may be only in fine-grained thought meanings needed to explain the person's behavior (4.17).

Faced by the four traditional problems, most philosophers abandoned 'Fido'-Fido. The Fregean alternative solved the problems by identifying a meaning with a property of referring by a certain descriptive mode. But some words must have causal modes, and those modes, will do just as well. Thus, IT yields the following solutions. The Identity Problem: '$a = a$' and '$a = b$' have different meanings because underlying 'a' and 'b' are d-chains of different types in virtue of being parts of different networks. In particular, the tokens in these networks will differ in being of different physical types.[36] The Existence Problem and the Emptiness Problem: The meaningfulness of a name does not depend on its having a referent; it is meaningful if it has an appropriate underlying network even if that network is not grounded in a referent.[37] The Opacity Problem: Substitutivity does not hold for a name in an opaque attitude ascription because the ascription depends for its truth on the mode of reference ascribed not simply on the reference ascribed.

This discussion of the Identity Problem may leave a lingering worry about a semantic theory that identifies meanings with properties of referring by causal modes. For, even though the difference in informativeness of '$a = a$' and '$a = b$' for a speaker does not establish a difference in meaning, the difference in informativeness *is* a fact. It has to be explained somehow. How can it be explained if the theory is correct?

There are two steps to the explanation. First, we explain the cognitive difference between 'a' and 'b' – why the names *seem* different to the speaker. Second, we explain why, given this difference, '$a = a$' and '$a = b$' differ so much in informativeness for the speaker. Only the first step draws on the semantic theory, and yet it is the second that does most of the explanatory work.

Much of the apparent difference between 'a' and 'b' is embarrassingly easy to explain: The names have different conventional forms involving different physical types; for example, the names *sound* different. So, *of course,* they will seem different to the com-

---

36 Takashi Yagasawa dismisses the idea of solving the Identity Problem with the help of causal chains, but, strangely, he takes the idea to identify meanings with *token* chains (1993: 144). This identification is indeed bizarre and, so far as I know, it is also a straw man.

37 Dealing with empty names is not easy for any causal theory, of course. My attempt is 1981a: Chap. 6

petent speaker. Any causal theory can accommodate this. Thus, according to IT, the very meanings that a speaker ascribes to '*a*' and '*b*' using opaque t-clauses, day in and day out, are modes of reference that essentially involve those different physical types. The names will seem even more different in a situation where the difference in informativeness of the two identity statements is most striking: the situation where the speaker does not already know that $a = b$. In this situation, according to IT, a speaker interpreting utterances involving the names will process the input from '*a*' to one "mental file," the input from '*b*' to another. Any causal theory will develop an account of inner mental processing along these lines. Because of this difference in processing, the names will seem very different at the conscious level.

The radical difference in informativeness of '$a = a$' and '$a = b$' is largely due to *the meaning of* '='. For it is this meaning that makes '$a = a$' *un*informative. To understand ' = ' is to master the law of identity. So any instance of the law will be an uninformative consequence of that understanding; self-identity is trivial. An instance of the law contains two tokens of the same name for the same object. So, provided '$a = a$' seems to be an instance,[38] it will be uninformative. Given the just noted difference between '*a*' and '*b*', '$a = b$' does not seem to be an instance and is informative. Hence '$a = a$' and '$a = b$' are not equally informative. The responsibility of ' = ' for this difference can be further demonstrated by comparing it with 'love'. To understand 'love' is not to master any analogous law of love. So '*a* loves *a*' is not an uninformative consequence of that understanding; self-love is not trivial. Hence '*a* loves *a*' and '*a* loves *b*' *are* equally informative. Thus, once a causal theory has accomplished the relatively easy task of explaining why different names appear different to the speaker, the difference in informativeness of '$a = a$' and '$a = b$' poses no special problem.

---

38 Given the ambiguity of names, it need not seem to be an instance, of course (1981a: 155–6).

My discussion of the Identity Problem has all been about names, but the Problem can arise also about other terms. I shall discuss it for demonstratives and pronouns (briefly, "demonstratives") later (4.17). Meanwhile, I note that evidence for the Problem with demonstratives, as with names, is best found by applying the methodology, not by attending to epistemic issues of informativeness and the like. Furthermore, the way in which the explanation of the cognitive significance of identities involving different demonstratives calls on the theory of meaning is straightforward: The possibility of tokens of different demonstratives having different referents is such an obvious and dominant fact about demonstratives. So any identity involving different demonstratives can be cognitively significant. Indeed, even one involving the same demonstrative can be.[39]

4.8. Direct Reference

Given the familiar problems with the 'Fido'-Fido theory of names, it is startling to find so many able philosophers recently insisting on it. They seem to be in the grip of what one of them, Nathan Salmon, has aptly called "direct-reference mania" (1986: 82). This insistence on the 'Fido'-Fido theory raises two questions, one of method and the other of motivation: How *can* the theory be maintained in the face of these problems? Why would anyone *want* to?

Method. Concerning the question of method, on the one hand, the direct-reference philosophers are prepared to bite bullets; for example, they are prepared to claim that '$a = b$' does mean the same as '$a = a$'. On the other hand, there is usually an attempt to

39 I argued along these lines in my 1989: n. 68. Taschek makes a similar point (1987: 175) in arguing against the epistemic principle that accompanies Kaplan's theory of demonstratives (1989a: 530). Kaplan's Cartesianism is weaker in "Afterthoughts": "I have become more sceptical about the competence of competent speakers and about our access to what our words mean" (1989b: 578n).

export the familiar problems from semantics either to the theory of mind or to pragmatics.[40]

Such export strategies cannot just be dismissed. Some linguistic phenomena will surely be in the province of the theory of mind or pragmatics. In particular, because I share the doubts of direct-reference philosophers about Fregean epistemic principles,[41] I must be sympathetic to the exportation of differences in informativeness from semantics. However, an export strategy always needs a principled basis for treating something as nonsemantic. Direct-reference philosophers do not in general have such a basis.

I shall examine one example of the direct-reference method in detail. It is provided by Salmon (1986). It is a striking example of bullet biting and of exportation to pragmatics. I shall refer to other examples in passing.

Salmon's discussion is actually about the Opacity Problem. However, as we have noted (4.2, 4.7), any discussion of the truth conditions of attitude ascriptions bears immediately on the theory of the meanings ascribed. Because Salmon's discussion is about ascriptions of *identity* beliefs, it bears immediately on the Identity Problem.

Salmon describes the problem carefully in a way that demonstrates its enormity for the 'Fido'-Fido theory (1986: 80–1, 87–92).[42] He notes that we always entertain "a singular proposition" under some "guise." Part of this guise is our "mode of acquaintance" with the object that the thought is about (pp. 107–9).[43] He acknowledges that these modes are "similar in some respects to

40 For examples of exportation to pragmatics, see Salmon 1986; Soames 1988: 104–5; Fodor 1987: 85–6. Salmon lists many others who have taken this path before (167n). For examples of exportation to the theory of mind, see Almog 1985 and 1986, Lycan 1985, Wettstein 1986, 1989a, and 1989b, and Fodor 1990: 166–72. Kaplan seems to be tempted (1989a: 529–40, 562–3).

41 Indeed, the doubts of at least one direct-reference philosopher have a similar anti-Cartesian basis to mine: Wettstein 1989a, 1989b (but cf. Perry 1993: 231–3).

42 See also Soames 1988: 105–6.

43 See also Soames 1988: 125.

Fregean senses" (p. 120). So Salmon has provided the motivation and the means to adopt a Fregean view. But his faith in 'Fido'-Fido does not waiver:

The ancient astronomer agrees to the proposition about the planet Venus that it is it when he takes it in the way it is presented to him through the logically valid sentence 'Hesperus is Hesperus', but he does not agree to this same proposition when he takes it in the way it is presented to him through the logically contingent sentence 'Hesperus is Phosphorus'. The fact that he agrees to it at all is, strictly speaking, sufficient for the truth of both the sentence 'The astronomer believes that Hesperus is Hesperus' and the sentence 'The astronomer believes that Hesperus is Phosphorus'. (p. 116)

Whatever she might say, Lois Lane really does know that Clark Kent is Superman (p. 83).

If modes are not relevant to the truth conditions of belief attributions, what is their significance? Salmon thinks that attributing them serves a "pragmatic function" (p. 117),[44] which makes

the first [way of attributing the belief to the astronomer] better than the second, given our normal purpose in attributing belief. Both sentences state the same fact . . . but the first sentence also manages to convey *how* the astronomer agrees to the proposition. Indeed, the second sentence, though true, is in some sense inappropriate; it is positively misleading . . . (p. 116)

Salmon accepts that the astronomer has his belief under a certain mode of acquaintance and not under others. He accepts that the best belief attribution conveys which mode the belief is under. He accepts that conveying this is important "given our normal purpose in attributing belief."[45] So Salmon agrees that we do, as a matter of fact, convey information about a mode (descrip-

---

44 See also Soames 1987: 67–9; 1988: 104–5, 117–25.
45 Wettstein inclines toward this view also. He accepts that substitutivity often does fail for these attributions. He finds the subject "difficult and messy" but seems to think that a context-relative account of these attributions will leave the 'Fido'-Fido theory unscathed (1986: 204–9). See section 4.11.

tive) and that we ought to do so because doing so serves our purposes (normative). What better evidence could he have that the mode is involved in the meaning attributed? But Salmon will have none of that:

it is no part of the semantic content of the sentence to specify the way the astronomer takes the proposition when he agrees to it. The 'that'-clause is there only to specify the proposition believed. (p. 117)

There should be no quarrel with Salmon's insistence that we distinguish what is semantic from what is merely pragmatic nor with the idea that merely pragmatic concerns may affect the way we ascribe beliefs (or anything else for that matter); see, for example, the earlier discussion of "getting the message through" (4.3). But to make good his position Salmon must show *that the normal purposes served by conveying information about modes are not semantic but merely pragmatic.* For this he needs an account of what purposes *are* semantic. So far as I can see, he never addresses this issue. He takes the semantic task to be explaining the natures of "cognitive semantic content[s]" (p.1) where I take it to be explaining the natures of "meanings," but that is an unimportant verbal difference. What he fails to do is to tell us what purposes are served by attributing these contents. This leaves the semantic task ill-defined and leaves no basis for the claim that conveying information about modes is not attributing contents.

Everyone agrees that the folk think that the t-clause 'that Hesperus is Phosphorus' does not apply to a belief that would be expressed, "Hesperus is Hesperus." Salmon thinks that the t-clause does apply and so the folk are wrong: They confuse semantic purposes with pragmatic ones. Other direct-reference philosophers (with weaker jaws?) think that the t-clause does not apply and so the folk are right; but, in applying the t-clause, the folk would not only have the semantic purpose of ascribing content but would have pragmatic, or whatever, purposes as well.[46] Both

46 I place the following among these other philosophers. (1) Adams, Stecker, and Fuller (1993) think that we need to ascribe a mode of presentation to a sentence for the purpose of explaining intentional behavior. Yet, on their

positions need a justification that explains our semantic purposes. Neither position gets one.

A constant refrain of the holism debate is that the molecular localist must provide a principled basis for her distinction between the inferential properties of a token that are alleged to constitute its meaning and all its other inferential properties (3.1). Properly understood, the demand is appropriate (3.2). It is noteworthy, therefore, that the direct-reference philosopher is not confronted with a similar demand that is equally appropriate. He must provide a principled basis for his distinction between the one referential property of a token that is alleged to constitute its content − its property of referring to x − and all its other referential properties − its modes of referring to x. In responding to such demands, a theorist needs an account of our semantic purposes in ascribing meanings or contents (3.10).

In my view, our semantic purposes are to explain people's behavior and to use others as guides to reality (2.5). Those purposes *are* served by ascribing modes of reference, as we have seen (4.2–4.3). *The very same considerations that lead us to ascribe meanings at all lead us to ascribe modes.*[47] Salmon is well aware that direct

direct-reference view, the mode is not part of the meaning of the sentence. So the purpose of ascribing meanings is not to explain behavior. They do not say what the purpose is. (2) Braun (1991) agrees that we need to distinguish the belief that Fred would express, "Twain is clever," from the one that he would express, "Clemens is clever," because of their different causal roles, but he insists that they do not thereby differ in "content." To claim otherwise, given that "the traditional notion of content is intimately connected with the notions of truth and reference," is "an abuse of terminology" and "conceptually misguided" (p. 296). He needs to say why this "traditional notion of content" is theoretically interesting. (3) Fodor (1990: 167–70) thinks that it serves our purpose in ascribing beliefs − implicitly, our purpose of explaining behavior, at least − to distinguish the belief that Jocasta is eligible from the belief that Oedipus' mother is eligible because their "vehicles" differ in the way in which they express a common "content." He does not tell us why that difference in vehicle does not *therefore* count as a difference of content (hence the irony referred to in sec. 3.12, n. 18).

47 For a reason that is obscure to me, Adams, Stecker, and Fuller (1992: 377–8) claim that an earlier version of this argument (1989b: 224–5) "begs the

reference flies in the face of folk theory (pp.83–5). However, its problems are much more serious than that. It flies in the face of a scientific methodology for semantics.[48]

Of course, the behavior we use modes to explain is opaquely described intentional behavior. Can we then save direct reference by seeking only to explain transparently described behavior, for which 'Fido'-Fido meanings will do? First, we should note that this rescue would be revisionist because we do, as a matter of fact, seek to explain intentional behavior. So we need an argument explaining why we should cease this practice. And the argument will have to be strong, given the apparent success of the practice. More importantly, we have seen that explanations of transparently described behavior are parasitic on explanations of opaquely described behavior, for the relevant generalizations advert to the latter (4.3). So, ascribing a 'Fido'-Fido meaning will do in the first instance only if it can be backed up by ascribing a mode.

Finally, it must be noted that direct-reference philosophers find support for their view in a variety of "puzzles." They think that consideration of these puzzles lessens, if not removes, the threat to their view posed by the apparent failures of substitutivity in attitude contexts. I think that they are wrong (4.18). Consideration

question." So let me emphasize why the present version, at least, does not. I call something "a meaning" if it serves certain purposes to ascribe it (2.5–2.6). I argue that ascribing modes does serve those purposes and so modes are meanings (4.2–4.3). Salmon has not presented a rival view of the purposes of ascribing meanings (or contents) to support the claim that modes are not meanings.

48 The dire need for a methodology is apparent in Mark Crimmins's (1992) response to Salmon. Crimmins shares Salmon's direct-reference view of names but not his pragmatic account of the difference between the two ascriptions of identity beliefs to the ancient astronomer. Crimmins has a hidden-indexical view of these ascriptions – to be discussed later (4.11) – that enables him to see the difference as semantic. He raises a very good question: "What would count as a reason to choose between" these two views? His answer is the usual disappointing appeal to intuition: "Only a simple criterion of reasonableness: Where you can adopt an account that is consonant with intuitions and there is no reason not to do so" (p. 34).

of these puzzles in part IV will take us even further away from direct reference. I will argue that the explanation of behavior sometimes requires the ascription of meanings that are finer grained than those I have already posited, hence more distant from the coarse-grained meanings of direct reference.

Motivation. Turn now to the question of motivation. This question is particularly pressing because direct-reference philosophers offer very little explicit argument for 'Fido'-Fido.

These philosophers start from the Representationalist insight that the referent of a word is central to its meaning. Next, they are very impressed by the refutation of description theories of names. Given that the meaning of a name is not descriptive, they see no viable alternative to taking the meaning to be the referent. The possibility that the meaning might involve a nondescriptive causal mode of representation is either ignored, set aside, or dismissed as preposterous. Salmon's discussion is most striking again. He describes my proposal as "ill conceived if not downright desperate . . . wildly bizarre . . . a confusion, on the order of a category mistake" (1986: 70–1). He says almost nothing in support of this. What he most needs to provide is some principled way of judging what goes into the category of meaning.[49]

In section 4.6, I raised the following question: Why is it the received view that the historical-causal theory of names is a 'Fido'-Fido theory? If the possibility that meanings involve nondescriptive modes is taken seriously, the view clearly requires argument. Yet the view is typically taken for granted, demonstrating that direct-reference theorists are not alone in overlooking the possibility.

Returning to the motivation for direct reference, the 'Fido'-Fido theory of names fits neatly into the tradition of formal semantics, a tradition that has no place for causal modes of repre-

---

49 Wettstein objects to meanings as causal modes on the Cartesian ground that competent speakers do not know about these modes (1986: 194). This is strange because he himself rejects Cartesianism. Almog assigns causal links only the "presemantic" role of preserving meanings (1984: 483–4; see also Kaplan 1989a: 558–63).

sentation. David Kaplan's work (1989a) has been particularly influential in this respect. However, the main concern of that work is with the semantics of demonstratives and indexicals. The 'Fido'-Fido theory is much more of a by-product of that semantics than it is something with independent motivation. In general, the bearing of formal semantic theses on the meanings of actual thoughts and utterances always needs to be demonstrated (2.7).

The property of referring to x under a certain causal mode and the property of simply referring to x are different, of course. Thus we could *define* 'meaning' so that it applied only to the latter and *define* 'semantics' so that it was a theory of only the latter. One could allow that the other property, and the problems it generates, may be very interesting while insisting that they are not the concern of semantics. Direct-reference philosophers often seem to be doing just this when they export the traditional problems from semantics.[50] However, defining away one's problems is clearly too easy an approach to intellectual life. And the approach has the disadvantage of making the 'Fido'-Fido theory trivial. What the theory needs in order to avoid this triviality is a justification for an export strategy that is based on an independent view of the semantic task. In the absence of this justification, the exclusion of modes from semantics is *theoretically arbitrary and ad hoc,* nothing but a verbal maneuver deserving of Lycan's mockery (2.3).

At bottom, I think that the popularity of direct reference arises from inattention to the methodological issues discussed in Chapter 2, in particular, the issue of semantic purposes. This inattention explains the attempt to export semantic problems, the dismissal of causal modes of reference, and the attachment to the formal tradition.

---

50 This appearance comes from the lack of theory-independent explanations of key terms like "cognitive content," "semantic value," "proposition," or "semantic function."

186

4.9. Semi-Representationalism: Two-Factor Theories

Direct reference is one alternative to my program. It is an extreme form of Representationalism. I shall now consider some alternatives that are not Representationalist. Verificationist and "use" theories tend to be positively *anti*-Representationalist, denying that truth conditions and reference are parts of meaning at all. Two-factor theories are *semi*-Representationalist: One "factor" of meaning is representational, the other is not. Setting aside the prejudice that a token can have only one meaning, this amounts to the view that a token has two meanings, one representational and one not.

I shall consider two-factor theories[51] in this section and anti-Representationalist ones in the next. I shall take these theories, as their proponents often may not intend, as *descriptive* theories, as partly theories of the properties we *do* ascribe for semantic purposes. I shall argue that they are not descriptively correct. Given the success of our ascriptions, this is evidence that they are not correct about what we *ought to* ascribe either (2.9). The descriptive failure of these theories thus increases the onus on them of showing that they are right about this normative issue and hence of showing that they are right about the basic issue of what meanings are. Why do our ordinary ascriptions *seem* to serve our purposes so successfully if they do not really do so? What reason have we for thinking that the ascriptions recommended by the theory will better serve our purposes of explaining behavior and guiding us to reality? The onus of answering these questions is heavy. There will be further discussion of the normative issue in the next chapter.

According to the two-factor theory, one meaning of a token – what the theory calls "one factor" of its meaning – is *representational*. If the token is a name then this meaning is, as the 'Fido'-Fido theory claims, its property of referring to its bearer; if it is a

---

51 Theories of the sort I have in mind are Block 1986; Field 1977, 1978; Loar 1981, 1982; Lycan 1988; McGinn 1982.

sentence, this meaning is its property of having certain truth conditions. The token's other meaning is its property of having a certain conceptual or, better, "functional" role, a property constituted by its inferential relations to other tokens and by its relations to proximal sensory inputs and/or proximal behavioral outputs. These functional-role meanings are not modes of *representation* (on my usage) because they do not determine reference; the Fregean assumption – inferential properties constitute meaning only insofar as they determine reference – is rejected. (Functional-role meaning is usually thought to be holistic, as we have noted [1.13], but we can prescind from that mistake.)

We might find evidence of two sorts for the descriptive two-factor theory. The best sort – type 1 – would be examples of the folk sometimes ascribing only the representational property and sometimes only the functional-role property. Because transparent examples rather clearly ascribe representational properties (if anything does; 4.10), any examples of ascribing functional-role properties will have to be opaque. Even if we cannot find this sort of evidence, we might find another sort – type 2: opaque examples that ascribe *both* sorts of property at once.

Some people think that we can find type 1 evidence. Consider the following:

Sometimes we group our tokens into types . . . according to the inferential roles they play within their authors' conceptual schemes . . . their *computational* roles. At other times we individuate them according to sameness of truth-conditions. (Lycan 1988: 73)

There is a preliminary problem with this that may be only terminological. For reasons to be discussed at some length in the next chapter (5.6–5.8), I think that Lycan's talk of "inferential" and "computational" roles is a mistake. Briefly, this talk implies that the non–truth-conditional typing is concerned only with the relations a token has to other tokens whereas the typing the two-factor theorist needs is concerned also with the relations the token has to proximal inputs and/or outputs. It is for a similar reason that I think that it is better for the two-factor theorist to talk of typing by "functional" rather than "conceptual" role. Rewritten in the preferred way, Lycan is claiming, in effect, that our ordinary attitude ascriptions sometimes ascribe a purely functional-role meaning.[52] However, he offers no examples to support his claim.

When we look at opaque ascriptions, we discover that (purported) reference always seems to be relevant: It does not matter how right the ascription is about the functional role of the subject's belief, for the ascription to be true it has to be right about the belief's reference. Even opaque ascriptions do not seems to classify beliefs simply by functional role.

As usual, Putnam's Twin-Earth fantasy helps to illustrate this. I am prepared to say (opaquely) of Ralph, "He believes that Reagan is a ham," even though I am not prepared to say the same of Twin Ralph. Yet I know that Twin Ralph on Twin Earth has a belief with a functional role identical to the one that makes my ascription true of Ralph. Twin Ralph's belief is not adequate because it is not about Reagan; it is about Twin Reagan. Consider a more down-to-earth example. I say, demonstrating a certain horse, "Tom believes that that horse is a winner." In fact, Tom has never spotted that horse but has another one, indistinguishable to Tom from the first horse, about which Tom has a belief that he expresses, "That horse is a winner." My ascription is false, and yet Tom does indeed have a belief with the right functional role. Finally, consider my saying, "Tom said that Bruce is a philosopher." I have the new Bruce in mind. Tom has never heard of him but has one of the other departmental Bruces in mind in saying, "Bruce is a philosopher." My ascription is false but, once again, it is right about everything except reference.

---

52 At one point, Lycan suggests that psychologists need a new form of ascription that would individuate according to his computational scheme; it would use "some appropriately neutral syntactic code" (1988: 77–8). Clearly, the psychologist needs this only if the psychologist does not already have a form that individuates according to this scheme; i.e., only if Lycan's two-factor theory is *not* descriptive. Yet the passage quoted in the text, and the surrounding discussion of Kripke's puzzle, show that the theory *is* intended to be descriptive.

Two of Stich's examples (offered for a somewhat different purpose) help to bring out the difficulty in finding type 1 evidence. The first concerns Mrs. T, who would say, "McKinley was assassinated," even though she was apparently unaware of the link between assassination and death, or indeed of the basic facts of death. Imagine that Mrs. T

is led into a room where she can see . . . Mr. T sitting in a booth wired to a chair. She is told that Mr. T is receiving painful electric shocks, and Mr. T goes along by screaming convincingly. We then tell Mrs. T that she can stop the shocks by pushing one of two buttons. If McKinley was assassinated, she must push the red button to stop the shocks; if McKinley was not assassinated, she must push the green button. On hearing this Mrs. T rushes to the red button. Why?. . . because she believes that McKinley was assassinated. (1983: 94)

Yet, it might be claimed, Mrs. T is too confused for her belief to refer to assassination. The second example concerns a child, Alice,

who accepts and repeats a few isolated sentences of a complex scientific theory . . . quiz show producers are pondering what questions to set for little Alice. Their plan is to allow her to win a small sum, but to be sure that she does not win the grand prize. "For the grand prize, how about asking her what E equals in Einstein's famous equation," proposes one producer. "No," protests the other, who has interviewed Alice at length, "she knows that $E = mc^2$." (p.86)

Yet surely, it might be claimed, someone as ignorant as Alice does not refer to E.

So it may seem that the truth of the ascription need not depend on the belief's reference. But the examples are not persuasive. First, it is not obvious that people *would,* on reflection, be prepared to ascribe the beliefs in these circumstances. Second, if they did, it is not obvious that the beliefs would not refer. Such examples leave us very uncertain.[53]

53 We do sometimes ascribe *sameness* of belief to two people despite a difference in the references of their beliefs. However, the sameness is in *reference-determining* functional role (5.12) and so is no help to two-factor theorists.

Even if (purported) reference is always relevant to ordinary ascriptions and so there is no type 1 evidence, two-factor theories could still get evidential support if there were examples ascribing a nonrepresentational functional-role property *as well as* reference: type 2 evidence. In a Representationalist theory, opaque examples ascribe a property that gets its "finer grain" from a functional role that determines reference. So, if two-factor theory is not to collapse into Representationalism, it needs examples where the finer grain comes from a functional role *that does not determine reference*.[54]

Once again, I know of no examples that will do the trick for the two-factor theory. And, once again, two Stich examples help to bring out the difficulty. One concerns the color-blind Peter: After carefully examining a green Christmas ball he places it in a box for red balls, and yet, Stich claims, we would not want to say in these circumstances that Peter believes that the ball is red (pp. 67–8). Another concerns Alice again: Where she needs the belief that $E = mc^2$ to solve an important problem, Stich thinks that we would not be prepared to ascribe it (p. 86). So the idea would be that our reluctance to ascribe beliefs is to be explained by the subject's failure to have a belief with the appropriate functional role and not the subject's failure to have a belief with the right reference. But the examples are not persuasive because it is not obvious that we *would not* be prepared to ascribe the beliefs; and if we were indeed not prepared to do so, this might be because we doubt that the subject's belief has the right reference.

These cases reflect a general problem in finding type 2 evidence for the two-factor theory. We do not know enough about what does determine reference to be confident that a functional role that seems to constitute the property ascribed does *not* determine reference.

---

54 Loar claims that ordinary ascriptions specify both functional roles and truth conditions, but the functional roles specified in his examples are ones that determine reference (1983a: 631). Similarly, the functional roles in the examples that motivate conceptual-role semantics for Field are all ones that determine reference (1977: 390–3; 1978: 50–2).

Even if we were to find type 2 evidence for two-factor theories, it would be worrying that we could find no type 1 evidence.[55] I have argued that attitude ascriptions serve two purposes: They help us to explain behavior and help to guide us to reality. Two-factor theorists tend to subscribe to some such dual-purpose view themselves. Furthermore, they tend to think that each purpose is served by a distinct meaning; in particular, functional-role meaning is to explain behavior (e.g., see Lycan 1988). Now, if this were so – a distinct meaning for a distinct role – we would expect to find examples where an attitude sentence ascribes *only* a functional-role property. For, when our purposes are simply to explain behavior, as they often are, we would be interested only in that property. (Note that there is no similar worry about failed expectations in the view I have urged. In that view, all meanings, whether transparently or opaquely ascribed, are representational and can, in certain circumstances, serve either purpose.)

In sum, we do not have *one clear* example where the property we ascribe for semantic purposes is not either the property of referring to something or a property that determines reference. So, the semi-Representationalist two-factor theories lack descriptive evidential support. The onus of showing that they are normatively right, hence right about meanings, is then heavy. In the next chapter, I shall argue that they do not come close to discharging this onus: It remains unclear what putative functional-role meanings are and how they could explain behavior (5.11–5.12).[56]

55 McGinn addresses this worry briefly (1982: 216).
56 Two-factor theories are sometimes accompanied by the view that an ordinary attitude ascription *indirectly* refers to the functional role of a representation by *directly* referring to a proposition. The proposition indexes the functional role because the semantic role of the proposition mirrors the functional role of the representation (see, e.g., Loar 1981, 1983a). The view is intuitively clear if we think of the causal relations between representations mirroring the logical relations between propositions (although the view is committed to an implausibly charitable view of human rationality). But what semantic role of a proposition is supposed to mirror the relation between a representation and proximal inputs and outputs? Aside from that, the view does not help with the evidential problem for two-factor theories.

4.10. Anti-Representationalism

I turn finally to anti-Representationalist alternatives to the theory I have urged: verificationist, use, and one-factor functional-role theories.[57] These theories deny that representational properties like **being true if and only if snow is white** or **referring to Cicero** constitute meanings at all. In coming to terms with these theories, it is important to consider three preliminary questions.

1. Must anti-Representationalism abandon truth and reference altogether? It need not, and it should not: Truth and reference can be taken to be *deflationary* (2.7). So, talk of truth and reference is perfectly acceptable; it is just that it has no role in explaining meaning. And this deflationism yields a neat way of explaining away the apparent fact that reference is always relevant to the meanings we ascribe, a fact that I have been making much of. First, the anti-Representationalist can accept the intimate link between the meanings ascribed and the meaning of the sentence in the ascribing t-clause. Second, given the nature of deflationary reference, the intimate link determines that any referring term in a sentence that has the meaning ascribed will share a reference with a term in the ascribing t-clause.

2. Must anti-Representationalism be verificationist? Anti-Representationalist theories, like Representationalist ones, must see meanings as constituted out of the relations that tokens have to each other, to proximal inputs and outputs, or to worldly objects and situations. According to a verificationist theory, the

---

The evidence suggests that reference is always relevant to the truth of an ascription, and so the ascription does not serve simply to index a functional role. The evidence suggests that any functional role relevant to the truth of the ascription determines reference, and so the ascription does not index non–reference-determining functional roles.

57   Theories of the sort I have in mind are Brandom 1988; Harman 1987; Horwich 1990. Some theories talk of "proper" use (e.g., Horwich 1990: 74). This talk could be appropriate only about *conventional* meaning: For a token to be properly used is for it to be used according to the convention for tokens of that physical type. So this talk has no bearing on our primary concerns, thought meaning and speaker meaning.

relations that constitute a token's meaning also constitute some epistemic condition like the condition in which the token would be verified or confirmed. In principle, an anti-Representationalist theory might not be verificationist, but in practice this is difficult. For, in discussing the normative issue, any theory must answer the following question about the properties that the theory alleges are meanings: What is it about those properties that makes them serve our semantic purposes and hence be meanings? I have already claimed that Representationalism can answer this question (4.1). Perhaps verificationism can too. It is hard to see how a theory that identifies sentence meanings with neither truth-conditional nor epistemic properties can begin to answer it.[58]

Two-factor theories face a similar normative problem with their functional-role meanings. In principle the meanings might not be verificationist, but in practice this is difficult.

3. Must verificationism be anti-Representationalist? No. It can endorse a truth-conditional, hence Representationalist, semantics *provided that it explains truth in terms of some epistemic notion.*[59] However, this explanation has a terrible price: When combined with "the equivalence thesis" according to which all appropriate instances of

s is true if and only if *p*

hold, it yields statements of the form,

p if and only if *s* is verifiable (or confirmable, or . . .)

This, I have argued, threatens antirealism (1991b: 44–6). Because realism is more plausible than any semantic doctrine, particularly from a naturalistic perspective, this sort of verificationism is not acceptable (1991b: 283–5).

What then does the evidence show about anti-Representa-

---

58 Harman (1993) admits that he does not know how to say fully what aspects of use determine meaning. What he does say suggests that his use theory is verificationist.

59 I take it that this is at least one strand in Dummett's work; see Kirkham 1989: 207–10.

tionalism as a descriptive theory? The evidence from our discussion of opaque ascriptions in the last section is not helpful. I argued that for a token to have a putative meaning, however fine grained, it must always have the right (purported) reference and that any additional property it must have would determine that reference. These "facts about reference" are just the sort that anti-Representationalism can easily explain away. For, on the deflationary view of reference, the facts are trivial consequences of the token having the right *non*referential meaning, whatever that may be. So the facts do not count against anti-Representationalism. However, they obviously do not count for it either because they fit Representationalism so well.

Of course, if an opaquely ascribed property is not a mode of reference, the anti-Representationalist needs to tell us what it is. I do not know what he could plausibly say. He has a special difficulty if he favors a version of verificationism that is otherwise attractive. If verificationism is descriptively correct then the folk use t-clauses to ascribe to a token epistemic properties like **being confirmed if and only if** *p*. Verificationists typically seem to have some sort of *subjective* confirmation in mind: confirmation-*to-x,* where the token to which the meaning is ascribed is *x*'s. The contrast is with *objective* confirmation: with what *really does* confirm a token, whatever anyone thinks. Our earlier discussion of the arguments from ignorance and error poses an immediate problem for the subjective version. Given the enormous differences in expertise among the people to whose tokens we ascribe the one meaning, any subjective confirmation condition *in common* with these tokens is unlikely (3.8).

The evidence from our earlier discussion of transparent ascriptions (4.2) is much more interesting. It counts decisively against anti-Representationalism. We saw that the 'Fido'-Fido theory seemed right for these transparent ascriptions: The *only* property that seemed to be shared by the singular terms to which we ascribe the one putative meaning was the property of referring to a certain object. Now if reference is taken to be deflationary, this property cannot be the shared meaning. *But we seem to have no other candidate.* Thus, consider the variety of tokens to which we apply (transparently) 'that Big Felix is insane'. These tokens involve 'Big Felix', 'Smith's murderer', 'I', 'he', 'you', 'the most successful mobster', 'the man seen at the bar', and any other way of referring to Big Felix. It is most unlikely that these share any epistemic or other functional-role property that could be the meaning.

In sum, the evidence counts against anti-Representationalism as a descriptive theory, a theory of the properties we do ascribe for semantic purposes, just as it did against semi-Representationalism. Of course, anti-Representationalism might still be normatively correct, correct about the properties we ought to ascribe for those purposes. But, given the success of our current practice of ascribing representational properties, it is going to be difficult to show this. The arguments in the next chapter that count against normative semi-Representationalism count also against normative anti-Representationalism (5.11–5.12).

I presented my Representationalist program in part I. In this part I have rejected rival programs. I turn now to developing my program further. In part III I consider the semantics of attitude ascriptions themselves; we move from discussing "first-level" meanings to discussing "second-level" ones. In part IV, we consider some interesting puzzles.

III. ATTITUDE ASCRIPTIONS

4.11. The Context Dependency of Meaning Ascriptions

The discussion so far has involved plenty of attention to attitude ascriptions. However, our focus has not been on *their* meanings, second-level meanings. It has been rather on what the folk use of those ascriptions shows about the meanings of simpler sentences, first-level meanings. This focus was dictated by the "ultimate" method. In using an attitude ascription, a person applies a certain property to a token for semantic purposes, she applies a putative

196

meaning. So, by considering such uses we can discover what tokens the folk apply the meaning to. Despite this focus, we could not avoid some second-level claims.

One such claim will be the concern of this section. I shall then address a methodological question about the relation of semantics to metaphysics that is raised by the usual second-level discussion (4.12). Against this background, I shall propose a theory of second-level meanings (4.13).

In my first-level discussion, I concluded that we ordinarily ascribe at least three different sorts of meaning to singular terms (4.2). This conclusion was based on a Quinean view of meaning ascriptions, a view that was supported by the discussion. The Quinean view makes meaning ascriptions like

(1) Ralph believes that Ortcutt is a spy

mildly context dependent: The context – in particular, the intention of the speaker – determines whether the ascription is transparent or opaque. Some philosophers think that these ascriptions are more radically context dependent. In this section I shall consider this issue of context dependency and its bearing on the conclusion about meaning.

It is important to start by noting that the context dependency of these ascriptions is *clearly* not *very* radical. Thus, on the one hand, if 'that Yeltzin has risen' is used according to the conventions of English, then there are indefinitely many meanings it could *not* be used to ascribe, however the context is varied, including all the meanings of the token I shall now utter: "Wittgenstein is a hero to many." On the other hand, there are only a small number of English t-clauses that could be used to ascribe any of the meanings of this utterance of mine, however the context is varied. If t-clauses are indexicals, they are certainly not nearly *as* indexical as demonstratives like 'this' and 'that'. The meanings of a t-clause limit the meanings it can be used to ascribe.

How? I have already suggested an answer: A t-clause can only ascribe a meaning that is closely related to one of the meanings of its content sentence; there is an "intimate link" between the two meanings. I have also suggested that the link is often the closest relation of all: identity.

The assumption that there is an intimate link is prima facie very plausible. Indeed, semanticists tend to take it for granted.[60] The present discussion yields a powerful argument for the assumption. We need the intimate link not only to explain the limitations on what meaning a t–clause can ascribe but also to explain how it can do its job of ascribing meanings at all. Hearers typically understand attitude ascriptions. So the meaning ascribed has to be such that hearers can readily tell that it has been ascribed. What does this show us about these ascriptions and their dependence on context?

To get a feel for the sort of answer we might give, we should remind ourselves of how hearers *generally* understand utterances. To understand an utterance is to associate the right set of meanings with it (4.2). In some cases, the hearer can understand with only minimal help from the context because, first, the right set of meanings is the *conventional* one for the sentence tokened in the utterance and, second, she participates in the convention; for example, an English speaker's understanding of an utterance of 'Dogs have fleas' in an English-speaking environment. But she may need substantial help from the context in other cases. Three sorts of help seem relevant. (i) An indexical has associated with it the convention that the meaning of a token is determined by a certain aspect of the context; thus, 'I' conventionally refers to the speaker; 'you', to an object addressed; 'he', to a perceived and/or demonstrated male. The hearer's understanding of a token indexical depends on detecting the appropriate aspect of the context. (ii)

---

60   As I pointed out before (2.12, n. 34), the assumption underlies Frege's view that expressions in a content sentence refer to their usual senses, Davidson's doctrine of "semantic innocence," and Kripke's "strengthened disquotational principle." My stance on these is as follows. I reject Frege's view, partly because it overlooks the transparent reading of (1) and partly on the ontological grounds set out in section 4.12. I accept semantic innocence. I accept Kripke's disquotational principle, opaquely construed (perhaps with a qualification because of the puzzles discussed in sec. 4.16).

The context has a more subtle role in removing ambiguities. An ambiguous sentence may have more than one convention covering its syntax ('Visiting relatives can be boring') or a contained word ('bank'). Which convention applies to a particular token of the sentence? That is determined by what the speaker has in mind, but the hearer must be guided in her understanding by aspects of the context that are more accessible to her. (iii) Many utterances are elliptical because the speaker omits what he thinks is too boringly obvious in the context. Thus he will omit 'in New York' from 'It's raining in New York' if responding to a question about the weather in New York. So, in understanding the utterance, the hearer must supplement it, guided by what is obvious in the context. The morals to be drawn from this brief reminder are first, the meaning of a token utterance (normally) depends heavily on the conventional meaning of its type, and second, insofar as the hearer's understanding must be guided by some aspect of the context, that aspect is usually *accessible to* the hearer.

In sum, a theory of attitude ascriptions must meet two constraints.

First Constraint: The theory must make the intimate link close enough to explain the limitations on what a t-clause can ascribe. The further this link departs from identity, the more difficult explaining this becomes.

Second Constraint: The theory must explain how hearers use linguistic conventions together with accessible context to understand ascriptions. The more numerous the meanings that a t-clause can ascribe, the more difficult explaining this becomes.

1. Consider how my Quinean theory fares. With ascriptions of two sorts of meaning, the intimate link is an identity, and so the theory readily meets the first constraint. (*a*) One meaning of a singular term is its property of referring to a certain object. When the term is in the t-clause of an ascription with a simply-transparent construal, that property is the meaning that the

199

t-clause ascribes; thus, in this construal, the t-clause containing 'Ortcutt' in (1) ascribes the property of referring to Ortcutt. (*b*) Another meaning of a singular term is its property of (purportedly) referring to an object by a certain mode. When the term is in an opaquely construed ascription, that property is the meaning that the term ascribes; thus, in that construal, the t-clause in (1) ascribes the property of referring to Ortcutt by the very mode that its token of 'Ortcutt' does.

The theory for ascriptions of these two sorts of meaning also meets the second constraint. The only thing noteworthy about understanding a sentence like (1) in this theory is that the sentence has a special sort of ambiguity.[61] In one convention, (1) is transparent and ascribes one meaning of its content sentence; on the other, it is opaque and ascribes another. So the context has role (ii): guiding the hearer to the meaning in mind. This role is subtle, as I remarked, but the context required for it in this case seems as accessible as normal.

(*c*) Ascriptions of the third sort of meaning, rapport-transparent ascriptions, do not meet the first constraint so simply. This is not apparent when we consider,

(2) Ortcutt is such that Ralph believes him to be a spy,

where the singular term in the t-clause, 'him', is designational (because the term on which it depends, 'Ortcutt', is designational). So the t-clause ascribes a meaning that the term has, the property of designating Ortcutt. But consider

(4) The shortest spy is such that Ralph believes him to be a spy.

Here 'him' is attributive (because, we are assuming, the term on which it depends, 'the shortest spy', is attributive) and does not have the meaning that the t-clause ascribes, the property of desig-

---

61 Is the ambiguity syntactic or lexical? Is it a matter of different "deep structures" yielding the one "surface structure," or is it a matter of different, although closely related, meanings of 'believes that'? I do not know. Presumably, we must look to our best syntactic theory for an answer.

nating whomever is the shortest spy. 'Him' does, of course, have the property of *referring to* that spy. So, although the intimate link here is not identity, it is close enough for the theory to meet the first constraint.

The theory easily meets the second constraint. The shift from reference to designation is achieved by the conventional syntax of ascriptions like (2) and (4), a syntax that distinguishes them from sentences like (1). This syntax determines that the t–clause ascribes the property of designating what 'him' refers to. The ascription adds no extra context dependency.

2. Let us now consider more extreme context-dependency theories. One theory does not depart much from my Quinean view. It takes the singular term in the t–clause to ascribe the property of (purportedly) referring to a certain object by a certain mode. The object in question is the (purported) referent of that singular term. The mode in question – and this is the big departure – is not necessarily the mode of that singular term: It can be *some other mode that the speaker has in mind*. The mode ascribed is not determined by the conventional meaning of the singular term in the t–clause but by a "hidden indexical" component of the ascription together with the context of utterance.[62] The theory tends to ignore Quine's discussion of the transparent-opaque distinction, and yet it could easily take account of the discussion. It could treat examples that suggest my Quinean opaque construal as the special case where the mode that the speaker has in mind happens to match the mode of the singular term in the t–clause. It

---

62 Schiffer 1979, Crimmins and Perry 1989, Richard 1990, and Crimmins 1992 are examples of this sort of theory; Fodor 1990 (pp. 171–2) comes close. Schiffer claims that the "essential idea [of the theory] must have occurred to almost anyone who has thought seriously about the semantics of belief sentences" (1992: 500). Quine (1979) himself has come to favor a context-dependency view of the examples he formerly thought of as transparent, renouncing many of the claims on which my Quinean theory is based (too many, in my view: 1981c). He is driven to this by two assumptions: that any transparent attitude ascription requires rapport and that the rapport required must be explained in terms of the context-relative notion, *knowing who*. I think that both these assumptions are wrong (4.2, 4.6).

could treat examples that suggest my Quinean transparent construals by allowing that a speaker may have no particular mode in mind: Either *any* mode (simply-transparent) or *any designational* mode (rapport-transparent) will do.[63] Given the arguments I have already presented, I think that the most plausible version of the "Hidden-Indexical" theory would treat these examples in these ways. So that is the version I shall discuss.

Although this version of the theory differs from my theory of how we ascribe meanings to a singular term, it is in agreement in being Representationalist about the meanings ascribed; thus, in the cases mostly attended to, meanings are properties of (purportedly) referring by certain modes (or, taking meanings as objects, the meanings are those modes). This version accepts the Fregean assumption that the only inferential properties that are parts of meaning are those that constitute modes of reference. Indeed, it agrees totally with my theory about the three sorts of meaning that get ascribed.[64]

Suppose Ralph is in a belief state that would lead him to say,

(12) Ortcutt is a spy.

Then, this version of the theory agrees with my theory that attitude ascriptions can ascribe three different meanings to 'Ort-

63 Schiffer 1979 did not allow this, and so, as I have argued with the help of an example due to Paul Reddam, is open to the objection that the speaker need not have any particular mode in mind (1981c: 219–20). Interestingly, Schiffer himself now offers a detailed objection along these lines to the Hidden-Indexical theory (1992: 512–8). The version of the theory I discuss is not open to this objection. Crimmins and Perry move toward this version in allowing for a second sort of ascription "in which notions [modes of presentation] are not provided" (1989: 705; cf. Crimmins 1992: 171–9). Richard near enough accepts the version (1990: 135–6).

64 This agreement may be obscured if the theory is presented, as it usually is, as part of a "propositional" view of thoughts, a view according to which a thought involves a relation to a *proposition*. This view is inessential to the Hidden-Indexical theory. The version of the theory I am discussing goes along with my view that thoughts are attitudes toward sentences. I shall consider the propositional view in the next section.

cutt' in (12): the property of referring to Ortcutt, the property of designating him, and the property of (purportedly) referring to him under the mode 'Ortcutt'. The version disagrees in thinking that this latter meaning can be ascribed not only by t-clauses containing 'Ortcutt' but by ones containing other terms that (purportedly) refer to Ortcutt. In brief, the most plausible version of the theory disagrees over the semantics of the likes of (1), not over the likes of (12). So, nothing very significant about meaning is at stake in this disagreement.

So much for the description of the Hidden-Indexical theory. What is its motivation? There is a serious problem with this. What we need are some examples that favor the extreme context dependency of the theory *over the mild context dependency of the Quinean theory*. That is not what we get. What we mostly get are standard examples like those that motivated the Quinean theory in the first place (part I).[65] These can, of course, be readily handled by that theory, and no attempt is made to show otherwise; for, as I have noted, the theory tends to ignore Quine's discussion. We also get post-Quinean "puzzling" examples, like Kripke's famous one.[66] However, as we shall see in part IV, these examples support, at most, a minor modification of the Quinean theory, not the Hidden-Indexical theory. Once again, no attempt is made to show otherwise. The motivation for the theory seems to come largely from other theoretical commitments.[67]

---

65 Schiffer 1979: 64–7; 1992: 509–10; Crimmins and Perry 1989: 698–9; Richard 1990: 133–41.

66 Schiffer 1979: 66; 1992: 510; Crimmins and Perry 1989: 706–9; Richard 1990: 179–96.

67 Consider Crimmins and Perry (1987), for example. They are committed to direct reference and to semantic innocence. This seems to have the highly implausible consequence that attitude ascriptions are not opaque after all. Crimmins and Perry are not prepared to join Salmon and Soames in biting that bullet. The Hidden-Indexical theory is their way of avoiding doing so. It enables them to locate the opacity not in the very words of the ascription but in "unarticulated constituents." The result is nicely criticized by Graham Oppy (1992). He recommends dropping semantic innocence. I recommend dropping direct reference.

To see the problem that the Hidden-Indexical theory has in standard situations, let us return to the Big Felix example (4.2). Mary, having learned the identity of the man she saw at the bar, says to a mobster (just as the moll did before),

(7) Ralph believes that Big Felix is insane.

In the original story, Mary has in mind that Ralph has his suspicions under the mode of 'Smith's murderer'. If the theory is correct, the conventions of English make it possible for (7), in some context, to ascribe to Ralph a belief under that particular mode. And in some other context, it could ascribe a different mode that Mary might have in mind, the mode 'the man seen at the bar', 'the most successful mobster', or whatever. So it has to be possible for (7) to be false in some context because the mode Mary has in mind is 'the man seen at the bar' whereas the mode under which Ralph has his suspicions is 'Smith's murderer'. In particular, it has to be possible for (7) to be false in some context *even though Ralph would assent to "Big Felix is insane"* because that is not the mode Mary has in mind. So far as I know, the literature contains no examples that support these possibilities, and I have been unable to imagine any.

How does the theory handle the constraints? It does well enough with the first because its intimate link is close enough to identity to explain the limitations on what a t-clause can ascribe: The mode of referring ascribed by a singular term in a t-clause must be a mode of referring to the object (purportedly) referred to by that term. But the theory has real problems with the second constraint, with explaining how hearers use linguistic conventions together with accessible context to understand ascriptions.

We note, first, that the role of the context here is unlike any of the three we outlined. It is unlike (i) in that, if anything directs the hearer of an attitude ascription to a particular aspect of the context in order to discover the intended mode, it is not a *convention* associated with the ascription that does this. No convention associated with (7) directs the hearer to something that picks out 'Smith's murderer' as the mode, in the way that the convention for the indexical 'you' directs the hearer to the person addressed as the referent. The role of the context is unlike (ii) in that ascriptions are not appropriately ambiguous. Thus, it is not the case that, according to one convention, (7) specifies the mode, 'Smith's murderer', according to another, 'the man seen at the bar', according to another, 'the most successful mobster', and so on through all modes of referring to Big Felix. So it cannot be the case that the context guides the hearer's choice of the convention that the speaker has in mind. Finally, despite suggestions to the contrary (Crimmins and Perry 1989: 699–700; Schiffer 1992: 504), the role of the context is unlike (iii).

The first respect in which it is unlike is that ascriptions do not seem to be elliptical. What, after all, is (7) an elliptical version *of?* Suppose that Mary has the mode 'Smith's murderer' in mind, then presumably she *could* ascribe this mode by asserting

(5) Ralph believes that Smith's murderer is insane.

It would be strange to see (7) as an elliptical version of (5). It would be even stranger to see (5),

(10) Ralph believes that the most successful mobster is insane,

or

(11) Ralph believes that the man seen at the bar is insane,

each of which, in the theory, could be used in some context to ascribe the mode 'Big Felix', as elliptical versions of (7).

The second respect in which the role of the context is unlike (iii) is that the mode that the context is supposed to supply does not seem *obvious* in the context. This raises a general problem for the theory.

In defense of the theory, it might be claimed that the role of the context with attitude ascriptions does not have to be (i), (ii), or (iii): It could be sui generis. Fair enough, but what then is the role? One way or another, the context must guide the hearer to the mode in mind. It is hard to see how *any aspect of the context accessible to the hearer* can do that. It is presumably not the case that *each* of (5), (7), (10), and (11) could be used in *any* context to ascribe *any* of the modes of referring to Big Felix, for then the hearer's task would clearly be impossible. In some way, the context must limit the ascriptions that can be used for a mode, so that the hearer can infer the mode from the ascription in the context. It is hard to see what the limitations could be. At least, the Hidden-Indexical theory is seriously incomplete without an account of the limitations.[68]

In sum, my Quinean theory accepts that attitude ascriptions have a small amount of context dependency of a familiar sort, that of the ambiguous. The Hidden-Indexical theory claims that the context dependency is much greater. There is no argument to support this claim. Furthermore, the theory badly needs to explain how it satisfies the second constraint; how some aspect of the accessible context could play the required role, a role other than the familiar (i), (ii), or (iii). I doubt that the theory can meet this constraint.

3. Finally, let us consider non-Representationalist views. My examination of attitude ascriptions yielded no clear evidence for such views; I found no evidence that we ever ascribe a meaning that is even partly a non-reference-determining functional role (4.9–4.10). But suppose I were wrong about this. What theory of the context dependency of attitude ascriptions might accompany the resulting view of meaning? There seem to be three sorts.

(*a*) One theory is no more context dependent than is mine. It assumes that an ascription can ascribe only a small set of meanings, some of which must of course be, at least partly, constituted by functional roles that are not determinate of reference. Each of these meanings is a meaning of the ascription's content sentence, and so the intimate link needed for an ascription to do its job is identity. Thus this theory would meet the first constraint. But how would it meet the second constraint? It could start by claiming that an ascription is ambiguous, having associated with it a

---

68 Crimmins and Perry frankly admit the failure of their own theory in this respect (1989: 711).

convention for each of the meanings it can be used to ascribe. My Representationalism makes me doubt this start, but, if it could be made good, then the context could have role (ii), guiding the hearer to the conventional meaning in mind.

(b) The next theory is much more context dependent. It also takes the intimate link to be identity, thus meeting the first constraint. But it differs from (a) in assuming that an ascription has, and hence can ascribe, an indefinitely large set of meanings. These meanings are constituted in many different ways out of a token's functional role and referential properties.[69] So, to meet the second constraint this theory must show how the accessible context enables the hearer to tell which of the meanings in this large set is ascribed. This time we cannot start by claiming ambiguity: An ascription surely does not have indefinitely many conventions. So the context does not have role (ii). The role of the context in choosing between many meanings is as mysterious here as it was with Hidden-Indexical theory.

(c) The last theory is also very context dependent. It differs from the previous one in not taking the intimate link to be identity. So a person can ascribe a meaning using a content sentence that does not have that meaning. To meet the first constraint, it seems that the meaning ascribed must include *at least part of* a meaning of the content clause. One candidate for that part is reference (cf. the Hidden-Indexical theory), but that candidate is not available if the meaning ascribed is entirely nonreferential. Aside from this difficulty with the first constraint, the theory has the same difficulty with the second constraint as does (b). How could the context accessible to the hearer guide her to what has been ascribed?

We earlier found no evidence that we ever ascribe meanings that were even partly non-Representationalist. We see now that if we do ascribe such meanings, our ascriptions are likely to be only mildly context dependent.

---

69 A theory along these lines is suggested by Stich (1983: 85–106), using, inter alia, the examples discussed in section 4.9.

I conclude that it is unlikely that attitude ascriptions are highly context dependent. Our consideration of this issue has not motivated any modification in our Quinean theory of attitude ascriptions nor in our theory of the meanings ascribed.

The discussion has provided persuasive evidence for the intimate link. Further evidence comes from a consideration of human babies and the higher animals. The nonlinguistic behavior of these creatures gives us reasons for thinking that they have thoughts. However, we feel (or should feel) uncomfortable in using ordinary attitude ascriptions to ascribe these thoughts (Armstrong 1973: 25–7; Stich 1979). Why? Because, given the intimate link, an ordinary ascription requires us to find a sentence that (near enough) shares a meaning with the creature's thought. We quite reasonably doubt that we have such a sentence. Even extensional ascriptions seem dubious: Are Fido's thoughts "about bones" *really* about *bones?* Thus, the intimate link helps explain our discomfort.

4.12. "Put Metaphysics First"

The second-level investigation of the meanings of attitude ascriptions raises an interesting methodological issue about the relation of semantics to metaphysics. Lycan has pointed out that

until recently, semanticists investigating belief sentences, particularly those semanticists working within the possible-worlds format, have paid no attention to the question of what psychological reality it is that makes such sentences true. (1988: 8)

He thinks that such attention is necessary for our theory of these sentences and thus for our theory of thought ascriptions generally. I agree. Indeed, I think that we should go further in criticizing the traditional approach to the semantics of thought ascriptions. This semantics should *start* with close attention to psychological reality (1984: 385–6). Semantics *generally* should give a certain temporal and explanatory priority to metaphysical concerns; it should be guided by the methodological slogan "Put metaphysics first" (2.12). And this should lead us to expect that the semantics of a sentence will be explained in terms of its relations to a reality that we already believe in for reasons independent of semantics.

The present concern is with second-level meanings. But note that my investigation of first-level meanings in parts I and II has already been in accord with this slogan. Our ascriptions of meanings to token thoughts and utterances committed us, of course, to those tokens. But my theory was not committed to any other peculiarly semantic objects. In considering what is common to word tokens that have a certain meaning, I found that they are (usually) related to other objects. But these objects were not ones posited especially for semantics. They were objects like Ortcutt and spies that we already had good reasons for believing in, reasons having nothing to do with semantics; they were already part of our metaphysics. And had I considered in more detail the syntactic structure that is common to sentence tokens that have a certain (first-level) meaning, no other objects would have been posited. Putting this together, there would be no need in explaining the meanings of those sentence tokens to posit any unfamiliar objects other than the sentence tokens themselves.

Apply the slogan now to the second-level investigation of thought ascriptions. What do we find when we look at the psychological reality that seems to be the concern of these ascriptions? We find a reality revealed by the earlier first-level investigation and by theories of the mind. There are people with mental states – beliefs, desires, and so on – that play certain causal representational roles. These states consist partly of tokens with first-level meanings. These meanings are properties that tokens have in virtue of their relations to a familiar, largely nonsemantic, world and to other tokens. A similar story holds for the *linguistic* reality that concerns our *utterance* ascriptions. That reality consists of meaningful linguistic tokens playing certain causal roles. The meanings of these tokens are like the meanings of thoughts. So far, then, the reality that concerns our attitude ascriptions is of a fairly unobjectionable sort: concrete physical objects with properties determined by relations to each other and the world. Does it consist of anything more?

The semantic investigation of attitude ascriptions is dominated by philosophers who think that this reality consists also of "propositions." Now, if talk of propositions were a mere manner of speaking to be paraphrased away, when the ontological chips are down, into talk about the properties of concrete thoughts and utterances, then I would have only the minor objection that it is unnecessary and misleading. But the talk usually involves a serious commitment to *Platonic objects* that are separate from the concrete spatio-temporal world of meaningful tokens, a commitment to "transcendent realism" about propositions.[70] Here is a typical statement:

the referents of 'that'-clauses are *propositions,* in the philosophical sense of that term: abstract mind- and language-independent objects. (Schiffer 1992: 506–7)

Guided by the slogan, I offer four reasons for resisting the positing of propositions in semantics. First, in semantics, as in everything else, we should follow Occam and Quine in positing only such objects as are needed to explain the phenomena. We found no need for propositions to explain first-level meanings. In a moment I shall argue that we do not need them to explain second-level meanings. Second, propositions are posited primarily to give meanings to t-clauses. This smacks of positing a golden mountain to give meaning to 'the golden mountain'. Part of what discredited this Meinongian procedure was that we had no *non*semantic reason for believing in golden mountains. And possible-worlds semantics, taken literally, should be similarly discredited if David Lewis (1986) is not right in arguing that there are good nonsemantic reasons for believing in possible worlds. Third, the nature of Platonic objects like propositions is very mysterious. Fourth, because propositions and the like can play no causal role in mind and language, we have the best of reasons for thinking that they are not part of mental and linguistic reality.

70 Cf. David Armstrong's definition of transcendent realism about universals: "The doctrine that universals exist separated from particulars" (1978: 140).

Objection 1: "If the third and fourth reasons were good, they should count equally against talk of numbers in physics. Yet physics is committed to numbers." I think that this commitment should be much more a source of discomfort about physics than it should be a source of comfort about propositions. We should seek some way of understanding physics that is not committed to Platonic objects, perhaps following Field (1980) in eliminating numbers altogether.

Objection 2: Mark Richard starts a recent book

with the assumption that attitude ascriptions are what they appear to be:... two-place predicat[ions] ... This assumption – that at a certain level of generality

> Iago hopes that Desdemona will betray Othello

is on a syntactic and semantic par with

> Iago kissed Desdemona

– saddles us immediately with t-clauses as names of entities of some sort. That is, it saddles us immediately with propositions. (1990: 5)

So, Richard's implicit response to my first reason is that semanticists do need to posit propositions because folk attitude ascriptions are committed to them. And Richard speaks for many here.

But are the folk really committed to propositions? I have already indicated a preference for an alternative construal of these ascriptions (2.2). On this alternative, the earlier hope ascription is on a par with

> Iago kissed a woman.

So, just as this sentence commits us to a token object with the property specified by 'woman', the hope ascription commits us to a token mental state with the property specified by 'that Desdemona will betray Othello'. The ascription does not commit us to propositions. And, despite what Richard says, an attitude ascription no more appears to have the logical form of 'Iago kissed Desdemona' than it appears to have that of 'Iago kissed a woman'.

In light of this alternative, the case for propositions seems to disappear. Applying our methodology to the second-level investigation, we are interested in what is common and peculiar to the tokens that we call "that Iago hopes that Desdemona will betray Othello"; Richard's ascription is an example of such a token. I have described the relevant reality that we, including Richard (pp. 37–57), *already* believe in – a reality of people in relations to sentences that are themselves related to a familiar world. Guided by the slogan "Put metaphysics first," we should expect to find that any relations that are common and peculiar to token attitude ascriptions will be relations to *this* reality. And we should require compelling reasons before concluding that we must take these tokens as sharing a relation to a proposition, an object we previously had no reason to posit. My alternative construal of the token ascriptions shows that Richard has not so far produced such a consideration.

However, there is more to be said. We have been discussing what we might call "particular" attitude ascriptions. Richard's case for propositions looks stronger when we consider "general" ascriptions, ones that seem to *quantify over* propositions. Consider, for example,

(13) There is something that Joe and Mary both believe.

Whereas there is nothing about the role of the form 'that *p*' that compels us to take particular attitude ascriptions as referring to propositions, the role of quantification does seem to compel us to take general ascriptions to be quantifying over propositions.

Suppose that this is so. It does not follow that *semanticists* are compelled to quantify over propositions to explain the meanings of general ascriptions. Consider an analogy. Sentences like the following were once common:

(14) There is someone who cast a spell over both Joe and Mary.

Just as (13) quantifies over propositions in that there have to be propositions for it to be true, so also does (14) quantify over

212

witches in that there have to be witches for it to be true. However, semanticists do not need to quantify over witches to explain the meaning of (14) if they are prepared to treat it as false, which they all are. No more do they need to quantify over propositions to explain (13) if they are prepared to treat it as false.

Treating general attitude ascriptions like (13) as false may seem a heavy price to pay for avoiding propositions. For, these ascriptions, unlike (14), seem to be explanatorily useful, generally successful, and needed. But we do not need to treat them, as we do (14), as *totally* misguided. There is another, less radical, way that they might be wrong. Quantifying over propositions may be a *mere manner of speaking* that is strictly false but that can be replaced, in the Quinean way, by a paraphrase that will serve original purposes well enough without the objectionable commitment. Situations of this sort are familiar enough. We say, "There's a chance he'll be late," quantifying over chances, and yet, when the ontological chips are down, we can paraphrase away our commitment with "He may be late." Sometimes the desired paraphrase is not so readily available; for example, it is not for numbers in physics, as the difficulties of Field's enterprise show. In the present case, however, paraphrases are easy to find. Instead of (13) we say:

Joe and Mary believe synonymous tokens.

This quantifies over sentence tokens, and yet it will do just as well as the quantification over propositions in explaining behavior and guiding us to reality. So we do not need to quantify over propositions. Given the objections to them, we should not quantify over them.

In terms of my methodology, what I have just proposed is that Richard is descriptively right about general attitude ascriptions but not normatively so. In these ascriptions the folk ascribe relations to propositions to serve their semantic purposes. But the folk should not do so: They should ascribe properties of the sort that we have been discussing in parts I and II. These properties, not relations to propositions, serve our semantic purposes and so are

213

meanings. This is revisionism, but it is revisionism of the mildest sort.

Return now to the semantics of *particular* attitude ascriptions. I argued that we do not need to take t-clauses as definite singular terms that purport to refer to propositions; we can take them as indefinite singular terms quantifying over sentence tokens. But suppose that I were wrong. So Richard would be descriptively right here too. The discussion of general ascriptions shows how we could still avoid commitment to propositions in semantics, so that Richard would again not be normatively right. Although t-clauses *purport* to refer to propositions, they *fail* to refer to them, in just the same way that 'Pegasus flies' purports to refer to a winged horse but fails to do so. And the problem of the semantics of t-clauses would be subsumed under the general problem of the semantics of empty singular terms. Of course, this treatment would have the seemingly unfortunate consequence that the folk's particular attitude ascriptions would all be false. Yet this would really be no more of a problem than the falsity of their general ones because, once again, a suitable paraphrase would be readily at hand. Even if I were wrong in thinking that folk attitude ascriptions have the form '*x R* an *F*', referring to tokens, ascriptions of that form would serve our purposes just as well as ones of the form '*xRy*' that name propositions. So we should replace ones of the latter form with ones of the former. In sum, if I were wrong, another piece of mild revisionism would be called for.

I have been arguing that "Put metaphysics first" spares us propositions in semantics. It has another advantage: Propositions are sometimes largely responsible for *generating* puzzles about belief ascriptions, as we shall see in section 4.15. Once propositions are dispensed with, the problems that remain seem more tractable.

Finally, many, perhaps most, philosophers of language will find my Quinean scruples about propositions and the like rather quaint. In part I think this reflects the history of semantics as a formal rather than an empirical science. I shall continue to stick to my scruples in presenting my theory, but those who do not share my taste for desert landscapes can often paraphrase the theory into jungle language, as I illustrate from time to time.

4.13. The Meanings of Attitude Ascriptions

I have argued so far that an attitude ascription has no more than a Quinean context dependency, that there is indeed an intimate link between the meaning it ascribes and the meaning of its content sentence, and that it has the form '*x R* an *F*' and so does not ascribe a relation to a proposition. On this basis, I shall now round out my account of the meanings of attitude ascriptions, of second-level meanings.

The straightforward way to start is to apply the "ultimate" method to putative second-level meanings by investigating ascriptions of attitudes *to attitudes:* We examine the token attitude ascriptions to which we do and do not ascribe a certain meaning. But the most popular way to start is, in effect, to apply the "ultimate" method to the *truth conditions* of attitude ascriptions: We examine the token ascriptions to which we do and do not ascribe truth. The problem with this way of starting, as I have pointed out (2.7, 2.12), is that it *presupposes* that the meanings of these ascriptions are truth conditional. This Representationalist view needs to be argued for. Truth might be deflationary, for example, having nothing to do with explaining meaning.

We have already noted that claims about the truth conditions of attitude ascriptions must bear on the investigation of the first-level meanings *ascribed.* For, to judge that '*x* believes that *p*' would be true in certain circumstances is to judge that we would call a token with certain properties "that *p*," *whatever* the notion of truth involved (4.2). Yet, paradoxically perhaps, it takes an argument to show that those claims bear on the investigation of the second-level meanings *of the ascriptions themselves.*

I take the case already presented for Representationalism to be such an argument. That case concerns first-level meanings. It is hardly conceivable that this case could be good and yet Representationalism not be true about second-level meanings. So I shall assume that it is true.

Using this assumption, we can make further progress before applying the "ultimate" method to second-level meanings. Consider the meanings of the moll's token utterance,

(7) Ralph believes that Big Felix is insane.

'Ralph' will have the usual three meanings: the property of referring to Ralph; the property of designating (en rapport reference) Ralph; and the property of referring to Ralph by the particular mode of 'Ralph'. In the light of what has gone before, that is not interesting. Interest begins when we consider the meanings of 'believes that Big Felix is insane'. If the logical form of (7) is '$x\ R$ an F' then we have to "locate the indefiniteness" in either 'believes' or 'that Big Felix is insane'.[71] If we locate it in 'believes' then one meaning of 'that Big Felix is insane' will be its property of applying to tokens with a certain meaning. If we locate the indefiniteness in 'that Big Felix is insane' then its property of applying to tokens with a certain meaning will be *part of* one of its meanings, the other part being its role as a quantifier. Corresponding remarks apply to 'believes'. I have no strong views on this subtle syntactic choice. However, ascriptions like 'Ralph believes Gödel's Incompleteness Theorem', where there is no t-clause, give a reason for locating the indefiniteness in 'believes'. And it will be convenient to locate it there because I shall be saying no more about the meanings of 'believes'. So one meaning of 'that Big Felix is insane' will be its property of applying to tokens with a certain meaning. And, given Representationalism, any other meaning it has will be a property of applying to those tokens by a certain mode.

According to the intimate link, a t-clause ascribes a meaning that is closely related to one meaning of its content sentence. Put this together with what we have just settled and we can conclude

---

71   Thanks to Eric Lormand for drawing my attention to this.

that the meanings of the token 'that Big Felix is insane' are its property of applying to tokens with a meaning of 'Big Felix is insane' and its properties of so applying by certain modes.

We have obtained these results without applying the "ultimate" method to second-level meanings. Applying it confirms the results. We consider ascriptions of attitudes to attitudes for evidence of what meanings we ascribe to attitude ascriptions; for example, consider

(15) The moll says that Ralph believes that Big Felix is insane.

Let us focus on the meanings we ascribe by 'Big Felix' in tokens of (15). On some occasions the context of 'Big Felix' in (15) is transparent, so that among the token ascriptions we are prepared to call "that Ralph believes that Big Felix is insane" are not only ones like (7) but ones that have in place of 'Big Felix' other terms that refer to Big Felix. So, the meaning we are ascribing to terms in the place of 'Big Felix' is that of referring to Big Felix. On other occasions, however, the context of 'Big Felix' in (15) is opaque, so that only tokens that are like (7) in having 'Big Felix' in the place of 'Big Felix' are called "that Ralph believes that Big Felix is insane." So, the meaning we are ascribing to terms in the place of 'Big Felix' is the property of referring to Big Felix under the mode of 'Big Felix'.

In describing all these properties that we ascribe to the likes of (7) as "meanings," I am assuming that ascribing them does indeed serve our semantic purposes. The assumption is reasonable in the light of our first-level investigation and could be supported by similar arguments to those used in that investigation (4.3). In ascribing attitudes to attitudes, we are interested in explaining the behavior of the person to whom we make the ascription; for example, our interest in the moll's behavior may lead to (15). And we are interested in using the ascription as a guide to the reality that is the subject of the attitude ascribed, (usually) someone else's attitude; for example, our interest in Ralph's beliefs – an interest we have because of our interest in explaining *his* behavior or our interest in the reality of Big Felix that the beliefs are about – may lead to (15). We could show how in some circumstances an opaquely construed, in other circumstances a transparently construed, ascription of an attitude to an attitude can serve one of these purposes.

I shall now develop the Representationalist program of part I by taking account of some interesting "puzzles."

IV. DEVELOPING THE PROGRAM[72]

4.14. Demonstratives

I have said little so far that is particularly about meanings ascribed by (deictic) demonstratives and pronouns (briefly, "demonstratives") in t-clauses. I remarked parenthetically that, in an opaque context, they ascribe the property of referring by a demonstrative but not necessarily by the particular demonstrative in the t-clause (4.2). (Let us call a mode of referring by some demonstrative or other, "a general demonstrative mode," and by a particular demonstrative, "a particular demonstrative mode.") And I have used IT as an illustration of how historical-causal links to reality might constitute the meanings ascribed (4.6). It is time to say more. (I postpone until the next section discussion of the meanings ascribed by reflexive pronouns.)

Richard has invented an example that generates some nice puzzles about belief ascriptions.

A . . . both sees a woman, across the street, in a phone booth, and is speaking to a woman through a phone. He does not realize that the woman to whom he is speaking – *B,* to give her a name – is the woman he sees. He perceives her to be in some danger – a run-away steamroller, say, is bearing down upon her phone booth. *A* waves at the woman; he says nothing into the phone. (1983: 439)

I shall be concerned with a puzzle about demonstratives.

72 The discussion in this part draws on several previous discussions, particularly in 1981a, 1984, and 1990b, but the methodology of Chapter 2 leads to a somewhat different line.

Suppose that C is with B in the phone booth and observes A waving. He says to B,

(16) That man waving believes that you are in danger.

At the same time, on the basis of information supplied to him by B, he would be prepared to say to her,

(17) The man on the telephone believes that you are not in danger.

(16) and (17) seem to ascribe contradictory beliefs to A and yet A is surely not irrational.

This confidence in A's rationality is quickly confirmed by following the slogan of putting metaphysics first. We start not by worrying about the second-level meanings of these ascriptions but by considering the psychological reality that concerns the ascriptions. That reality is not puzzling. A has two tokens in his belief box. One he has formed on the basis of his perception of B in the phone booth, which disposes him to say, "She is in danger." The other he has formed on the basis of his conversation with B, which disposes him to say, "You are not in danger." The singular terms 'she' and 'you' in these belief tokens are syntactically quite distinct and have different modes of reference. Furthermore, the example forces us to accept something that is congenial anyway: Because of the different modes, tokens of 'she' and 'you' have different meanings even if they are coreferential. For, the difference in modes makes a behavioral difference and hence a difference in semantic role. Thus, A's belief, "She is in danger," leads him to wave at B. Had he not seen B across the street but rather had heard a story that led him to a belief that he could express to B over the phone, "You are in danger," he would not have waved at her but *would have* expressed this belief and doubtless several others. Finally, although A's two actual belief tokens are, in a sense, contradictory, he is not in the least irrational because he has no access to the facts that make them so. To suppose otherwise is to adopt Cartesianism (1.7, 1.8, 2.2, 4.7).

The puzzle is not at the level of beliefs but at the level of

219

ascriptions of beliefs. We appear to be truly ascribing contradictory beliefs, and hence irrationality, to A.

To avoid overreacting to this, it helps to remember Quine's original discussion of transparent ascriptions. On the basis of Ralph's beliefs about a man in a brown hat, it is true to say, transparently,

(1) Ralph believes that Ortcutt is a spy.

But on the basis of his beliefs about a man seen at the beach, it is also true to say, transparently,

(18) Ralph believes that Ortcutt is not a spy.

That a person can have opposite beliefs about a person under different modes of reference, together with the fact that we can abstract from the modes by ascribing beliefs transparently, immediately opens up the possibility of appearing to ascribe irrationality. In Quine's example, the appearance can easily be removed by making the appropriate opaque ascriptions using 'the man in the brown hat' and 'the man seen at the beach'.

In Richard's example, the appearance is not so easily removed because (16) and (17) *are* the appropriate opaque ascriptions. The puzzle comes from our standard opaque way of informing a person we are addressing of demonstrative beliefs that someone has about her:

X believes that you are F.

This ascribes to X a belief, about the person addressed, under a *general* demonstrative mode but not under any *particular* demonstrative mode; thus the mode might be that of 'she' or 'you'. So, the meaning we ascribe is not as fine grained as the meanings we have just described. This is not to say that the folk would not ascribe the finer grain in unusual circumstances like Richard's example. They might resort to a more complex nonstandard form of ascription like the following:

X believes that you, qua the person (s)he is addressing, are F.

220

Much the same could be said about ascriptions involving any of the demonstratives.

It is obvious, of course, that 'she', 'you', and other demonstratives have slightly different modes of referring. And, on this basis, we are used to assigning them different meanings in our semantic theorizing. It is interesting, then, that the folk do not have standard forms of ascription that distinguish the meanings. The reason for this is not hard to find: In the usual circumstances of folk explanations of behavior, that fine a grain is not significant.

In light of this discussion, we must of course conclude that (16) and (17), although inadequate as explainers of behavior, are both true.

But perhaps this is too hasty. It might plausibly be objected that, in situations like this, the *context* determines which finer grained particular demonstrative mode is ascribed; the context "supplies the qua." Thus the context determines that (16) ascribes the mode of 'she' and (17) the mode of 'you', and they both explain *A*'s behavior well. In this situation, (16) and (17) are elliptical versions of nonstandard ascriptions, omitting the "qua-clauses" that are obvious in the context. The context plays what we earlier called "role (iii)," the paradigm of which is its contribution to the meaning of "It is raining" (4.11).

So, according to this objection, (16) and (17) have a "hidden-indexical" element. Indeed, Richard's example is one of the "puzzling" ones that motivate the Hidden-Indexical theory (4.11). It is insufficient motivation. If we accept the objection, as I am inclined to, the example shows that in situations like Richard's the context selects which particular demonstrative mode is ascribed by an attitude ascription involving a demonstrative. It does not show that the context plays this role in more usual circumstances. It gives no reason for us to reverse our view that such an ascription usually ascribes the general demonstrative mode. Probably *any* sentence can be elliptical *sometimes,* but *all* sentences are not elliptical *always.* More importantly, the example does not support the view that the context can determine that an ascription involving a demonstrative ascribes a particular *non*demonstrative mode, one

221

involving a particular *name* or *definite description*. Yet the Hidden-Indexical theory is committed to that view. The theory holds – implausibly, I have argued – that the conventional meaning of the singular term in the t-clause places no constraint at all on the modes that might be ascribed given the proper context; the conventional meaning constrains the reference ascribed but not the mode of reference.

The objection does not support the Hidden-Indexical theory. Rather, it supports a minor modification of my Quinean theory. A demonstrative in an opaque ascription usually ascribes the general demonstrative mode; so the mode ascribed is determined by convention. In unusual situations like Richard's, the context may "narrow down" the mode ascribed to one particular demonstrative mode; thus the mode ascribed is largely determined by convention but a little determined by the context.

We shall later consider another puzzle that motivates the Hidden-Indexical theory, Kripke's puzzle involving names (4.17). My conclusion will be similar: It does not support that theory but rather a minor modification of my Quinean theory.

My earlier discussion of singular terms in general (4.2–4.3) showed that we may have an interest in ascribing any of three different meanings to a demonstrative token. In order of increasing fineness of grain these were the property of referring to a specified object, ascribed by a simply-transparent ascription; the property of designating (en rapport reference to) a specified object, ascribed by a rapport-transparent ascription; and the property of (purportedly) referring to a specified object under the general demonstrative mode, ascribed by a standard opaque ascription. We see now that we may also have an interest in an even finer grained fourth meaning: the property of (purportedly) referring to a specified object by a specified demonstrative.[73] Perhaps we

---

73 Kaplan (1989a) holds that a demonstrative type has a "character" that determines its referent in varying contexts and that a demonstrative token has a "content" that is its referent. He prefers not to talk of the character of a token. And he prefers to talk of the content of a token as its "meaning" and the character of a type as its "meaning" (pp. 523–4). But it seems that

should say that we lack a standard form for ascribing this, or perhaps that the standard opaque ascription can do the job with the help of the context.

Clearly, the proposal of this fourth meaning should not count as revisionist. The meaning has been long recognized in semantic theory and is acknowledged by the folk in nonstandard ascriptions, at least.

To complete the semantics of demonstratives, it remains to give a theory of reference explaining the different ways in which demonstratives utilize the context to determine reference. It still seems to me that a theory along the lines of IT is correct.

4.15. First-Person Pronouns

Among people's thoughts are some they have of themselves. The following story, taken from John Perry, illustrates the special role these thoughts can play.

I once followed a trail of sugar on a supermarket floor, pushing my cart down the aisle on one side of a tall counter and back the aisle on the other, seeking the shopper with the torn sack to tell him he was making a mess. With each trip around the counter, the trail became thicker. But I seemed unable to catch up. Finally it dawned on me. I was the shopper I was trying to catch.

I believed at the outset that the shopper with a torn sack was making a mess. And I was right. But I did not believe that I was making a mess. That seems to be something I came to believe. And when I came to believe that, I stopped following the trail around the counter and rearranged the torn sack in my cart. My change in beliefs seems to explain my change in behavior. (1993: 33)

> he could accept, on *my* usage of "meaning" (2.6), that the meaning of a token is the combination of its content and the character of its type. If so, taking account, as he does, of the differing characters of demonstratives, this would identify the meaning with the fourth fine-grained meaning. This identification would be prevented, of course, if he took attitude ascriptions involving demonstratives as always transparent and hence as not ascribing a character. Perhaps he does (p. 554n). Certainly some other direct-reference philosophers do; e.g., Soames (1987: 66–7).

223

It is common to call beliefs of the sort that dramatically changed Perry's behavior *"de se."* I shall not follow this usage because clearly people can have beliefs that are *of themselves* that are not of that sort; Perry's initial belief of the shopper with a torn sack is an example. What is peculiar about the beliefs in question is that they include first-person pronouns like 'I' and 'myself'. So I shall call the beliefs "first person."

If we take beliefs to be relations to propositions and if we focus on the ascription of beliefs, first-person beliefs can seem very puzzling (e.g., Perry 1993: 33–52; Lycan 1988: 85–7). What exactly did Perry's change of belief consist in? How can we identify or express the proposition that Perry came to believe? It seems as if that proposition is mysterious and inaccessible to us.

Yet if we set aside propositions and belief ascriptions and focus, once again, on the psychological reality that the ascriptions are about, there is no puzzle. Perry's initial belief about a person making a mess involved 'the shopper with a torn sack'. The change in Perry's behavior came with a change in belief: He came to token a belief involving 'I'. The story vividly illustrates that these two coreferential singular-term tokens play different roles and have different meanings. This is no more surprising than the difference in meaning between Ralph's belief involving 'Smith's murderer' and one he might come to have involving 'Big Felix'. Our inability to express Perry's first-person belief is just what we should expect. For that belief has a meaning that includes a first-person mode of referring to Perry, manifestly something that only a token produced by Perry could have.

Turn now to the level of belief ascription. Is there a standard form for ascribing first-person thoughts to a person? The question is interesting, but not of great importance. We have already noted that there are standard forms for ascribing thoughts about a person under the mode of his name and under the general demonstrative mode, but perhaps not one under the mode 'you'. Given the special role that first-person thoughts play in the explanation of behavior, we should expect to find a standard way of ascribing them. Hector-Neri Castañeda (1966; 1967) has argued convinc-

224

ingly that there is such a way using pronouns that are implicitly or explicitly reflexive:

X believes that he himself is F.

(Similarly, there is a way with 'I myself', 'you yourself', and so on.) This ascribes a belief that the person would express "I am F." It cannot therefore be reduced to the standard opaque or transparent forms of attitude ascription that we have already discussed.[74]

I have claimed that an opaque ascription containing a demonstrative ascribes a general demonstrative mode, instances of which include the modes of 'you' or 'she' (4.14). We must count the mode of 'I' as an instance too (although 'I' is not strictly a demonstrative). In light of this, it is clear that we ascribe each of the three meanings we discovered in part I to 'I'. In this section, we have seen that we also ascribe to it a fourth meaning: the property of referring to a specified object under the first-person mode, ascribed by an ascription of the preceding form. This meaning has a similarly fine grain to those we posited for 'you' and 'she' in the last section. It differs from them only in having a standard form of words reserved for its ascription,[75] reflecting our much greater interest in the first-person mode.

4.16. Speaker Meaning and Conventional Meaning; Partial Reference

I have earlier claimed that we should follow Grice in distinguishing speaker meanings from conventional meanings (4.4) but have not brought the distinction to bear on the meanings of singular terms. As usual, metaphor and irony provide examples of the need for the distinction. Thus, a cynical journalist, observing General Westmoreland at his desk during the Vietnam War, comments:

---

74 Boër and Lycan (1980: 432) disagree; see my 1984 (p. 399) for a response. Lycan has since changed his mind (1988: 85–7).

75 Not quite reserved, perhaps. Ernie Sosa has constructed an ingenious example suggesting that this form is also open to a transparent construal (1970: 893).

"Napoleon is inventing his body count." We can report the comment in a way that acknowledges the Gricean distinction by saying, "The journalist said that Napoleon was inventing his body count but he meant that Westmoreland was." Other examples of name tokens with different conventional and speaker meanings are provided by the sort of "crossed wires" for which Canon Spooner was famous. And the first use of a nickname for an object, without a dubbing, will have the object as its speaker referent but will not have any conventional referent.

Our semantic purposes make us interested in utterance meanings because they are indicative of thought meanings (2.5). The speaker meaning of an utterance is *immediately* indicative because it is the meaning of the thought that produced the utterance (4.4). The conventional meaning of an utterance is *mediately* indicative because it is a guide to the speaker meaning.

Acknowledging the Gricean distinction requires a modification in IT. According to IT, the opaquely ascribed meaning of a name token is a property it has in virtue of having underlying it a certain sort of network, a network of d-chains involving tokens of certain physical types linked together by the sort of mental processing I described (4.6). The Gricean distinction brings out that networks underlie tokens in two ways: In one way, networks determine the meanings of *mental* tokens and hence the *speaker* meanings of *linguistic* tokens; in the other way, networks determine the *conventional* meanings of *linguistic* tokens by determining which convention the speaker "participates in." Consider the journalist, for example. One network determines that he meant **WESTMORE-LAND** by his token of the sound type /Napoleon/ and that this is the meaning of the thought token that the sound expressed. Another network determines that the journalist participated in a convention that gives his sound the conventional meaning **NA-POLEON.** Usually, of course, speaker and conventional meaning are the same, and so the one network is involved in both determining relations. Clearly, more needs to be said about these two relations. I shall say only one obvious thing about the participating relation. A linguistic name token can have the conventional

226

meaning, M, as a result of the speaker's participation in a convention only if *there is* a convention of using tokens of that physical type to mean M. So, not only did the journalist's token not conventionally mean **WESTMORELAND,** it could not have conventionally meant that.

Here is a puzzle that needs the Gricean distinction. Henry is competent with the name 'Nana' solely as a result of reference borrowing. Finally he meets a cat he takes to be its bearer, Nana. But the cat he meets is actually Jemima. Partly prompted by this encounter, partly by his prior beliefs about Nana, he uses 'Nana'. What is the referent of this token? There is only one relevant convention, which settles that the conventional referent is Nana. But what about its speaker referent (and the thought referent that underlies it)? There seems to be no fact of the matter about whether Henry meant Nana or Jemima. We are tempted to say he meant both. This gets support from IT: The network of d-chains underlying the token is grounded in Nana via the reference borrowings and in Jemima via the encounter. Yet the reference relation for name tokens is supposed to be one-one. As a result of this "confused" meaning at the first level, we have a problem at the second level: Because *our* uses of 'Nana' and 'Jemima' are not confused, we have no standard way to ascribe a speaker meaning to Henry's token. We need to enrich the theory to deal with this puzzle.

We need to enrich it also to deal with the next one. A name type is usually ambiguous: It has many conventional meanings in that it has many bearers; think, for example, of a popular name like 'Bruce'. This can lead to an interesting mistake: A person treats two conventions as one; in terms of IT, he processes tokens from each convention into the one network. Consider an example. Joe has a number of politically well-informed friends who frequently discuss the history of socialism. They often use the name 'Liebknecht', sometimes to designate Wilhelm, the father, and sometimes Karl, the son. Joe, who knows little of politics, takes all of these uses of the name to designate one person. In time, Joe forms some opinions that he airs using 'Liebknecht'.

There seems to be no fact of the matter about whether these tokens refer to Wilhelm or refer to Karl. And the problem here is with both their conventional and speaker meanings. Once again, the confusion at the first level leaves us with no standard way to ascribe meanings to Joe's tokens.[76]

I have argued (1981a: 138–48) that we need Hartry Field's notion of "partial reference" (1973) to deal with these confused meanings. Using this notion we can say that although Henry's token did not speaker refer to either cat, it partially speaker referred to both. And, although Joe's token did not (speaker or conventionally) refer to either Wilhelm or Karl, it partially referred to both. We have no more reason to be gloomy about explaining partial reference than we have about explaining reference. So we can expect to be able to explain the meanings of Henry's and Joe's tokens. Our standard forms will still, of course, fail to ascribe these meanings.

This failure raises the question whether these confused meanings really deserve to be called "meanings" at all. I think they do. First, we can ascribe them in nonstandard ways and doing so can serve our semantic purposes: Tokens with these meanings can explain nonstandardly described behavior and even guide us to reality (Field shows how tokens with these meanings can be true). Second, they are very closely related to paradigm meanings.

4.17. Kripke's Puzzle and Very Fine-Grained Meanings

Joe makes the mistake in processing tokens of the sound /Liebknecht/ of assuming a certain identity and hence creating one "file" where he should have created two: Joe treats tokens that are not conventionally synonymous as if they were synonymous. This leads to serious confusion in Joe's thinking, as we have seen. The opposite mistake in processing is failing to assume a

---

76 If Henry and Joe count as "normal English speakers" then their cases require a modification in Kripke's disquotational principle: They are disposed to sincere reflective assent to 'p' but do not believe that p.

certain identity and hence creating two files where one is appropriate: Tokens that are conventionally synonymous are treated as if they were not. This is the mistake that generates one version of Kripke's puzzle.

This version, unlike the more famous one about Pierre, arises in one language:

Peter . . . may learn the name 'Paderewski' with an identification of the person named as a famous pianist. Naturally, having learned this, Peter will assent to 'Paderewski had musical talent'.. . . Later, in a different circle, Peter learns of someone called 'Paderewski' who was a Polish nationalist leader and Prime Minister. Peter is skeptical of the musical abilities of politicians.. . . Using 'Paderewski' as a name for the *statesman,* Peter assents to, 'Paderewski had no musical talent.' (1979: 265)

Given what Peter was first ready to assent to, we feel entitled to claim:

(19) Peter believes that Paderewski had musical talent.

Yet given what he is later ready to assent to, we feel entitled to claim:

(20) Peter believes that Paderewski had no musical talent.

Thus, we seem to be ascribing contradictory beliefs to Peter even though he is surely not irrational.

There is clearly a puzzle here at the second level, the level of our ascriptions of beliefs. But, guided by our slogan, we should start at the first level, the level of the beliefs themselves.

We see immediately that Peter is no more irrational than was Quine's Ralph or Richard's *A* (4.14). In Peter's belief box, as in theirs, we can distinguish two sets of mental sentences. In each case the sentences in one set contain tokens that lead occasionally to the utterance of a singular term, and the sentences in the other set contain tokens of a syntactically distinct type that also lead occasionally to the utterance of a singular term. There is a difference between the cases, of course. With Ralph and *A* the two types of token lead to the utterance of singular terms that *sound different* – /the man in the brown hat/ and /the man seen at the beach/, and /she/ and /you/, respectively – whereas with Peter the two types of token lead to singular terms that *sound the same* – /Paderewski/. But this difference does not reflect on Peter's rationality any more than his having as many as thirty distinct types in his beliefs, all of which lead him to utter singular terms with the sound /Bruce/. Syntactically distinct types *often* lead to the utterance of the same sound. Peter's beliefs about Paderewski are like Ralph's beliefs about Ortcutt in that they involve distinct coreferential types. Peter's beliefs about Paderewski are like his own beliefs about thirty different Bruces in that they involve distinct types that lead to the utterance of the same sound. There need be nothing irrational in Ralph's beliefs about Ortcutt or in Peter's beliefs about the various Bruces. No more need there be anything irrational in Peter's beliefs about Paderewski. To suppose otherwise is to assume that Peter has Cartesian access to the facts that make his beliefs, in some sense, contradictory.

But what about the *meanings* of the two types of 'Paderewski' tokens in Peter's thoughts and utterances? Are they the same or not? To answer this we have to consider our semantic purposes, particularly our purpose of explaining behavior. And we must go back to the beginning.

The generalizations that support our explanations of behavior advert to thoughts and actions *opaquely* described (4.3). Why must we describe them in this way to get our generalizations and explanations?[77] I think that the answer starts with the following view: To be a certain opaquely described action an event must have a certain opaquely described intention as its immediate cause.[78] Thus, to be the event of opaquely avoiding Smith's murderer, an event has to be immediately caused by an intention

---

77 We can ignore explanations that advert to transparently described behavior because they are parasitic on explanations that advert to opaquely described behavior (4.3).

78 This is what Bratman calls "the Simple View" (1984). Adams (1986) defends the view from Bratman's criticisms.

that means opaquely **AVOID SMITH'S MURDERER.** Now, it is not difficult to see how a belief like Ralph's that means opaquely **SMITH'S MURDERER IS INSANE** can have a role in causing that intention. So we can then understand the role of that belief in explaining the behavior partly constituted by its relation to that intention. It is partly because of similar relations between intentional behaviors and thought meanings that the generalizations hold.

The moral to be drawn from this is that these psychological generalizations and explanations depend on a certain matching of meanings: the matching of a meaning in the intention that must cause the behavior to be explained with a meaning in the explaining thought.

How fine grained must these matched meanings be for the generalizations and explanations to be good? The question arises because the meanings are properties of referring by certain modes, and such modes vary in their fineness of grain; for example, a particular demonstrative mode involving 'she' is more finely grained that the general demonstrative mode, which might involve any demonstrative whatsoever; similarly, for names. Our earlier discussion suggests an answer to the question. I have argued that the folk are right to distinguish the modes of particular names in their use of opaque ascriptions to explain intentional behavior. Richard's puzzle brings out that the folk may not similarly distinguish the modes of particular demonstratives (except first-person pronouns), and yet, in certain circumstances, the distinction is significant in explaining behavior. The circumstances are ones where the subject has more than one demonstrative mode for an object and has not made the appropriate identity assumption; thus, A does not think to himself, "You, the person I am addressing, are she, the person I am waving at." Let us say that a person's mode of referring to something is "unified" with another if she makes the appropriate identity assumption. Let us say that a person's mode, x, is a "species of" another, y, if any of her tokens that have x have y (but not vice versa); thus, A's *particular* demonstrative modes of referring to B by 'you' and by 'she' are species

231

of his less finely grained *general* demonstrative mode of referring to her by some demonstrative or other. Using this terminology, the suggested answer is this: For a psychological generalization or explanation to be appropriate, *a mode involved in a matching meaning must have no ununified species*. Thus, we cannot explain *A*'s waving by adverting to a property of referring to *B* by the general demonstrative mode because that mode has two species, his mode for 'you' and his mode for 'she', which *A* has not unified. Normally, however, a person's particular demonstrative modes of referring to something *are* unified, and so her behavior can be explained by adverting to the property of referring by the general demonstrative mode. Thus it is not surprising that our ordinary explanations of behavior do not distinguish among the particular demonstrative modes (except first-person pronouns). In contrast, it is common for a person to have more than one name for something and not to unify the modes for those names; so it is not surprising that our ordinary explanations do distinguish these modes. (But we shall soon have to modify these claims.)

A token's property of referring by a certain mode will sometimes be too coarse grained to explain intentional behavior. An example is the property shared by *A*'s 'you' and 'she' of referring to *B* by the general demonstrative mode. However, given appropriate identity assumptions, such properties can explain behavior. And they are as good as any at guiding us to reality. So, properties of referring by certain modes, whatever their grain, have semantic roles and are thought meanings and speaker meanings. And, the token has as many such meanings as we can distinguish modes (as well as its transparently ascribed property of simply referring to something). Similarly, where the token is the result of participation in a convention, the token can have many conventional meanings.

Before applying this discussion to Kripke's case of Peter, I shall apply it to some other cases that are interestingly similar and different.

I start with the case of Pierre and the well-known city with the English name 'London' and the French name 'Londres'. This yields the more famous version of Kripke's puzzle (1979: 254–65). (Cases involving closely related names in the one language would probably do as well: for example, the cases of one well-known philosopher with the names 'Ruth Barcan' and 'Ruth Marcus' [Soames; 1987: 67] and of another whose name is sometimes pronounced /*don*-al-n/ and sometimes /don-*nell*-n/ [Richard 1990: 189].) This case, like the standard one of two names for the one object, involves two different conventions, each with its own set of physical types. So, even though a particular token of /London/ and a particular token of /Londres/ may be alike in having the conventional meaning of referring to London, they are different in that one has the conventional meaning of referring to it by the mode for 'London', the other, by the mode for 'Londres'.[79] Similar remarks apply to thought and speaker meanings. The interesting thing about this case is that our opaque ascriptions of meanings using one of these names do not fit what I have claimed in that they do not normally distinguish between the two names: 'Pierre believes that London is pretty' could be true on the strength of Pierre being prepared to affirm "Londres is pretty"[80] or "Londres est jolie." So, in a t-clause, each name ascribes in a standard way a meaning involving the "disjunctive" mode of 'London' or 'Londres'[81] rather than a finer-grained meaning involving one of the disjuncts. And my recent claim about our ordinary ascriptions involving names needs to be modified accordingly.

79 Any vagueness in the identity conditions for a physical type will carry over to the convention for that type. So there will not always be a determinate matter of fact about whether two tokens share the same set of conventional meanings.

80 I assume that there are no good semantic objections to this mixing of languages. "Londres is pretty" has speaker meanings that are as unobjectionable as any. Its participation in the conventions of both French and English may be offensive to the Académie française but nevertheless yields straightforward conventional meanings.

81 Or, indeed, the "translation" of 'London' in any other language. I shall ignore this, taking 'Londres' to represent all those translations. A modification along the lines in the text is necessary, of course, to handle Church's objection (1950) to Carnap.

It is not surprising that our ascriptions should be like this because almost everyone either has unified the modes for 'London' and 'Londres' or else has only one of these modes. As a result, explanations adverting to properties of referring by the disjunctive mode will usually be good ones. Kripke's Pierre is a problem because he is unusual. On the basis of what Pierre has heard while living in France he asserts, "Londres est jolie." He moves to London without realizing that this is the city he referred to earlier. He has some unpleasing experiences that lead him to assert, "London is not pretty." On the basis of his assertions, we feel entitled to say both of the following.

(21) Pierre believes that London is pretty.
(22) Pierre believes that London is not pretty.

Indeed, we *are* entitled on the assumption that the meaning ascribed by 'London' in (21) and (22) is the property of referring to London by the disjunctive mode, for, on that assumption, (21) and (22) are both true. Pierre is unusual in not having unified his modes for the two names, and so the meaning ascribed is not fine grained enough to explain his behavior. And if we want to advert to the meanings that will do the explanatory job, we have to resort to a complex nonstandard ascription, instead of (22), for example:

(23) Pierre believes that London, qua city he is living in, is not pretty.

Perhaps not. Perhaps in this situation, as in Richard's (4.14), the context of (22) "supplies the qua"; (22) has a hidden-indexical element; and (22) is elliptical for (23). Suppose this is so. It still does not support the Hidden-Indexical theory (4.11). It does not undermine our view that a t-clause containing 'London' *usually* specifies a disjunctive mode and is not elliptical. More importantly, it does not give any reason to believe that the t-clause might, given the right context, specify a *demonstrative* or *descriptive* mode of referring to London. What it does support is a minor modification of my Quinean theory. In unusual situations like Pierre's, the context may "narrow down" the mode ascribed by a name from a disjunctive mode to one of the disjuncts.

In all respects so far, Pierre's case is analogous to Richard's one about demonstratives. We shall soon see that there is one interesting disanalogy.

Although the meaning ascribed by 'London' in a t-clause is not normally the fine-grained property of referring to London by the mode of 'London', there do seem to be exceptions. Consider:

(24) Pierre believes that London is not Londres.

This sentence seems to be true, and yet it would not be if the two names both ascribed the coarser grained meaning involving the disjunctive mode. Given the triviality of self-identity, the sole interest that we are ever likely to have in ascribing an attitude to a (positive or negative) identity is one that can be served only by adverting to the finer grained meanings. An utterance of

(25) Pierre believes that Londres is pretty but London is not

is also likely to be an exception. In these contexts, 'London' and 'Londres' specify different meanings, and so substituting one for the other may not preserve truth.

I have indicated the similarity between demonstratives and names. One aspect of this is that the meaning ascribed by a demonstrative in an ordinary ascription is not the fine-grained property of referring by a particular demonstrative. Do ascriptions of attitudes to identities provide an exception to this too? In general, no. Thus, if we want to describe A's mistake to B, we have to resort to something nonstandard such as:

(26) A believes that you, qua person waved at, are not you, qua person addressed on the telephone.

But then consider a situation where Flora observes the bow and stern of what, unbeknownst to her, is one very long ship the middle of which is obscured by a large building. Pointing to the bow, she says, "This ship is Japanese"; pointing to the stern, she says, "That ship is not Japanese."[82] Just as in A's case, our ordinary practices justify us in ascribing beliefs that appear to be contradictory. But in this case, we can describe Flora's mistake in a standard way:

(27) Flora believes that this ship (pointing to the bow) is not that ship (pointing to the stern).

Indeed, the meanings ascribed here are *more* fine grained than the properties of referring by the mode for 'this' and the mode for 'that', modes that hardly differ anyway. This point becomes obvious when we note that we could serve the purposes of (27), albeit less comfortably, using only the demonstrative 'this ship' to identify the ship. The meanings ascribed involve certain "perspectives" on the ship, perspectives that could fix the reference of either 'this ship' or 'that ship'.

I return at last to Peter's case. I have already argued that to suppose that the case implies irrationality in Peter is to assume Cartesianism. In this respect the case is like all the others we have considered. It is like them also in drawing attention to meanings that are more finely grained than those we can normally ascribe by the standard opaque forms, setting aside for a moment the possibility of hidden indexicals. We cannot explain Peter's behavior by either of the following,

(19) Peter believes that Paderewski had musical talent,
(20) Peter believes that Paderewski had no musical talent,

just as we cannot explain A's by (16) or (17) nor Pierre's by (21) or (22), even though all these ascriptions are true.[83] We cannot do so because these ascriptions advert to meanings involving modes that have ununified species. Thus, Peter has two ununified

---

82 The case is based on one of Perry's (1993: 12–13).
83 This is in agreement with claims that Loar (1988) and Patterson (1990) make about similar cases but not with some of my own earlier views (1984: 409–11; 1990b: 174).

modes of referring to Padereweski by the name 'Paderewski', both of which are species of the mode adverted to by (19) and (20). But Peter's case is *unlike* all the others in that the crucial difference between the fine-grained thought and speaker meanings of the name are not mirrored by a difference in their conventional meanings. Whereas there are, for example, distinct conventions for 'London' and 'Londres' relevant to Pierre's case, and distinct conventions for 'she' and 'you' relevant to *A*'s case, there is only one convention for 'Paderewski' relevant to Peter's case.

As a result of this, we cannot describe Peter's mistake, as we could Pierre's, with a simple standard ascription of an identity belief like (24). We have to resort to a complex nonstandard form like

(28) Peter believes that Paderewski, qua pianist, is not Paderewski qua politician.

This is like (26), the description of *A*'s mistake, but in that case we were driven to the 'qua' locution by a different reason ('she' and 'you' *are* conventionally different) − that ordinary ascriptions ascribe general demonstrative beliefs, not particular ones.

Perhaps, once again, this is too hasty. Perhaps (19) and (20) can be taken as elliptical sentences with the context "supplying the qua." But if so, once again, there is no support for the Hidden-Indexical theory; there is simply support for a minor modification of my Quinean theory.[84]

In light of all this, what should we say about the meanings of the two types of 'Paderewski' tokens in Peter's thoughts and utterances? First, the two utterance types share all conventional meanings from the coarsest to the finest. Second, the two thought types share all meanings from the coarsest to those ascribed by the standard opaque forms, for example, by (19) and (20); and these

---

84 Richard holds the Hidden–Indexical theory (4.11). He also loves propositions (4.12). In other respects, however, his handling of some of the puzzles that I have discussed in this part (1990: 179–96) is very similar to mine.

meanings will be shared speaker meanings of any utterances that express those thoughts. The two thought types differ in the very fine-grained meanings needed to explain Peter's behavior; and this difference will carry over to the speaker meanings of any utterances that express those thoughts.[85]

This discussion reveals a truth underlying the Fregean epistemic principle:

> 'S1' and 'S2' mean the same only if they are alike in informativeness and cognitive significance to all competent speakers.

The truth is that a competent speaker's failure to accept an identity is sufficient for a difference in thought meaning. Usually this difference is accompanied by a difference in conventional meaning; for example, the case of 'Hesperus' and 'Phosphorus'. Sometimes the difference is very fine grained and is not accompanied by such a difference; for example, the case of Peter and 'Paderewski'. Earlier, I doubted the Fregean principle because it rested on the Cartesian assumption that the linguistically competent have privileged access to meanings (4.7). The underlying truth does not rest on any such assumption.[86]

A person who thinks of a token as having just one meaning is right to be disturbed by Peter's case. She will naturally object to

85 In my previous discussions of Kripke's puzzle I have said simply that the two types differ in speaker meanings (1984: 408; 1990b: 173). This is inadequate: They share many speaker meanings differing only in the very fine-grained one.

86 Owens (1989) criticizes attempted solutions to Kripke's puzzle that imply a Cartesian access to speaker meanings. My appeal to speaker meanings does not imply such access. I applaud the criticism, of course. Boghossian (1994) argues that we need the Cartesian assumption that the meanings of a person's thoughts are "epistemically transparent" to her in order to explain her rationality or lack of it in puzzle cases: In particular, it is only when the relevant meanings are epistemically transparent that she can be convicted of irrationality. A consequence of my discussion is that she can be convicted if she accepts the appropriate identities. Accepting identities is not a matter of having any beliefs about meanings and so does not require that meanings be transparent.

taking the very fine-grained meanings of Peter's 'Paderewski' tokens as a general model for the sole meaning of a name, for such fineness of grain is mostly irrelevant to our semantic purposes.[87] By accepting that a token has more than one meaning, we can sympathize with this objection while allowing the relevance of very fine-grained meanings in unusual cases.

These meanings, ascribed with the help of qua-clauses, will prove a challenge to a semantic theory. For, what does the difference consist in? What indeed are these meanings? We have much less initial grip on the answers to these questions than we have on the analogous ones for 'you' and 'she' tokens, the meanings of which are also ascribed by qua-clauses (although our initial grip on the answers to the analogous questions about the "perspectival" meanings of Flora's 'this ship' and 'that ship' seem equally infirm[88]).

The questions expose the lack of resources of IT, for example (4.6). The meanings cannot be explained simply by relations to the actual tokens (in reference borrowings and groundings) processed to Peter's two 'Paderewski' networks, for it must be possible for somebody who has not experienced those very tokens to make Peter's mistake and share his meanings. And not any old splitting of the 'Paderewski' network into two will yield these meanings: Somebody might make a different mistake yielding a

---

87 If she is a lover of propositions, she will object to the general view that the sole object of a thought is a proposition with a grain as fine as that ascribed by (28).

88 Taschek's discussion (1987) brings out the problem nicely. He describes a situation where a person in a room in Ann Arbor assents to "That is F" on one occasion, but dissents from it on a later one, even though the one object has been demonstrated on both occasions and his perspectives on it are qualitatively identical (cf. the long ship example). Part of the explanation is that he falsely believes that he has been moved from Ann Arbor to Baltimore between the occasions. The meanings of the two belief tokens that the person has about the object must be distinguished because they are apt to cause different behaviors (when combined, for example, with his belief that he is in Baltimore). What could this difference in meaning consist in?

different pair of fine-grained meanings. IT needs to be developed by focusing on Peter's *disposition* to respond selectively to tokens of 'Paderewski'; the meanings are to be found not simply in what historically was done but also in the explanation of why it was done. (In thinking about this development, it will be helpful to remember the case of George – a person leading a double life each under the name 'George' (4.6) – because in that case *everyone* makes Peter's mistake, yielding two conventional meanings.)

In conclusion, the cases of Peter and Pierre have led us to say more about the first-level meanings of beliefs that explain behavior and have laid bare some problems in explaining those meanings. But the cases do not primarily pose a first-level "puzzle about belief" (cf. Donnellan 1989); rather they present a second-level puzzle about the ascription of beliefs. In this respect Kripke's puzzle is like Richard's.

The second-level puzzle of appearing in certain cases to ascribe irrationality to subjects arises from the fact that the meanings ascribed by our standard forms are too coarse grained to explain behavior in these cases. We should not be bothered by this fact. For, as I have pointed out, these cases are rare. And when they do occur, we can manage with more complex nonstandard forms.

4.18. Direct Reference Again

The direct-reference view that a name has only a coarse-grained 'Fido'-Fido meaning is threatened by apparent failures of substitutivity in attitude contexts. I noted earlier (4.8) that direct-reference philosophers think that this threat is lessened, if not removed, by consideration of the sorts of cases discussed in this part of the chapter. If my argument is good, they are wrong. I shall respond briefly to the three distinct strains in their thinking about these cases.

First, and least interesting, direct-reference philosophers find evidence for substitutivity in cases where, in ascribing a belief to a person, there seems room for plenty of variation in the singular term we would use.[89] From my perspective, these cases are of two sorts. (i) Some are cases of transparent ascriptions, hence cases where substitutivity does indeed hold. But, of course, this does not show that substitutivity holds in all cases. I accept that sometimes it suits our purposes to ascribe 'Fido'-Fido meanings but have argued that many times it does not. (ii) Some are cases of ascriptions using demonstratives to ascribe belief under the general demonstrative mode. There is indeed room for some variation here, but, as we have seen in discussing Richard's puzzle (4.14), the variation is rule governed and is not a sign of full substitutivity.

Second, direct-reference philosophers are encouraged by a moral that Kripke draws from his puzzle: that an argument against substitutivity, which he thinks is widely accepted, is dubious (1979: 253–4, 267–70).[90] The argument starts by inferring

(29) Jones believes that Cicero was bald

on the basis of Jones's sincere assent to 'Cicero was bald'; and by inferring

(30) Jones believes that Tully was not bald

on the basis of his sincere assent to 'Tully was not bald'. If substitutivity applied to these ascriptions, we could infer that Jones was irrational, believing that Cicero was bald and that Cicero was not bald. Yet Jones is not irrational. So, the argument concludes, substitutivity does not apply. Kripke's doubt arises because his puzzle derives the same mistaken charge of irrationality in Peter without invoking substitutivity; see (19) and (20). So substitutivity is not to blame for the mistaken charge. But my earlier argument against substitutivity (4.2) is different, resting nothing on a mistaken charge of irrationality. I argue that, in Jones's circumstances, (29) is true, but there is a way of construing

(31) Jones believes that Tully was bald

that makes it false. So substitutivity fails.

89 See, e.g., Soames 1987: 64–7; 1988: 118–19; Salmon 1990: 223–7.
90 See, e.g., Soames 1987: 61–4.

Third, and most interesting, direct-reference philosophers argue that the inference from the apparent failure of substitutivity in, say, (29) to the conclusion that 'Tully' and 'Cicero' differ in meaning (or, as they would say, "content") must be faulty. For, substituting "straightforward (strict) synonyms" (Salmon 1990: 220) can yield the same apparent failure. Consider, for example, 'London' and 'Londres' earlier, or 'doctor' and 'physician', or 'ketchup' and 'catsup', or 'fortnight' and 'fourteen days'.[91] These sorts of cases lead Salmon to conclude that the apparent failures of substitutivity do not count against his view at all: They are "in fact evidentially irrelevant and immaterial" (p. 217).

It is a consequence of my argument that tokens of the expressions in each pair of alleged synonyms do not in fact share all their meanings. So there is a sense in which the expressions in the pair are not really synonyms. Soames thinks that this view "would wreak havoc with our intuitions about meaning" (1988: 108). I think that it is a mistake to rest so much on these intuitions. When we look at the purposes served by ascribing meanings, when we look at what meanings actually do, we see that there is indeed a sense in which, say, 'London' and 'Londres' are not synonymous: They play slightly different roles in *the explanation of behavior*. Despite this, Soames's intuitions can be accommodated. With the recognition of the many meanings of a token goes a recognition of several notions of *synonymy*. When we are *translating* a name, it will suit our purposes to treat as synonymous a term in another language that is both a name and coreferential;[92] for example, 'London' and 'Londres'. And, when we are *writing a dictionary entry* for a term covered by a description theory, it will

---

91 See, e.g., Soames 1988: 106–8; Salmon 1990: 220–21; Fodor 1990: 164–6; Adams, Stecker, and Fuller 1992: 382–3. Mates 1952 is the *locus classicus*.

92 Should there be two such terms, then each of them will be treated as synonymous with the original. Thus, according to Kripke (1979: 268), Hebrew has two names, 'Ashkenaz' and 'Germaniah', coreferential with 'Germany'. So they are both synonyms of 'Germany' in the sense in question. But in the earlier sense they are not, for they differ in modes just as 'Cicero' and 'Tully' do.

suit our purposes to treat it as synonymous with its "definition": for example, 'fortnight' and 'fourteen days'. There is no harm in this flexibility: All these notions of *synonymy* are open to theoretical explanation.

In sum, substitutivity often does fail for attitude ascriptions, and this failure indicates meaning differences. However, my argument against direct reference does not rest simply on the failure of substitutivity; it rests on the *explanation* of that failure. When our purpose is to explain a person's behavior, the role of a name in the content sentence of an ascription is to specify a certain mode under which the person refers to the name's bearer. The name has this role because *the goodness of the explanation depends on the mode.* The name specifies that mode in virtue of the fact that it, itself, refers to the bearer by that mode. Hence, substituting for that name any other term with a different mode of referring to that object may not save the truth of the original ascription.

The conclusion that the direct-reference philosophers draw from the puzzles discussed in this part are "in the wrong direction." The puzzles do not supply evidence that meanings are coarse grained but rather supply evidence that some meanings are *more* fine grained than those ascribed by standard attitude ascriptions. The puzzles show that we sometimes need to ascribe these very fine-grained meanings to serve the semantic purpose of explaining behavior.

This concludes my description of the broad outlines of a Representationalist semantic program. Most of the discussion has been concerned with the descriptive semantic task: exploring the nature of the properties the folk ascribe for semantic purposes. I have argued that these natures are all Representationalist. In part I, I argued that we ascribe at least three sorts of putative referential meanings to singular terms. In part II, I first rejected an extreme Representationalism: the direct-reference view that we ascribe to a name only its property of designating its bearer. I then rejected the semi-Representationalism of two-factor theories and the anti-Representationalism of verificationist and use theories. In part III, I considered the putative meanings we ascribe to attitude

243

ascriptions – second-level meanings – rejecting the view that these meanings are heavily context dependent. In part IV, a consideration of various puzzles led to the view that we ascribe other sorts of putative referential meanings to singular terms (as well as the aforementioned three), sometimes very fine-grained ones.

The main argument for Representationalism on the normative/ basic issue has been as follows: Because folk ascriptions of Representationalist properties for semantic purposes are successful, we probably should ascribe those properties, and so those properties probably are meanings. We have found further support for this conclusion by considering *how* these properties serve semantic purposes. It remains to defend the program from various revisionist and eliminativist criticisms.

5

Eliminativism and revisionism

I. INTRODUCTION

5.1. What Are Eliminativism and Revisionism?

The view of meanings that has emerged in the last chapter is realist and conservative: Thoughts and utterances have meanings, and meanings are, minor revisions aside (4.12), the properties that we already ascribe for semantic purposes. And meanings are, as many suppose, truth referential, "Representationalist." But I have not yet seriously considered the radical alternatives of eliminativism (or nihilism) and revisionism. In this chapter, I shall do so. We need to start by clarifying both these alternatives.

Eliminativism. Eliminativism about *F*'s is the doctrine that there are no *F*'s. It is important to note that this eliminativism needs to be accompanied by a background assumption about *what it would be like* for there to be *F*'s, about what is *essential* to being an *F*, about the *nature* of *F*-hood. For, it is not sufficient simply to *say* there are no *F*'s; one needs an *argument*. And that argument will have the following form:

If anything were an *F* then it would be *G*.
Nothing is *G*.
So, there are no *F*'s.

The first premise is the background assumption. A possible realist response is then to deny the assumption: *F*'s are not essentially *G*. How do we settle this disagreement? That is precisely the methodological issue discussed earlier (2.10). We saw then that it may be difficult to settle the issue even by the "ultimate" method.

Indeed, settling it may be impossible because there may not be any determinate matter of fact about the assumption. If there is not, then there is no determinate matter of fact about whether the absence of G things requires eliminativism about F's. The vagueness of **F-hood** leads to the vagueness of eliminativism.

Consider some examples. Most people are eliminativists about witches because they believe that nothing casts spells, rides on a broomstick through the sky, and so on. Some people may be eliminativist about God because they are convinced by the Problem of Evil that nothing is both all powerful and all good. But these are grounds for eliminativism only if the casting of spells, riding on broomsticks, and so on, and the being all powerful and all good are essential to **being a witch** and **being God,** respectively. And those may be difficult matters to settle, and there may be no settling them.

The problem of vagueness is particularly acute for meanings. We are taking meanings to be properties (2.4). So our concern is with the eliminativist view that nothing *has* meanings.[1] The problem is that it is far from clear, in advance of some explication, what should count as having a meaning (2.3) and hence what is the appropriate background assumption for discussing eliminativism about meanings. I argued earlier for a certain explication of our talk of meanings that makes semantics worthwhile (2.4–2.6). Perhaps a good argument can be given for another explication (2.7). That remains to be seen. Meanwhile, the background assumption for the following discussion of eliminativism and revisionism reflects my view.

My background assumption is that something is a meaning if and only if it plays a "semantic role," that is, if and only if it is a property of the sort specified by t-clauses that can explain behavior and/or can be used as a guide to reality. If this is accepted then there seem to be two ways to be an eliminativist about meanings. First, one can deny that anything has the sort of properties speci-

---

1 The issue of the existence of meaning properties, part of the realism-nominalism issue, does not concern us.

fied by t-clauses. Second, even if some things have such properties, one can deny that the properties are meanings on the ground that they do not explain behavior or guide us to reality.[2]

This background assumption removes a lot of the vagueness from eliminativism, but certainly not all: In particular, talk of properties "of the sort" specified by t-clauses is obviously vague.

Quine is a famous example of an eliminativist. Under the influence of a radical behaviorism, he holds that stimulus meaning is the only "objective reality that the linguist has to probe." He rightly thinks that the ordinary view of meaning, reflected in "intentional usage," is far richer (1960: 39, 221). Something close to this is probably Davidson's view also (2.7).

We have been considering eliminativism about meanings. It is usual, and surely right, to relate this closely to eliminativism about *thoughts*. In particular, it is plausible to think that eliminativism

---

2   The intimate link between the putative meaning ascribed by a t-clause and a putative meaning of the content sentence of the t-clause (4.11) poses a small but interesting problem for eliminativism. Consider the following argument.

> It cannot be denied that people talk, saying things like 'Yeltsin has risen'. And it cannot be denied that this utterance has some properties or other. Given the intimate link, it cannot then be denied that this utterance has the sort of property specified by a t-clause. For, the property specified by 'that Yeltsin has risen' is a property closely related to one that its content sentence, hence the utterance, has. In using the t-clause to ascribe a property to the utterance, we are not committed to any assumption about the *nature* of this property; perhaps, for example, it is only Quine's "stimulus meaning." So, the first way of being an eliminativist is ruled out.

> The point is well taken: Short of implausibly rejecting the intimate link, it is hard to see what basis there could be for denying that the utterance has the property **YELTSIN HAS RISEN** (or one very like it). But the problem is only a small one for eliminativism for two reasons. First, the argument does not count against the denial that there is any *thought* with that property. So it does not count against the first way of being an eliminativist about *thought* meanings. Second, and more important, the argument does not count against the denial that the property can explain behavior or guide us to reality. So it does not count against the second way of being an eliminativist.

about meanings is sufficient for eliminativism about thoughts; having meanings is essential to thoughts. And it might be argued that if nothing has a meaning, then nothing is really an *utterance* either: The sound /Yeltsin has risen/ may have a property ascribed by a t-clause but because that property is not a meaning, and none of its other properties are meanings, it does not count as an utterance. In effect, this is to take utterances as essentially *mentalistic*. (For the sake of argument, I shall not adopt these essentialisms about thoughts and utterances in this chapter.)

I have followed Fodor in arguing for "the language-of-thought hypothesis" (4.4) According to this hypothesis, the things in our heads that *have* thought meanings are "mental sentences," complex sentencelike structures of distinct items each of which has a simple meaning out of which the complex meanings of thoughts are composed. The hypothesis is about the *implementation* of meanings in the head: It concerns "cognitive architecture." Clearly one could be eliminativist about mental sentences without being eliminativist about thought meanings; one could think that the vehicles of meanings have a different form.

I have argued for a particular sort of compositional meaning: *truth-referential meanings*. One could be eliminativist about these. And if it is assumed that the meanings of thoughts and utterances are essentially truth referential, eliminativism about truth-referential meanings amounts to eliminativism about meanings in general. But the assumption might be rejected and certainly needs an argument.

Revisionism. A doctrine is revisionist in a certain area if it revises the current theory, the status quo, in that area; it claims, normatively, that we ought not to do what, descriptively, we do do. Once again, there is vagueness: What is to count as "the current theory"? We have noted that it is doubtful whether much of the explicit semantic theory offered by philosophers and linguists has the credentials to be included (2.11). The status quo is to be found mostly in "folk semantics," in particular, in the implicit theory reflected in the folk practice of attempting to ascribe meanings to thoughts and utterances using t-clauses. (So folk semantics is part of intentional folk psychology.) There is room to argue about what is implicit in folk practice.[3] I take a minimal view of folk semantics, but I shall arrive at the status quo by adding one substantial philosophical thesis. This is the main descriptive thesis that I hope to have established: that the properties the folk ascribe are all truth referential and hence Representationalist. So I shall take the semantic status quo to involve commitment, first, to thoughts and utterances having the properties ascribed to them by the folk using t-clauses; second, to those properties being Representationalist; and, third, to those properties having semantic roles and hence being meanings. I shall call any theory that revises this status quo, "Revisionist."

Revisionism about meanings comes in degrees. Eliminativism is one extreme form: If nothing has a meaning then our implicit theory that something has a certain meaning must be mistaken. Another extreme form is the view that tokens have meanings, but these meanings are none of the properties we currently ascribe. More moderate Revisionism allows that tokens have some of the meanings we ascribe while insisting that they have others as well. Most moderate of all is a position like mine in the last chapter that urges only minor changes in the status quo (4.12).

5.2. Transcendentalism

From the naturalistic perspective, the question whether eliminativism about meanings or thoughts is correct is an empirical one. Many philosophers doubt this. They are impressed by "transcendental" arguments to the effect that such eliminativism is not simply false as a matter of empirical fact, it is in some sense "incoherent," "contradictory," "unstable," and so on and so *must*

---

3 For arguments that not much is implicit, particularly not a language of thought, see Loar 1983a and 1983b; Bogdan 1993; Horgan 1993.

be false. We can put the view in Kantian terms: It is "a condition on the possibility of theorizing at all" that people have thoughts and that tokens have meanings. To deny this is, in Lynne Rudder Baker's vivid phrase, to commit "cognitive suicide" (1987: 148). Transcendental arguments are thought to establish the case against eliminativism a priori.

Transcendental arguments are particularly popular in support of beliefs. Here is a naive example:

1. The eliminativist sincerely utters, "There are no beliefs."
2. So, the eliminativist believes that there are no beliefs.
3. So, eliminativism about beliefs involves realism about beliefs.
4. So, eliminativism is incoherent.[4]

Why is this argument so footling? *Because it starts by ignoring what the eliminativist actually says.* Because she *is* an eliminativist, she rejects the established intentional way of talking. So she will not describe any utterance, *including her own in stating eliminativism,* as expressing a belief. So step 2, which saddles her with precisely what she is denying, is blatantly question begging.

To say this is not to deny that the eliminativist has a problem. She owes us an alternative description to that in step 2. This debt is part of a quite general one. The eliminativist must provide an alternative way of talking that will enable us to describe, explain, and predict mental and linguistic phenomena in other terms. It is

---

4   Baker comes close to urging arguments of this sort (1987: 113–48); see also, Malcolm 1968; Gasper 1986. Barbara Hannan points out how common such arguments are. She discusses one sympathetically but does not endorse it (1993: 171–2). My discussion draws on my 1990c, which is mostly a critique of an extremely complicated transcendentalist argument in Boghossian 1990a. Boghossian 1990b is a response to the critique. Devitt and Rey 1991 is a response to that response. Taylor 1994 is a nice critique of transcendental arguments. Such arguments find sympathy in surprising places; see, e.g., Fodor and Lepore 1992: 207.

reasonable to think that eliminativism has not been made plausible. But this does not show that eliminativism *could not be* right. At most it shows that eliminativism *probably is not* right. The slide from charging that eliminativism is implausible to charging that it is incoherent is totally unwarranted.

A certain myopia afflicts transcendentalists: They do not see that the theory that the eliminativist must provide, *transcendental argument or no transcendental argument,* would supply alternative ways of talking that could be used quite generally, including to describe eliminativism and the eliminativist. The eliminativist's theory, or lack of it, is open to criticism, but there is no room for a transcendental "first strike" against her.

Some also seem to think that the eliminativist denies herself the right to talk. For, according to her, talking "does not really say anything; it is mere gibberish." This simple confusion is an indication of the entrenchment of folk theory. Talking is one thing, the folk theory of talking another. So you can talk without holding the theory. The eliminativist does not recommend silence. She recommends different talk about talk. The eliminativist is not committed to the view that all talk is "mere gibberish." A plausible eliminativist theory would surely distinguish, in nonintentional terms, between gibberish and what we regard as genuine utterances.

Finally, it is futile to keep emphasizing how shocking eliminativism is and how difficult it would be to live with. The eliminativist is thoroughly aware of this. She is fond of pointing out how often in the history of science the truth has been shocking. This is a very good point. What eliminativism calls for in response is neither transcendentalism nor cries of horror, but arguments aimed at what the eliminativist actually says.

Transcendental arguments against eliminativism may take many forms and may involve any of the intentional notions.[5] However, they all share the question-begging strategy with the naive argu-

5   As Baker illustrates; 1987: 113–48.

ment. The strategy is to start the argument by applying notions to the eliminativist that are laden with precisely the theory that she thinks should be abandoned and to overlook that she would think that notions from a replacement theory were the appropriate ones to apply.

In sum, eliminativism is a perfectly coherent position: If it is eliminativism about meaning, it can deny that any attitude ascription is true, and/or it can deny that any such ascription serves our semantic purposes. This is not to say that eliminativism is plausible. I think that neither it, nor any other Revisionism except a mild one, is plausible. An important aim of what follows is to show this.

5.3. A Brief Assessment of Eliminativism

The semantics I proposed in the last chapter is very mildly Revisionist. My primary aim in this chapter is to defend the status quo from any Revisionism that is not similarly mild, particularly from any that proposes a semantics that is not purely Representationalist. In this section, I shall make a brief assessment of eliminativism, an extreme Revisionism.

If the view that there are Representationalist meanings and only such meanings is indeed in accord with the status quo, then that alone is some evidence for the view. And the less we have a worked-out and viable alternative to this view, the stronger is that evidence. So the onus is on Revisionism to produce the alternative. However, Representationalism has much more to be said for it than this.

My second methodological proposal was that we should look to the descriptive task for evidence for the normative/basic one (2.9). Following this proposal supplies the main support for Representationalism, a point much harped upon in the last chapter. For, our ordinary attitude ascriptions are apparently *successful* at serving our semantic purposes. This is evidence that thoughts and utterances have the properties ascribed and that the properties are meanings. And we have already established, I claim, that the properties ascribed are Representationalist. In the face of this, anyone who wants to overthrow Representationalism needs both a powerful argument and a plausible alternative. This makes the onus on Revisionism heavy.

Three sorts of evidence would count in favor of Revisionism: (1) Evidence that the apparent success of our ascriptions was not real or was greatly exaggerated. (2) Evidence that a naturalistic explanation of Representationalist properties was not available or likely; so we would not be entitled to ascribe those properties. (3) Evidence that we could serve our purposes better in some other way; so we would not need to ascribe Representationalist properties.

In a series of papers and books over the last fifteen years, Patricia and Paul Churchland have offered evidence of all three sorts.[6] Their critiques of the status quo from a neuroscience perspective constitute the most sustained and radical Revisionism, rejecting not only folk psychology but any sort of intentional psychology at all. With this goes a rejection of any of the usual mental semantics, including Representationalist ones. The Churchlands accept, I take it, that mental states have representational properties of *some* sort but not ones anything like those we ordinarily ascribe in t-clauses. Given my earlier explication of our talk of meanings, this amounts to denying that there are any meanings at all; it amounts to eliminativism. Doubtless, they would want to offer another explication that would motivate a different semantics.

I applaud the Churchlands' insistence – in the face of obdurate transcendentalism – that whether or not intentional psychology is true is an empirical matter. And I agree with them that we should let neuroscience expand our imaginations in thinking about cog-

---

6 See, e.g., Patricia Churchland 1986; Paul Churchland 1981, 1989; Churchland and Churchland 1983. Paul Churchland 1993 is a nice summary of their critique.

nitive matters. Nevertheless, I do not share their pessimism about the intentional. I shall briefly indicate why.

Concerning (1), I share the doubts of others[7] that the evidence adduced by the Churchlands should really count as failures of intentional psychology and hence of a truth-referential semantics for the mental. More importantly, these alleged failures pale into insignificance alongside the extraordinary success of that psychology and semantics: Our ascriptions of Representationalist meanings, parts of our ascriptions of thoughts and utterances, appear to do a remarkably good job of explaining and predicting behavior and of enabling us to learn about the world. We do not have anything close to a convincing explanation of why there would be this appearance of success if things did not really have those meanings. In sum, I think that the Churchlands' case is weak here.

Concerning (2), what we look for are physical states of the brain that are the vehicles of Representationalist meanings. Yet, the Churchlands insist, current research on the brain shows no sign of representational states with the sentencelike structures that this requires. Now, one response to this would be to disagree about the requirement. Certainly, there is no inconsistency in accepting a truth-referential semantics for thoughts while denying that the vehicles of thoughts must be mental sentences; the semantics is one thing, the language-of-thought hypothesis, another. And if the hypothesis should turn out to be false, it would surely be more plausible to think that Representationalist meanings have other vehicles than that there are no such meanings. Nevertheless, I am sufficiently persuaded of the language-of-thought hypothesis to grant that the absence of mental sentences would be very bad news for the meanings. But I doubt that we know anywhere near enough about the brain and about what the required mental sentences might look like to despair of finding them in the brain.

7   E.g., Kitcher 1984: 90–8; Horgan and Woodward 1985: 401–3. The latter paper also contains criticisms of two of Stich's arguments against folk psychology that I shall not discuss.

In sum, I think that the Churchlands' case is much stronger here, but not nearly strong enough to be decisive.[8]

Concerning (3), we note that the Churchlands' neuroscience alternative to intentional psychology is, at this stage, little more than a gleam in their eye. But we should not make much of this because we can surely expect a fuller account along those lines to be forthcoming soon. The problem with such an account is rather that, to a considerable degree, it changes the subject and so does not serve our original purposes; it is "at a different level." In particular, although we can expect it to explain behavior in some sense – "mere bodily movement" – it will not explain *intentional* behavior – "actions." And, although we can expect it to explain brain processes, it will not explain *thought* processes.[9] Now, of course, the Churchlands think that there is no level of intentional behavior and thought processes, and so there should *be* no purpose of trying to explain such matters. But their ground for that must depend almost entirely on (1) and (2). So I do not think that their sketch of a neuroscience alternative adds much to their case.

5.4. More Moderate Revisionism

In the rest of this chapter I shall be concerned with other, more moderate, Revisionisms.[10] The general inspiration for these is the functionalist theory of the mind. More particularly, the inspiration is the arguments from "methodological solipsism" and autono-

---

8 Kitcher 1984 and von Eckardt 1984 contain interesting defenses of the scientific respectability of intentional psychology from the Churchlands' criticisms.

9 As Fodor and Pylyshyn's critique of connectionism demonstrates (1988).

10 I shall draw on my 1989a and 1991a in places (particularly in sections 5.4–5.7), but I am now much less sympathetic to Revisionism. In those papers I was impressed by Burge's argument for the status quo (1986), but insufficiently so. I was led astray by my conflation of the two views of narrow meanings: as functions from contexts to wide meanings and as functional roles. Fiona Cowie's skepticism about my former position helped me to sort out this confusion.

mous psychology and from the analogy between the mind and a computer.[11] Revisionism sometimes holds that cognitive psychology should explain the interaction of mental states with each other and the world by laws that advert only to "formal" or "syntactic" properties, not to Representationalist ones. Revisionism at other times holds that psychological laws advert only to "narrow" meanings not "wide" ones.[12]

These more moderate Revisionisms can sometimes be seen as offering evidence of sort (1): that the apparent success of our attitude ascriptions is either not real or is exaggerated. But what they mainly offer is evidence of sort (3): arguments that our psychological purposes would be better served by ascribing something other than the Representationalist meanings we do ascribe. I shall focus on these arguments.

These arguments, like those of the Churchlands, are all concerned with what is needed for psychology and the explanation of behavior. Yet that is not the only purpose for which we ascribe meanings: We do so to use others as guides to how the world is. So even if we did not need wide Representationalist meanings for psychology, we might need them for this purpose. Two-factor theorists (e.g., Loar 1981; Schiffer 1981) tend to think that we do. Other Revisionists owe us a story about how we can use the beliefs of others to learn about the world if there are no wide meanings. I set this matter aside in what follows.

Stephen Stich's "Syntactic Theory of the Mind" ("STM") is a clear example of Revisionism:

cognitive states . . . can be systematically mapped to abstract syntactic objects in such a way that causal interactions among cognitive states, as well as causal links with stimuli and behavioral events, can be described in terms of the syntactic properties and relations of the abstract objects to which the cognitive states are mapped. (1983: 149)

---

11 I shall be considering only empirically based arguments for Revisionism. So I shall not be considering arguments for, say, verificationism that seem to be based on a priori commitments to behaviorism or Cartesianism.

12 On the terminology "narrow" and "wide," see Putnam 1975: 220–2.

A similar view has been urged by Hartry Field (1978: 100–2) and Stephen Schiffer (1981: 214–15).

It is natural to take many writings of Jerry Fodor and Zenon Pylyshyn as powerful defenses of Revisionism. Fodor urges the "formality condition," which is definitive of "the computational theory of the mind" ("CTM"):

> mental processes have access only to formal (nonsemantic) properties of the mental representations over which they are defined (1980a: 63).

Pylyshyn endorses this condition (1980a: 111–15; 1980b: 158–61). He believes that "cognition *is* a type of computation" (1984: xiii). Because CTM is about mental processes, it seems to be about the lawlike generalizations of psychology. It seems to agree with Stich that these laws may advert only to syntactic properties. CTM has been taken this way by friend and foe alike.[13] However, this is not the way Fodor and Pylyshyn take it. Although they (Fodor, at least) are slightly Revisionist, they are basically in favor of psychological laws that advert to full truth-conditional meanings. This leads Stich to accuse Fodor of trying to "have it both ways" (1983: 188): the intentional talk of folk psychology on the one hand, and the formality condition on the other. Fodor thinks that he can have it both ways because CTM is concerned with a different level from that of the laws: the level of their implementation (1987: 139–40, 166n). CTM certainly does suggest a claim about a level of physical implementation, as we shall see (5.6). However, it is largely concerned with a psychological level, which Fodor thinks of as between the physical and the folk-psychological. I shall consider Fodor's attempt to have it both ways later (5.9). Meanwhile, for the sake of argument, I shall write as if there were only one psychological level, treating CTM as if it were a Revisionist doctrine like STM.

---

13   E.g., Baker 1986: 41; Demopoulos 1980; Kitcher 1985: 89; Lepore and
     Loewer 1986: 598–9; Lycan 1984: 91–2; McGinn 1982: 208; Schiffer 1981:
     214–15; Stich 1980: 97.

In part II, I shall argue that the mind is not purely syntactic at any level, even the implementational. In so doing, I shall emphasize three distinctions: that between formal properties and syntactic properties, that between thought processes and mental processes in general, and that between syntactic properties and putative narrow meanings. (*Putative* meanings are *really* meanings only if they play semantic roles: Section 2.6. Whether or not putative narrow meanings play the semantic role of explaining behavior is a good deal of what is in contention.)

In part III, I shall reject the idea that psychology should advert to narrow meanings. There are two views of narrow meanings. According to the more popular view, the narrow meaning of a sentence is a *functional role* involving other sentences, proximal sensory input, and proximal behavioral output. I shall argue that these meanings are unexplained and unmotivated. Furthermore, there is nothing to show either how these meanings might explain intentional behaviors or, alternatively, that there are no such behaviors to be explained. According to the other view, the narrow meaning is a function taking an external context for an argument to yield a wide meaning as a value. These meanings are unobjectionable enough, but I shall argue that we have decisive reasons for choosing not to ascribe them but to ascribe wide meanings.

II. SYNTACTIC PSYCHOLOGY

5.5. 'Syntactic' and 'Formal'

I have described a Revisionism committed to the view that psychology adverts only to the "formal," "syntactic," or "narrow meaning" properties of a token. Sometimes the properties needed for psychology are described as "nonsemantic" (e.g., by Fodor earlier). Sometimes psychology is said to treat tokens as "meaningless" (Field 1978: 101) or "uninterpreted" (Schiffer 1981: 214–15). These various descriptions are often used in cognitive science as if they were rough synonyms (e.g., Fodor 1982: 100). This usage leads to confusion and blurs important distinctions. I am

258

concerned to draw these distinctions and so will try to be very precise about my usage.

In this section I will discuss 'formal' and 'syntactic'. Prior to this debate about the mind, these two terms had fairly clear "ordinary" meanings, and I shall start with those. I shall then consider a technical meaning of 'formal', stemming from the study of "formal languages," which also precedes the debate. I will discuss the other terms in section 5.7.[14]

Ordinarily, a form of an object is a "shape, arrangement of parts, visible aspect." A property of an object is formal if it concerns "the outward form, shape, appearance, arrangement, or external qualities." A form of a word is "one of the shapes [it takes] in spelling, pronunciation, or inflexion" (*Concise Oxford Dictionary*). So the formal properties of an object are some of its *intrinsic* and fairly brute-physical properties. A formal property of the inscription *'Fa'* is that of beginning with an inscription shaped such and such (replace 'such and such' with a description of the shape of *'F'*). A formal relation between *'Fa'* and *'Fb'* is that of both beginning with an inscription of the same shape. A formal property of a symbol in a computer is that of being a certain pattern of on-off switches. A formal property of a symbol in the brain is a certain array of neurons.[15]

Syntax is "sentence-construction, the grammatical arrangement of words in speech or writing, set of rules governing this" (*COD*). Linguists use the term 'syntax' to refer also to the study of such matters. "Syntax is the study of the principles and processes by which sentences are constructed in particular languages" (Chomsky 1957: 11). Syntactic properties and relations are ones that bear on that construction and are talked about in that study. A syntactic

---

14 Some of the points in my discussion are similar to ones made independently by Crane (1990: 193–5).

15 Note that a sentence or word can appear in indefinitely many forms; it is medium independent. A letter can be similarly characterized, if letters are taken to make up a word in all its forms. However, letters are often taken to be restricted to inscriptions, in which case a letter can appear in a more limited number of forms.

property of 'Ron' is that of being a noun; of 'loves', that of being a two-place predicate; of 'Ron loves Maggie', that of being a sentence.[16] A syntactic relation between 'Ron loves Maggie' and 'Maggie is loved by Ron' is that of the latter being the passive of the former. Syntactic properties are ones that a token has in virtue of its role in relation to other tokens in the language; they are functional properties and *extrinsic* to the object.[17]

If the terms 'formal' and 'syntactic' are used in the way I have just explained, they refer to very different types of properties and relations. They have their places at different levels, the one physical, the other functional. It is not even the case that formal and syntactic properties of tokens match up, so that whenever there is a difference in one there is a difference in the other.[18] Written and spoken tokens of the one sentence are syntactically alike but formally very different. Two tokens of 'Dad is cooking' printed out by the same machine are formally alike but may be syntactically different.

Aside from this "ordinary" sense of 'formal' there is a very different technical sense that arises out of the notions of a *formal language* and a *formal system*. Formal properties and relations, in this technical sense, are functional just as are syntactic ones.

A *formal system* is like a game in which tokens are manipulated according to rules, in order to see what configurations can be obtained. (Haugeland 1985: 48)

Chess is a good example of such a system. In a realization of the system, a token of any type – for example, a pawn or a bishop –

---

16 I do not mean to suggest that properties like **being a noun** may not *also* be semantic; see section 5.6.

17 This is the deep truth in the structuralist tradition in linguistics. For the deep falsehood, particularly in the French version, see Devitt and Sterelny 1987: Chap. 13.

18 Formal and syntactic properties obviously do not match up if we remove the restriction to linguistic tokens. Objects like the Harbor Bridge and the Opera House have forms but no syntax.

is, of course, a physical entity of a certain form in the ordinary sense. It is usually important that tokens of each type differ in their brute-physical properties from those of any other type, but, beyond that, it does not matter what form the tokens have in the ordinary sense. So far as the system is concerned, all that matters about a token is its role in the system. To be a token of a particular type is simply to be covered in a certain way by the rules. So a pawn is a pawn, however it is physically realized, because it plays the role of a pawn in the game. It is common to call types or properties, like **being a pawn,** "formal." Such properties abstract from the brute-physical properties of any realization of the system; that is, from the formal properties in the earlier ordinary sense. They are functional, structural, or relational properties. Note finally that nothing outside the system has any bearing on these properties. In particular, meaning is irrelevant to them.

The contrast between this sort of formal property and the earlier sort might be brought out as follows. Properties of the earlier sort characterize the "shape" of *an object*; they are intrinsic to the object. Properties of the present sort characterize the "shape" of *a structure of objects*; they are intrinsic to the structure but not to any object.

Some formal systems are or contain languages. Such a language consists of a set of basic symbols classified into various types – for example, names, variables, one-place predicates, a conjunction symbol – together with *formation* rules for combining symbols of various types to form other symbols (e.g, sentences). The system containing the language also includes *transformation* rules for "deriving" some symbols from others in an inference. Properties like **being a name** are just like **being a pawn**: They are functional. They are properties that a token has not in virtue of its brute-physical makeup but in virtue of its role in the system. So what matters to being a conjunction symbol is not whether a token looks like '&' or '.', but that it is governed by certain rules. Such properties of tokens in a formal language are also commonly called "formal."[19] And, of course, any meaning a token may have is irrelevant to its having one of these properties.[20]

The formal properties of symbols in a formal language, in the technical sense, are clearly similar to the earlier-described syntactic properties of symbols in a natural language; and formal relations are similar to syntactic relations. Indeed, formal properties and relations are often called "syntactic," most notably by Carnap (1937).[21] They are quite different from formal properties in the earlier "ordinary" sense.

Just how similar are properties and relations that are formal in the technical sense to the earlier syntactic ones? All those that concern the formation rules are obviously very similar. Some that concern the transformation rules are less obviously so. Thus the formal relation, *being derived from,* has nothing to do with sentence construction and so is not obviously syntactic in the earlier sense. And the transformation rules, unlike the formation ones, are concerned with sameness and difference of types *within the basic types.* It matters to the transformation rules not only whether a token is a name but also whether it is a token of the *same* name type as, or of a *different* name type from, another token. Consider, for example, the transformation rule *modus ponens,* which we might express:

> Given both a conditional and its antecedent, derive its consequent.

---

19 This usage relates to that of 'logical form'. To say that these properties are formal is not, of course, to make a claim about what 'name' and 'conjunction symbol' "ordinarily mean"; their ordinary meaning is surely also semantic (see 5.6). It is to say what they mean in discussing a formal language.

20 For more on the matter of the last three paragraphs, see, e.g., Haugeland 1978: 5–10, 21–2; 1985: 4, 50–2, 58–63, 100–3.

21 It is natural to think of syntactic properties as a subclass of formal properties (in the senses specified): They are the formal properties of *symbols* (but not, say, of pawns). However, Haugeland extends 'syntactic' to cover all formal properties (1985: 100).

What is meant by "its antecedent"? It means, of course, a token of the same type as that of the token that is the antecedent of the conditional. But it means this not merely in the sense that the token must also be a sentence. The token has to be a token of the *same* sentence as the token antecedent; that is, it has to have the same structure and have tokens of the same name, predicate, and so on occupying that structure. For example, if the conditional is a token of '$Fa \rightarrow Fb$', then what is referred to by 'its antecedent' is a token of 'Fa'. So, *relations of* sameness and difference of sentence, name, predicate, and so forth are also formal relations of the system. (However, note that the *properties of* **being a certain sentence, being a certain name, being a certain predicate,** etc., are not formal properties, because such properties play no role in the system.)

So I think that we should see the technical 'formal' as going beyond the earlier 'syntactic'. Yet it seems appropriate to lump all the properties they describe together: These properties are all functional ones that a token has simply in virtue of its relations to other symbols within a system of symbols. The token's relations to anything outside that system are irrelevant to these properties.

From now on I shall use 'formal' in the "ordinary" sense explained first, referring to a fairly brute-physical intrinsic property. And I shall use 'syntactic' to cover not only properties involved in sentence construction but also functional properties referred to by 'formal' in the technical sense to be found in the study of formal languages. I am thus going against the practice in cognitive science of using the two terms as rough synonyms. My point in so doing is not to make a fuss about usage but to mark an important distinction in a convenient way. This distinction is the first of the three that I wish to emphasize.

A problem in discussions of doctrines like STM and CTM is that the uses of 'syntactic' and 'formal' do not clearly distinguish the syntactic from the formal. When the terms 'syntactic' and 'formal' seem to refer to formal (intrinsic, fairly brute-physical) properties, as they sometimes do,[22] it would be appropriate to interpret statements of the doctrines as

FORMAL IMPLEMENTATION: Psychological laws should advert to properties of tokens that are implemented only by formal properties of tokens.

(The "psychological laws" in question are only those concerned with cognition. If one property "implements" another, then something has the latter property in virtue of having the former one; the latter "supervenes on" the former.) Interpreted in this way the discussions are at the implementational level and so, of course, not Revisionist at all. On the other hand, when the terms seem to refer to syntactic (functional) properties, which they usually do,[23] it is reasonable to interpret the statements as

SYNTACTIC PSYCHOLOGY: Psychological laws should advert to properties of tokens that are only syntactic.[24]

This very different doctrine is, of course, Revisionist.

(In expressing this doctrine, why not place the 'only', more pleasingly, after 'advert'? Because psychological laws will obviously advert to some properties that are not syntactic: the proper-

---

22 E.g., Fodor 1980a: 64; 1980b: 106; 1982: 102. See also the following commentaries, with which Fodor largely agrees: Haugeland 1980: 81–2; Rey 1980: 91. Stich also sometimes seems to have this interpretation in mind; see 1983: 44.

23 E.g., Fodor 1985: 93; 1987: 18–19, 156n. In comments on Fodor 1980a, with which Fodor also agrees (1980b: 105), Loar distinguishes the two senses and takes Fodor to intend the functional one (1980: 90). See also Pylyshyn 1980a: 111–15 (but note that Pylyshyn takes syntactic properties to be intrinsic to a representation); Stich 1983: 152–3. Many show no interest in the distinction; e.g., Baker 1986: 27; Block 1986: 616. It often seems as if people using the terms have in mind properties that are in limbo between levels, part brute physical and part functional (thanks to Georges Rey). See also n. 31 and accompanying text.

24 See n. 13 for examples of people who seem to interpret the formality condition in this way.

264

ties of inputs and outputs. The doctrine is concerned only with the properties of token symbols.)

In the next two sections, I shall consider the bearing of the two main arguments for Revisionism on SYNTACTIC PSYCHOLOGY and FORMAL IMPLEMENTATION. This will lead to the introduction of further doctrines.

5.6. The Argument from the Computer Analogy

The argument from the computer analogy has a dual aspect that is brought out nicely in the following passage from Pylyshyn (although it will be remembered that he and Fodor do not present this position as Revisionist; secs. 5.4, 5.9):

> the most fundamental reason why cognition ought to be viewed as computation . . . rests on the fact that computation is the only worked-out view of *process* that is both compatible with a materialist view of how a process is realized and that attributes the behavior of the process to the operation of rules upon representations. (1980a: 113)

The aspect of the computer analogy that concerns the "behavior of the process" bears on SYNTACTIC PSYCHOLOGY; the aspect that concerns materialism or, as I would prefer to call it, physicalism, bears on FORMAL IMPLEMENTATION.

Consider, first, the aspect that concerns the behavior of the process. It is argued that we should take the computer analogy seriously and so see thought processes as computational. Now computational processes are defined syntactically; they are "syntactic operations over symbolic expressions" (Pylyshyn 1980a: 113); they are "both *symbolic* and *formal*" (Fodor 1980a: 64). So we should see thought processes as defined syntactically. A typical example of a law that satisfies this requirement might be one for *modus ponens* inferences:

> Whenever a person believes both a conditional and its antecedent, she is disposed to infer its consequent.

265

What we have learned from formal logic is that all the properties of tokens adverted to in such rules – for example, **being a conditional** – which might ordinarily be thought of as semantic, can be defined syntactically. Examples like this lead Stich to STM (1983: 154–6), committed, in effect, to a "meaningless language of thought."

This may seem to be a good argument for SYNTACTIC PSYCHOLOGY. However, it is an argument only if we overlook a crucial distinction: the distinction between thought processes and mental processes in general. The mental processes that concern (cognitive) psychology come in three sorts, as the passage from Stich displayed in section 5.4 brought out:

processes from thoughts to thoughts ("Thought-Thought processes");

processes from sensory inputs to thoughts ("Input-Thought processes");

processes from thoughts to behavioral outputs ("Thought-Output processes").

What I have been calling "thought processes" are Thought-Thought processes: inferential processes (assuming, as everyone seems to, that we are not interested in mere "associations of ideas"). Computation does indeed seem a good analogy for these. I shall consider an objection to this analogy at the end of this section but meanwhile will go along with it. So:

SYNTACTIC THOUGHT PROCESSES: The laws of thought processes advert to properties of tokens that are only syntactic.

SYNTACTIC *PSYCHOLOGY* is much stronger than this doctrine. It requires that the laws for Input-Thought and Thought-Output processes also advert to properties of tokens that are only syntactic. Because the literature provides no reason to believe that a computer's input and output processes are analogous to Input-

Thought and Thought-Output processes nor, if they were, that such processes would advert to properties of tokens that are only syntactic, the argument from the computer analogy gives no reason to believe the stronger doctrine. Thus the argument has no bearing on whether psychological laws *in general* have to advert to semantic properties of tokens.

Not only is there no argument for the more extensive computer analogy required to support SYNTACTIC PSYCHOLOGY, that analogy seems very unlikely. The problem is that computers do not have transducers anything like those of humans and do not produce behavior in anything like the way humans do. Computers move from symbolic input via symbolic manipulation (computation) to symbolic output. Humans, in contrast, move from largely nonsymbolic sensory stimulation via symbolic manipulation (thinking) to largely nonsymbolic action. Any interpretation a computer's symbols have, *we* give them. In contrast, a human's symbols have a particular interpretation in virtue of their causal relations to a reality external to the symbol system, whatever we theorists may do or think about them. Furthermore, it is because of those external links that a symbol has its distinctive role in causing action. I shall say more against SYNTACTIC PSYCHOLOGY later (5.8).

The distinction between thought processes and mental processes in general is the second distinction that I wish to emphasize. Participants in the debate about the mind are strangely uninterested in this distinction. The problem is not that they are unaware of it: Typically discussions will start with what amounts to an acknowledgment of the distinction – as, for example, in the displayed passage from Stich (5.4). The problem is that from then on all processes except Thought-Thought ones tend to be ignored. Thought-Thought are treated as if they were representative of them all. Fodor is particularly striking in this respect. He begins his discussion of CTM by distinguishing the three sorts of process, referring to Thought-Thought as the "most interesting" (1987: 12). Yet a few pages later, in a passage important enough

267

to be displayed, he describes "the nature of mental processes" in a way that applies only to Thought-Thought:

Claim 2 (the nature of mental processes)
Mental processes are causal sequences of tokenings of mental representations. (p. 17)

The most interesting ones have become the only ones.[25] Despite this, it is clear that he takes CTM to cover all mental processes.[26]

Consider, next, the aspect of the argument from the computer analogy that concerns physicalism. Computers are undoubtedly physical things. So, by seeing the mind as like a computer, we can make our theory of the mind conform with the very plausible overarching principle of physicalism. However, the move from the computer analogy to the physicalistic doctrine,

FORMAL IMPLEMENTATION: Psychological laws should advert to properties of tokens that are implemented only by formal properties of tokens,

25 See also the transition in Fodor 1985 from a start in which thinking is "the paradigm of mental process" (p. 78) to an ending in which it is as if thinking were the only such process. For an example of a swifter transition, see Block 1986: 628.

 Note that the common view that the mind becomes representational very soon after receiving a sensory input (to be discussed in sec. 5.8) does not save Claim 2. Certainly all processes from then until the formation of a thought are, in this view, causal sequences of representations. However, the total Input-Thought process is not such a sequence, for that process has a beginning – the sensory input – that is not representational. Whether or not Input-Thought processes should be broken down into subsidiary processes involving representational states that are prior to thoughts is beside the point.

26 Some evidence for this: (i) Fodor takes the formality condition to show that prima facie mental states involving semantic notions – like *knowledge* and *perception* – have no place *in psychology* (1980a: 64). (ii) He argues that we need a *psychology* that accepts the formality condition and that this is all we can have (1980a: 66). (iii) He takes CTM to tell "the whole story about mental causation" (1987b: 139). (iv) He relates CTM to methodological solipsism (1980a: 64–5; 1987: 43), which concerns psychology in general, not just thought processes.

is too swift. What the analogy shows is that syntactically defined processes are implemented formally, for that is how they are implemented in a computer. If SYNTACTIC PSYCHOLOGY *were* true then FORMAL IMPLEMENTATION *would be* true. But, as I have pointed out, the computer analogy gives no reason to think that SYNTACTIC PSYCHOLOGY is true. I shall argue that it is false.

If SYNTACTIC PSYCHOLOGY is indeed false (though SYNTACTIC THOUGHT PROCESSES is true), Input-Thought and Thought-Output laws involve *non*syntactic properties of tokens. Such properties, unlike syntactic ones, cannot be implemented in the formal (intrinsic, fairly brute-physical) properties of tokens. Syntactic properties, we have noted, are constituted solely by relations among tokens. The computer analogy shows that these relations are implemented in formal relations that hold in virtue of the formal properties of the tokens (shape, etc.). Nonsyntactic properties, in contrast, are constituted partly by relations between tokens and other things. These relations cannot be implemented in formal relations that hold solely in virtue of the formal properties *of tokens.* Of course, a physicalist (who is prepared to use 'formal' generously) will think that these relations are implemented in formal relations that hold in virtue of the formal properties of tokens *and of other things,* for example, of perceptual causes. Strictly speaking, then, FORMAL IMPLEMENTA-TION, is false. However, if its talk of the "formal properties of tokens" is extended to cover their formal relations, *including their relations to other things,* a physicalist will think it true. But that is a lot to read out of the computer analogy. The analogy supports FORMAL IMPLEMENTATION only insofar as it concerns thought processes.

So far, I have gone along with SYNTACTIC THOUGHT PROCESSES, the view that the laws of thought processes are syntactic. I conclude this section by considering an objection to this doctrine.

It surely might be the case that instances of the following are laws:

269

Whenever a person believes that x is an F, she is disposed to infer that x is a G.

Consider, for example, substituting 'man' for 'F' and 'mortal' for 'G'. Certainly this possibility cannot be denied by anyone who thinks that some words are covered by description theories of reference. For, those theories *require* that some laws of this form (but not all) constitute meanings (4.5). Prima facie, these laws advert to *semantic* properties of tokens, contrary to SYNTACTIC THOUGHT PROCESSES: For example, a law may relate tokens meaning **MAN** to tokens meaning **MORTAL.**

One response to this[27] is to see laws of the form just noted as lower-level ones holding in virtue of upper-level laws like

Whenever a person believes that all F's are G's and that x is an F then she will tend to believe that x is a G.

Such upper-level laws are the concern of the theory of thought processes, and they advert only to syntactic properties of tokens. So, the semantic content comes in at the level of the application of the laws. The problem with this response is that some of these allegedly lower-level laws may not, as a matter of cognitive fact, hold in virtue of a higher-level law: For example, there may simply be no involvement of the belief that all men are mortals in the cognitive process of moving from believing that x is a man to believing that x is a mortal.

A better response is to resist the prima facie claim. Think back to the *modus ponens* law,

Whenever a person believes both a conditional and its antecedent, she is disposed to infer its consequent.

We treated **being a conditional** as a strictly syntactic property. In so doing, we take it to be a property that a token has solely in virtue of its role in a system of tokens, abstracting from the *meaning* that is, as a matter of fact, shared by all tokens that have this property. What we have already done for **being a**

27   Which I took in 1991a.

conditional, **a conjunction symbol**, and so on, we can also do for **being a 'man' predicate**, **being a 'mortal' predicate**: Treat them as strictly syntactic, abstracting from meanings. To mark this abstraction, we might call the syntactic properties "**being a 'man'$_s$**" and "**being a 'mortal'$_s$**." And we could express the law along these lines:

> Whenever a person believes a sentence token including a 'man'$_s$, she is disposed to infer one obtainable from that token by substituting a 'mortal'$_s$ for the 'man'$_s$.

This does, of course, introduce some unfamiliar syntactic properties. Yet these properties do not differ in kind from the familiar ones. All of them get their natures from their roles in the system. Just as one logical particle is distinguished syntactically from another by its inferential role, so also one predicate may be distinguished from another.

The availability of this maneuver takes some of the glamour out of being syntactic and hence may make SYNTACTIC THOUGHT PROCESSES seem less significant. Take any Thought-Thought law inferentially linking '*F*' tokens to '*G*' tokens. Consider now the property **being an '*F*'$_s$**, that these '*F*' tokens have in virtue of being inferentially linked to '*G*' tokens (and perhaps also to other tokens); similarly, the property **being a '*G*'$_s$**, that the '*G*' tokens have. These properties are of the sort we are calling "syntactic," for they are ones that a token has simply in virtue of its inferential role. Now, the syntactic **being an '*F*'$_s$** and **being a '*G*'$_s$** may not be the same properties as **being an '*F*'** and **being a '*G*'**, respectively, for the latter pair may be semantic, but there is a thought-process law, adequate to our purposes, that can be stated by adverting to **being an '*F*'$_s$** and **being a '*G*'$_s$**. We were, in effect, exemplifying this when we displayed the law for *modus ponens* inferences and claimed that it adverts only to syntactic properties. We see now that it can be exemplified also in a law for inferences from 'man' predicates to 'mortal' predicates. We have a general device for stating these laws that abstracts from the meanings of tokens, focusing simply on their syntactic properties.

271

In this way, semantic laws can be "mimicked" by syntactic ones.[28]

So I am inclined to think that SYNTACTIC THOUGHT PROCESSES survives the objection that we have been considering. Perhaps this is too optimistic, given the shortage of completeness proofs in logic.[29] Nevertheless, for the sake of argument, I shall accept SYNTACTIC THOUGHT PROCESSES.

My main aim in this section has been to argue that the computer analogy does not support SYNTACTIC PSYCHOLOGY, the view that *all* psychological laws, including those for Input-Thought and Thought-Output processes, advert to the properties of tokens that are only syntactic. Nor, strictly speaking, does it support FORMAL IMPLEMENTATION, the physicalist view that the properties of tokens adverted to in those laws are implemented only by formal properties of tokens.

5.7. The Argument from Methodological Solipsism

The second main argument for Revisionism is the argument from methodological solipsism (and psychological autonomy). At the bottom of this argument, there is a conviction:

the conviction that the best explanation of behavior will include a theory invoking properties supervenient upon the organism's current, internal physical state. (Stich 1978: 576)

beliefs play a role in the agent's psychology just in virtue of intrinsic properties of the implicated internal representations . . . those properties of representations that can be characterized without adverting to matters lying outside the agent's head. (McGinn 1982: 208)

This prima facie plausible view is supported by the idea that a person and her functional duplicate must be psychologically the same:

28 And the semantic property of **being a conditional** is "mimicked" by the syntactic one adverted to in the *modus ponens* law. In my 1991a (pp. 112–14) I wrongly claimed that the semantic property is reduced to a syntactic one.

29 As Georges Rey has emphasized to me.

we expect a psychological theory which aims at explaining behavior to invoke only the "purely psychological" properties which are shared by a subject and its replicas. (Stich 1978: 574)

This idea is often reinforced by a consideration of Putnam's famous Twin Earth:

Twin-Earth cases strongly suggest a natural abstraction from [the] referential apparatus. (Loar 1983b: 665)

Finally Stich uses examples of people who deviate from the normal adult – people with exotic beliefs, people with brain damage (Mrs. T), and children – to argue that a psychology that adverts to wide meanings will miss significant and powerful generalizations that can be captured narrowly (1983: 135–48). The conclusion is that psychology should advert only to meanings that are determined by what is in the head or, at least, inside the skin; it should advert only to narrow meanings.

Clearly, the argument counts against the view that a thought's property of having certain truth conditions is relevant to psychology, for that property is not supervenient on what is inside the person's skin, may not be shared by a duplicate, and is the paradigm of a wide meaning.

I shall later reject this argument (5.12). But suppose it were good. Then it would establish that truth-conditional (and other wide) properties are irrelevant to psychology, for these do not supervene on the brain. The point to be made now is that the argument would *not* establish SYNTACTIC PSYCHOLOGY. Certainly syntactic properties are narrow and are relevant to psychology. But the argument would not establish that *only* syntactic properties are relevant. To establish that, we need the further premise that there are *no other* narrow properties that are relevant. To my knowledge, no argument has ever been given that a narrow meaning going beyond syntax is irrelevant to psychology. However, I shall consider one later (5.8).

Further, the argument from methodological solipsism alone would not establish that only "nonsemantic" properties are relevant to psychology, nor would it establish that tokens are "meaningless" or "uninterpreted" so far as psychology is concerned. To establish this we would need the further premise that properties that are not truth conditional (or otherwise wide) are not meanings.[30] This is not something to be taken for granted or settled by ad hoc definition. It is an empirical matter to be argued by attending to which properties play semantic roles (2.6–2.7).

To bring out the contrast between a merely syntactic property and a putative narrow meaning consider the most popular theory of narrow meaning. According to this theory, a sentence's narrow meaning is a *functional role* involving other sentences, proximal sensory input, and proximal behavioral output. This meaning will be partly constituted by the sentence's syntactic structure. *But it will also be partly constituted by the narrow meanings of the words that go into that structure.* To some degree, these narrow word meanings are clearly syntactic. For example, part of the meaning of a token may be that it is a noun, which is partly a syntactic matter. And if the token is covered by a description theory then the inferential dependency of its meaning on other meanings can be seen as a syntactic matter, as I have just argued (5.6). But, in the end, we must come to tokens with meanings that are not covered by description theories, meanings that "stand on their own feet" (4.5). These narrow meanings are *hardly syntactic at all:* For the most part, tokens have them not in virtue of their relations to other tokens, but in virtue of their actual or potential relations to things outside the symbol system. Thus, what makes a token narrowly mean **ECHIDNA** and not **PLATYPUS** may be the fact that the token has some sort of noninferential causal link to echidna-ish not platypus-ish inputs and/or outputs.

If the argument from methodological solipsism were good then it would establish that psychology needs at most a narrow semantics. So the argument is compatible with

---

30 It is common to use 'semantic', 'meaning', and 'content' as if they must involve truth and reference, as Loar (1980: 90) and Rey (1980: 91) note in their commentaries on Fodor 1980a.

NARROW PSYCHOLOGY: Psychological laws should advert to properties of tokens that are only narrow semantic.

This should be read as a commitment to laws that advert to properties that are not syntactic, for example, to narrow word meanings. Hence it is inconsistent with SYNTACTIC PSYCHOLOGY. However, it should also be read as allowing that *some* laws of mental processes may advert only to syntactic properties; narrow semantic should be taken to *include* syntactic. So NARROW SEMANTIC is consistent with SYNTACTIC THOUGHT PROCESSES. This is as it should be because the argument from methodological solipsism does not count against SYNTACTIC THOUGHT PROCESSES.

The distinction between syntactic and putative narrow meanings, hence the distinction between SYNTACTIC PSYCHOLOGY and NARROW PSYCHOLOGY, is the third distinction that I wish to emphasize. There is nothing in the argument from methodological solipsism to suggest that SYNTACTIC PSYCHOLOGY is correct.

The contrast between NARROW PSYCHOLOGY and folk theory can be brought out neatly by the following statement of folk theory:

WIDE PSYCHOLOGY: Psychological laws should advert to properties of tokens that are wide semantic.

I shall argue later that this doctrine is correct.

Though Revisionist doctrines are most frequently urged using 'syntactic' and 'formal', so that the doctrines seem to be SYNTACTIC PSYCHOLOGY, they are sometimes urged, often in the same breath, as if they were committed to functional-role properties of the sort that many would call narrow "meanings" or "contents."[31] And Stich has claimed (1991) that his earlier talk of

---

31 Fodor sometimes has narrow functional-role properties in mind in using 'syntactic' and 'formal'; see Loar's commentary (1980: 90) and Fodor's response (1980b: 105); Fodor's response to Geach (p. 102); and Fodor (1991: 281, point 1). Note further that Fodor takes the formality condition as "a

'syntax' in proposing STM should be taken to refer to "fat syntactic" properties that are, in fact, narrow functional-role properties. So SYNTACTIC PSYCHOLOGY is being conflated with NARROW PSYCHOLOGY. Yet, as we have seen, these two doctrines are very different. Narrow functional-role properties involving sensory inputs or behavioral outputs are not syntactic in any ordinary sense of that term. Nor are they like the properties of symbols in a formal system. Perhaps we should see the Revisionists as giving 'syntactic' and 'formal' new meanings. If so, this novelty should be resisted because it blurs an important distinction. I shall continue to resist it.

Finally, FORMAL IMPLEMENTATION is unsupported by the argument from methodological solipsism just as it was by the earlier argument from the computer analogy. The present argument is for mental supervention on the brain, but FORMAL IMPLEMENTATION requires something much more restrictive: supervention on the formal properties of mental tokens. The putative narrow meanings do not supervene on those properties (though a physicalist may think they supervene on the formal properties of tokens *and other things*).

In sum, the arguments from the computer analogy and methodological solipsism establish neither SYNTACTIC PSYCHOLOGY nor FORMAL IMPLEMENTATION. The argument from the computer analogy might plausibly be seen as establishing SYNTACTIC THOUGHT PROCESSES and the related, more restricted, version of IMPLEMENTATION. If the argument from methodological solipsism were good it would support NARROW PSYCHOLOGY and the irrelevance of truth-conditional properties to psychology, but it would not establish that only syntactic ones are relevant. In the next section I shall argue that

sort of methodological solipsism" (1980a: 65) and takes the ordinary opaque taxonomy of mental states as roughly the same as that according to the formality condition (pp. 66–70). See also Block and Bromberger's commentary (1980: 74) and Fodor's response (1980b: 99); Rey's commentary (1980: 91) and Fodor's response (1980b: 106). For evidence in some others, see Field 1978: 100–101; Baker 1986 (a critic of CTM and STM): 27.

SYNTACTIC PSYCHOLOGY is false. I shall argue later that NARROW PSYCHOLOGY is false also.

I think that the failure to attend sufficiently to the three distinctions I have been emphasizing has led to considerable confusion in the discussion of doctrines like CTM and STM. Each failure confuses the false SYNTACTIC PSYCHOLOGY with a different plausible doctrine. (1) Failing to attend to the distinction between formal and syntactic properties confuses the doctrine with FORMAL IMPLEMENTATION. Though this doctrine is strictly false, it is close to one that a physicalist will find plausible. (2) Failing to attend to the distinction between thought processes and mental processes in general, a failure encouraged by the computer analogy, confuses the doctrine with SYNTACTIC THOUGHT PROCESSES, which I am accepting as true. (3) Failing to attend to the distinction between syntactic properties and narrow semantic ones confuses the doctrine with NARROW PSYCHOLOGY, which is plausible although, I shall argue, false.

5.8. Against SYNTACTIC PSYCHOLOGY

Once SYNTACTIC PSYCHOLOGY is distinguished from NARROW PSYCHOLOGY, perhaps nobody will subscribe to it. In any case, I have argued elsewhere that it is false (1989a: Sec. 5). I shall first summarize that argument and then consider a response.

Summary. The problem with SYNTACTIC PSYCHOLOGY is that it makes Input–Thought and Thought–Output laws impossible. Input–Thought laws must explain the *distinctive* role of a certain input, in conjunction with certain thoughts, in forming other thoughts; for example, they must explain why the sight of Ron riding leads to a certain belief that, according to folk theory, refers to Ron and does not lead to a belief referring to any other person. Thought–Output laws must explain the *distinctive* role of a certain thought, in conjunction with certain other thoughts, in causing output; for example, they must explain why a certain belief that, according to folk theory, refers to Ron leads to the

277

opening of a gate in the path of the mounted Ron and not to behavior involving any other person. Laws that advert only to the syntactic properties of tokens cannot possibly account for these distinctive roles. For, syntactic properties are constituted solely by relations *among tokens*. To explain the distinctive roles, we need to advert to properties of tokens that are constituted partly by relations between tokens *and other things*. In our example, if folk theory is right, we must advert to the wide property of referring to Ron; or, if folk theory is wrong, we must advert to some narrow meaning, perhaps one involving sensory input.

Response. Consider Stich's introduction of STM. All his examples of laws countenanced by STM are Thought-Thought laws (1983: 154–6). In order to test these laws, we need to relate thoughts to inputs and outputs. What we would like for this purpose are Input-Thought and Thought-Output laws. But, Stich claims, we will not get these in "the foreseeable future" (p. 156).[32] As a result, we have to make do with "ad hoc assumptions" to test the Thought-Thought laws (1983: 156–7; see also: 134–5). Indeed, it is an embarrassment of this whole debate that it is hard to think of even roughly plausible Input-Thought and Thought-Output laws. And if we look at what actually goes on in cognitive psychology, we do not find attempts at such laws. Nor do we find examples of belief-desire explanations of behavior, the sort of explanation so common in folk psychology and so beloved by philosophers.[33] This suggests an interesting fall-back position from SYNTACTIC PSYCHOLOGY.

32 Later, in responding to an objection by Patricia Churchland, Stich predicts that Input-Thought and Thought-Output laws will collapse into vacuity; the terms to which they will apply will be defined as the ones to which they apply (1983: 180–1). But there is no more danger of vacuity here than anywhere in science. Our theory of tigers does not become vacuous because, in some sense, tigers are "defined" as what the theory applies to.

33 See, e.g., John Anderson's textbook (1980). Barbara von Eckardt remarks that "cognitive psychology is not interested in explaining why people perform certain *actions* at all. Rather its focus is on the explanation of certain of our *capacities,* specifically cognitive capacities" (1984: 75).

One fall-back position is too extreme to be interesting: Psychology should restrict itself to Thought-Thought laws. The interesting position restricts psychology to *symbolic* processes. It is plausible to suppose that input becomes representational and symbolic very soon after it enters the mind; soon after the transducers go to work on it. The fall-back position says that the input does not become the concern of psychology until that point, that the link between sensory stimulation and the representation formed by the transducer is outside psychology. This representation is not part of a thought, but it is via such representations that the world influences thought formation. A similar story is told about output: Psychology stops at the final representation, not at the behavior itself. We have earlier allowed that Thought-Thought processes might advert only to syntactic properties. If the fall-back position were correct, we would then have to allow that the laws of psychology in general advert only to syntactic properties.[34]

We should note first that this interesting position does not save SYNTACTIC PSYCHOLOGY. That doctrine – based on the claims of Stich and others about psychology – is about laws that do concern sensory stimulations and behavior. The position really is a fallback.

Second, the position is not in any way Revisionist. Stich might think otherwise because he claims that the "ad hoc assumptions" that need to be added to Thought-Thought laws are syntactic. But this is wrong for the same reason that SYNTACTIC PSYCHOLOGY is wrong. The ad hoc assumptions we need are drawn straight from folk psychology. So on this fall-back position, scientific psychology makes its findings about the workings of the mind relevant to the explanation of behavior by a liberal supplementation of folk psychology. Most strikingly, it uses folk psychology, and semantics, to interpret linguistic input and output.[35] Scientific psychology could not, therefore, imply any criti-

34 This paragraph was stimulated by the comments of Norbert Hornstein and Georges Rey.
35 *All* Stich's examples of ad hoc assumptions concern linguistic input or output.

cism of folk psychology's ascription of wide meaning to explain behavior.

Finally, even if psychology were now restricted in the way required by the fall-back position, there seems no reason why it ought to be in the future. The more ambitious task of folk psychology is surely what psychology ought to aspire to. The difficulties in satisfying those ambitions may be a reason for being modest at present, but they can hardly be a reason for restricting the future. I suggest that the main reason that we are so distant from Input-Thought and Thought-Output laws is that they depend on elements of meaning beyond syntax that are, at best, poorly understood, at worst, denied. In any case, I shall continue to take the unrestricted view of psychology, for the sake of argument.

5.9. Can Fodor Have It Both Ways?

In rejecting the two main arguments for Revisionism, I have treated CTM as a Revisionist doctrine like STM. This is not the way Fodor sees it, as we noted (5.4).[36] Fodor is an enthusiast for folk psychology. He does not think that the laws of the mind advert to wide meanings, but he does think that they advert to narrow meanings *as functions*. These meanings are *proto-intentional*, yielding an intentional wide meaning given a context. How then can he also believe in CTM, according to which the laws of mental processes advert only to "formal"/"syntactic" properties of tokens? "How can Fodor have it both ways?" as Stich asks. Fodor could have it both ways, of course, if CTM simply concerned the level of fairly brute-physical implementation. But it does not; it largely concerns a *psychological* level. The answer is that Fodor, in urging CTM, mostly has in mind a different implementational level from the brute-physical one. It is a level "between common-sense belief/desire psychology, on the

36 Nor Pylyshyn. He shares many of Fodor's views discussed in this section, but perhaps not all.

one hand, and [the brute-physical one] on the other" (1985: 82). It is not the intentional level of psychological laws that advert to meanings, but it is nonetheless psychological. It is the level of the psychological theory of "mental processes," or "mental causation." Though this is not at the brute-physical level, it "worries about mechanism and implementation" (1987: 153–4). It is a psychological level that implements the semantic properties of intentional psychology in syntactic properties.

From Fodor's perspective, my discussion of CTM collapses three levels into two. And my talk of "psychological laws" equivocates between talk of the semantic level of *intentional laws of the mind* and of the syntactic level of laws of *mental processes*. In this section, I shall consider CTM as Fodor understands it.

With one small proviso, I have no objection to his CTM *if it is restricted to thought processes*. The computer analogy suggests that there is room for a Thought-Thought level between that of intentional psychology and the brute-physical level (indeed, it suggests there is room for several levels). And, I have allowed, the laws at this level will indeed advert only to the syntactic properties of tokens. My proviso is this: In accepting SYNTACTIC THOUGHT PROCESSES I have argued that we can serve our purposes *even at the highest intentional level* with Thought-Thought laws that advert only to syntactic properties (see the discussion of **being a conditional** and **being a 'man' predicate,** 5.6). But then syntactic properties at the CTM level would not implement semantic ones as Fodor suggests they do; they would implement other syntactic ones. However, we saw that these syntactic Thought-Thought laws mimic ones that advert to semantic properties. So perhaps we can see the CTM laws as implementing the mimicked semantic ones.

The difficulty in having it both ways is with CTM as a theory of Input-Thought and Thought-Output processes.

Two things are required if there is to be the distinct syntactic psychological level of CTM: There must be some explanatory task performed by the theory at this level that is not performed by the intentional theory of the mind, and that explanatory task must be psychological. Fodor's picture of the task at this level is as follows.[37] Input-Thought laws explain the formation of syntactically described thoughts as the result of physically described inputs. Thought-Thought laws explain the formation of syntactically described thoughts as the result of other syntactically described thoughts. Thought-Output laws explain physically described outputs as the result of syntactically described thoughts. This whole level implements the laws of the mind, which are intentional throughout: Intentionally described inputs lead to semantically described thoughts that lead to intentionally described outputs.

In a paper criticizing Fodor, I claimed that these psychophysical Input-Thought and Thought-Output laws do not, together with Thought-Thought laws, form a psychological level: They are between levels, bridging laws (1991a: 109–10). Fodor disagrees (1991: 283). I am still inclined to think that I am right, but the issue comes close to being "merely verbal," and I shall concede the point. My major objection to Fodor's CTM was that the Input-Thought and Thought-Output laws at this "level" advert to properties of tokens that are not merely syntactic. *The mind (as a whole) is not purely syntactic at any level.*

The argument is simple (1991a: 111). At the level of intentional psychology, the semantic properties adverted to in Input-Thought and Thought-Output laws differ from syntactic ones in not being constituted simply by relations that tokens have to each other; they are mostly constituted by relations that tokens have to other things. In discussing FORMAL IMPLEMENTATION, I claimed that such properties cannot be implemented in the formal (intrinsic, fairly brute-physical) properties of tokens (5.6). *No more can they be implemented in their syntactic properties.* Implementation of these properties requires relations to *non*tokens, hence *non*syntactic properties, *all the way down.* Consider the property of **designating Maggie,** an example of the sort of semantic property adverted to

---

37 Fodor 1975: 42–51; 1983: 38–52; 1987: 112–22; 1991: 281–4; Fodor and Pylyshyn 1981. See also Pylyshyn 1984: 147–91.

in intentional psychology. Whatever *constitutes* this property must involve a relation to Maggie, and so the property is not syntactic. *For the very same reason,* whatever *implements* the property at any level is not syntactic.

In his response to this criticism, Fodor makes an important concession that seems to me to grant the point, viz., that the Input-Thought and Thought-Output laws at the CTM level advert to nonsyntactic properties of tokens.[38] Indeed, he thinks that they advert to *representational* properties. However, this does not undermine his picture of two psychological levels because

I[nput]-T[hought] laws provide access *only* to representations of the

---

38 But three things make me wonder whether I have interpreted the concession correctly. (i) Shortly after making it, Fodor repeats the preconcession position that "if CTM is true" "mental representations enter into mental processes . . . under *syntactic* descriptions" (p. 283; my emphasis). (ii) Fodor alleges a "curious misreading" in which I "beat [him] over the head" for believing that denotation can be implemented syntactically. (He actually says that the head beating is for believing that denotation *is* a syntactic relation, but I take it that this is a slip.) The concession, on my interpretation, would yield Fodor a ready response to the beating: Implementation is in syntactic *and psychophysical* properties. But Fodor does not give this response. Instead he talks about the implementation of intentional Thought-Thought laws, which is beside the point because the issue is over intentional Input-Thought and Thought-Output laws (p. 284). (iii) Finally, in his most recent book (1994), Fodor describes his project as that of reconciling the old idea that psychological laws are intentional with the new idea that mental processes in which they are implemented are computational. If I have interpreted the concession right, it is difficult to see why he would regard this project as worthwhile. For, according to my interpretation, the concession allows that intentional Input-Thought and Thought-Output laws are implemented in *non*syntactic properties of tokens, and so, I have argued, the idea that they are implemented in computational processes is hopeless. One wonders whether Fodor's project concerns not mental processes in general but only Thought-Thought ones; cf. n. 26 earlier and accompanying text. But then the desired reconciliation seems to have *already* been achieved (setting aside worries about completeness).

physical properties of proximal stimuli; and T[hought]-O[utput] laws provide access *only* to representations of basic motor gestures. I take it to be simply obvious that this vocabulary is not remotely rich enough to state the full range of intentional psychological laws..... So, what you end up with is: one level at which the available vocabulary is whatever you need to state whatever intentional laws there turn out to be; and another level at which the available vocabulary is exhaustively psychophysical and syntactical; and [CTM] is the idea that the (mental) processes specifiable at the second level implement the intentional laws specified at the first. (1991: 282–3)

I assume that the implementation of a semantic property like **designating Maggie** must also involve some contribution from the environment, perhaps, that Maggie causes certain proximal stimuli. If so, then, given my earlier concession, I have no objection to Fodor's modified CTM. With the two concessions we are in agreement.

With acceptance of this modified CTM must go rejection of a view that it is easy to take from Fodor's writings (although it is doubtless not his): the view that the real causal work of the mind is done by syntactic properties but that we should, nevertheless, be interested in the intentional level because of "some pre-established harmony between syntax and semantics" (as Dretske nicely puts it; 1990: 8). So the intentional level seems, on this view, epiphenomenal, albeit predictive. The view must be rejected, first, because the causal work at the CTM level is not done by purely syntactic properties of representations but by syntactic *and psychophysical ones*. Second, such harmony as there may be between these properties and semantic ones arises from the former *implementing* the latter in the usual robust sense (whatever that may be). Third, our interest in the implemented level *should* not come here, any more than it *does* come anywhere else, from some happy harmony with the implementing level, but from the implemented level offering genuine explanations with a generality that is not available at the implementing level. Semantic properties should not be mere epiphenomena; they should do causal work.

III. NARROW PSYCHOLOGY

5.10. Narrow Meanings as Functions

We have seen that for the purposes of psychological explanation, we need to advert to more than the syntactic properties of a token: SYNTACTIC PSYCHOLOGY is false (5.8). The argument from methodological solipsism attempts to motivate NARROW PSY-CHOLOGY, the doctrine that we should advert only to narrow meanings to explain behavior. I have noted two views of narrow meanings. According to one, the narrow meaning of a sentence is a function taking an external context as argument to yield a wide meaning as value. Although NARROW PSYCHOLOGY is Revisionist in this view (because the folk do not ascribe these functions to explain behavior), it is still Representationalist according to our definition (3.11), for these putative narrow meanings determine truth conditions and reference. According to the other view, the narrow meaning of a sentence is a functional role involving other sentences, proximal sensory inputs, and proximal behavioral outputs. NARROW PSYCHOLOGY is much more Revisionist in this view because it is not even Representationalist: It is definitive of these putative narrow meanings that they do not determine truth conditions and reference (4.9). I shall consider the first view in this section, the second, in the next. In the final section, I shall reject the argument for NARROW PSYCHOLOGY.

I have argued, in effect, that we (correctly) ascribe more than one wide meaning to a token (Chap. 4). So, for example, a simply-transparent belief sentence ascribes to a singular term the property of referring to a specified object; an opaque sentence, the property of referring to the object under a specified mode. I argued, further, that opaquely ascribed wide meanings are the ones that ultimately explain intentional behavior. In light of this, if the argument from methodological solipsism motivates a move to narrow meanings as functions – the first view – it will be to the narrow ones that yield these opaquely ascribed wide ones as values. So those are the narrow meanings I shall be talking about, unless otherwise noted.

On the first view,[39] a narrow meaning is *proto*-intentional: In any context it yields an intentional wide meaning. But what precisely is a narrow meaning? What constitutes this function? Consider what must be the case for any token to have a certain wide meaning. Part of the answer is that the token must have some properties that it has solely in virtue of facts internal to the mind containing it. Those properties constitute its narrow meaning. So, if we had a *theory* of its wide meaning, we would know all that we needed to about its narrow meaning.[40] The theory will explain the narrow meaning by explaining *the way in which* the mind must take a fact about the external context as the function's argument to yield a wide meaning as its value. (Analogously, we explain the function SQUARE when we say that it takes a number as its argument and multiplies the number by itself to yield the function's value.) Thus someone who believes in wide meanings, as I do, is in no position to object to the first view of narrow meanings on the ground that it leaves these meanings mysterious.

Nor is there any problem about *ascribing* these narrow meanings: We simply introduce a method for ascribing them that is

---

39   To be found, e.g., in White 1982; Fodor 1987: 44–53. Because of his direct-reference view of the wide meanings of names and various other "simple" tokens, Fodor thinks that psychology should advert to narrow meanings that yield *transparently* ascribed wide ones. I think that psychology should not, because such meanings would not explain behavior; we need finer-grained meanings for that purpose. The direct-reference view is theoretically arbitrary (4.6–4.8).

40   Cf. Block, who claims that giving a theory of narrow meanings as functions, what he calls "the Mapping Theory," is "a *terrible problem*" (1991: 38). It is so only if the theory of *wide* meaning is. And that theory will supply two things that he rightly insists on: the restriction on "input contexts" (p. 39), and the way to continue the series "Earth/water, Twin-Earth/twin-water" (p. 42). Given the close relation of narrow meanings as functions to wide meanings, the Mapping Theory will be a corollary of the theory of wide meaning.

parasitic on the standard method of ascribing wide meanings. Consider, for example, the opaquely construed

(W) Oscar believes that water is wet,

which ascribes a wide meaning. Let us adopt the convention that

(N) Oscar believes *that water is wet

ascribes a narrow meaning; that is, it ascribes whatever mental property a token has to have that is intrinsic to the mind in order to have the wide meaning ascribed by (W), **WATER IS WET.** By using the *-operator in (N) we abstract from the external facts that go into determining that a token has that wide meaning. In a sense, of course, we do not know what the narrow meaning is, but, in the same sense, we do not know what the wide meaning is either: We do not have much of a theory of either of them. Yet we can still refer to them both.

An anticipated consequence of the first view of narrow meaning is that Oscar's 'water', referring to water on Earth, shares a narrow meaning with Twin Oscar's 'water', referring to *XYZ* on Twin Earth. An apparently unanticipated consequence is that it may also share a narrow meaning with the following tokens of duplicates on other planets: *W1*-Oscar's 'water' referring to milk on *W1, W2*-Oscar's 'water' referring to gin on *W2,* and so on, perhaps, through all the stuffs. Of course, given that all the Oscars are duplicates, *W1*-Oscar's *theory of* milk, *W2*-Oscar's *theory of* gin, and so on might then be rather bizarre. But, then again, it might not be, because the context may change the reference of *other* words in a way that brings the theories back toward the truth. In any case, if we take seriously, as we should, the arguments from ignorance and error (3.8, 3.11) and the fact that we can often borrow reference (4.5), bizarreness of theory alone does not count against the possibility.

I am raising the possibility that narrow meanings may be "coarse grained" in that there is not much to them and "promiscuous" in that they can yield any of a vast range of wide meanings as values by changing the relevant external context as argument. It is probably uncontroversial that the possibility is realized by demonstratives like 'this' and pronouns like 'she'. *Historical-causal* theories make the possibility vivid for other terms. According to a historical-causal theory of names, Oscar can have a token of 'Reagan' that refers to Reagan via the mechanism of reference borrowing despite Oscar's false beliefs about Reagan, lack of true beliefs about him, and lack of an ability to recognize him. Take IT, the theory outlined earlier (4.6), as an example. The opaquely ascribed wide meaning of Oscar's token is a property of referring to Reagan by a certain mode. According to IT, this mode is constituted by d-chains that are grounded in Reagan; that involve tokens of certain physical types – the sounds, shapes, and so on that are the conventional formal properties of the name; and that are linked together by a certain sort of mental processing. Oscar's token has the property of referring by this mode partly, of course, in virtue of certain facts internal to Oscar, including the token's having links to proximal input and output that mediate its links with those particular formal properties. These facts will constitute the narrow meaning of the token. Now compare this token with Elmer's token of 'Bush'. There is a striking difference in their wide meanings because they refer to different people. But what about their narrow meanings? The only difference in these meanings is that one links tokens to one set of formal properties – for example, the sound /Reagan/ – and the other, to another – for example, the sound /Bush/. So, suppose that there is a world, *W1,* where the conventions are different and Bush is called "Reagan." Then Oscar's 'Reagan' referring to Reagan on Earth shares a narrow meaning with *W1*-Oscar's 'Reagan' referring to Bush on *W1*. And consider a name that is actually ambiguous on Earth: Oscar's 'Bruce' referring to x on Earth shares a narrow meaning with Elmer's 'Bruce' referring to y on Earth because they are linked to the same formal properties. Indeed, for the same reason, Oscar's 'Bruce' referring to x shares a narrow meaning with *his own* 'Bruce' referring to y. Of course, Oscar's two uses of 'Bruce' will have different properties as a result of internal facts about the ways in which Oscar processes the two uses. But these internal properties have no role in determining that the opaquely ascribed wide meaning of a token of 'Bruce' involves x rather than y. That is determined by the external context of the token, in particular by its history. So these internal properties do not constitute the functions that are the opaquely ascribed narrow meanings.[41]

In sum, according to IT, the narrow meaning of a name token places only a trivial constraint on what the token refers to in a context: It must refer to something that has a certain conventional name in that context. As a result, given the right context, including the right conventions, any object at all can be the referent of a token with a certain narrow meaning.

The following "picture" may help. Think of a person as starting with many unused name "files," some linked to the conventional formal properties of 'Tom', others to those of 'Dick', others to those of 'Harry', and so on. Any of the files linked to the properties for 'Tom' can be used for any person called "Tom" in the external context. However, one of those files is as a matter of historical fact used for a certain Tom. It is in virtue of this external fact that the tokens in that file refer to that person and not any of the other Toms in the context. But the file might have been used to refer to any of the other ones. And in another context where different people are called "Tom," it might have been used to refer to them.

Now, of course, historical-causal theories of names may be faulty. But in precisely what respect are they faulty? Pending an answer, it remains to be seen whether the narrow meanings of names are significantly less coarse grained – hence less alike – and less promiscuous than just suggested. Even if a historical-causal

41 However, the earlier discussion of the case of Peter and 'Paderewski' (4.17) implies that the internal properties of the two uses of 'Bruce' *do* constitute narrow meanings that are *more* fine grained than the opaquely ascribed ones we are discussing. For these finer-grained narrow meanings yield the very fine-grained wide meanings needed to explain behavior in unusual circumstances like Peter's.

theory of names is sound, it does not, of course, follow that a similar theory is correct for any other term and hence that any other term's narrow meaning is similarly coarse grained and promiscuous. For one thing, the narrow meaning of a term covered by a *description* theory of reference will be partly constituted by some inferential properties that will constrain what it could refer to in a context; thus, perhaps 'bachelor' could refer to something in a context only if 'unmarried' refers to it in that context. For another thing, the narrow meaning of any term covered by a *reliablist* theory (4.5) is likely to place significant constraints on reference, for such a term depends for its reference on covariance. But it remains to be seen, again, how many terms are covered by these theories and how extensive such constraints are. Historical-causal theories for names and natural-kind terms like 'water' and 'tiger', together with uncontroversial views of demonstratives and pronouns, make it plausible to think that the narrow meaning of many a token places very little constraint on what it could refer to and that its reference is largely determined by the external context.[42]

So, on the view that narrow meanings are functions, it is an

42 This discussion supports my earlier doubts about step (i) of Block's Ruritania argument for holism (1.14–1.15). At stage one, Bruce and Barry's narrow meanings of 'grug' are the same even though Bruce's refers to beer and Barry's to whisky. By stage two, Bruce and Barry have learned several different things about their respective grugs. Block makes the claim that, as a result, their narrow meanings of 'grug' differ. If their wide meanings are explained by a historical-causal theory and their narrow meanings are functions and not functional roles, this claim is probably false. (How does the Ruritania argument fare on the functional-role view of narrow meanings? See n. 48.)

In a later version of the Ruritania argument, Block (1994–5) gives a new argument for his claim that the narrow meanings **BRUCE'S GRUG$_B$** and **BARRY'S GRUG$_W$** are not the same at stage two. He supposes that, at that stage, Bruce and Barry each *also* acquire the other's use of 'grug'. Block's argues for his claim from:

(1) **BRUCE'S GRUG$_B$** is not the same as **BRUCE'S GRUG$_W$**.
(2) **BRUCE'S GRUG$_W$** is the same as **BARRY'S GRUG$_W$**.

open question, to be settled with the help of future theories of reference, how coarse grained and promiscuous narrow meanings are. This is likely to raise an objection of the sort that Block has pressed (1991): If the narrow meanings of words like 'water' and 'Reagan' really were as coarse grained and promiscuous as I have been suggesting, how could they serve the needs of psychological explanation? One of my own objections to ascribing these meanings is related to this one, as we shall see in discussing the argument from methodological solipsism (5.12).

I have been talking of narrow meanings that yield opaquely ascribed wide meanings, a reference to something under a specified mode. Narrow meanings that yield transparently ascribed wide meanings, a reference to something regardless of mode, will place even fewer constraints on what a token could refer to. This can be illustrated by the Big Felix example (4.2, 4.7). The following tokens are coreferential and so have the same transparently ascribed wide meaning: Ralph's 'Smith's murderer' and 'Jones'; the moll's 'Big Felix', 'you', and 'the most successful mobster';

But (1) is equally suspect in a historical-causal theory. Block supports (1) with an assumption he calls "DIFFERENCE": "If at one time, a person has substantially different beliefs associated with term t_1 and t_2 then t_1 differs in narrow content from t_2 for that person at that time." This is another assumption that is probably false in a historical-causal theory.

Block goes on to contemplate a third version of the Ruritania argument. This version supports (1) with a principle that differs from DIFFERENCE in not appealing to a difference in beliefs: "If at one time a person thinks Xs are distinct from Ys, then 'X' differs from 'Y' in narrow content for that person at that time." This difference in narrow meaning is the very fine-grained difference accepted in n. 41 earlier on the basis of the argument about the wide meanings of Peter's 'Paderewski' (4.17). A Ruritania argument about *these* narrow meanings – meanings related to wide ones that are needed to explain behavior in very unusual circumstances – may be acceptable. But there would be nothing holistic about its conclusion: The change in the very fine-grained narrow meaning of Bruce's 'grug' from stage one to stage two would be required by his acquiring a second use of 'grug' whether or not there was any substantial change in his beliefs about beer, or indeed, any change at all (cf. my criticism of step (ii) of the original argument).

Big Felix's "I"; Mary's 'the man seen at the bar'. They share the "disjunctive" narrow meaning constituted by "the internal part" of the property of referring to Big Felix by any of his names, or by any true description of him, or by any demonstration of him, and so on. Clearly a token that had such a narrow meaning might refer to *anything* given an appropriate change of context: total promiscuity. If such meanings were supposed to explain behavior, Block's objection would surely have force against them.

In conclusion, narrow meanings as functions are proto-intentional and unmysterious, albeit, perhaps, coarse grained and promiscuous. When considering the argument from methodological solipsism, I shall argue that something, although not enough, can be said for a NARROW PSYCHOLOGY committed to these meanings (5.12).

5.11. Narrow Meanings as Functional Roles

I turn now to the second, and more popular, view of narrow meaning: nonrepresentational functional roles. It is much more problematic. I shall first consider the nature of these putative meanings, then the behaviors that they are alleged to explain, and finally the relation between the meanings and the behaviors.

On the second view,[43] a narrow meaning of a token is its property of having certain causal relations, including dispositional ones, to other things. Some of these things are other tokens, which are clear enough, but some are proximal inputs and outputs. What are the natures of these inputs and outputs? Implicitly, if not explicitly, their natures are fairly brute physical: excitations of the sense organs on the one hand, and bodily movements with straightforwardly physical natures, on the other. Certainly these inputs and outputs do not have intentional natures.

How, *precisely,* are narrow meanings constituted by causal relations to these things? Any token is causally related to indefinitely many other tokens, inputs, and outputs. Which ones constitute a

---

43 To be found, e.g., in Loar 1981 and 1982, McGinn 1982, Block 1986.

narrow meaning? What are its "identity conditions"? To answer these questions we must consider our semantic purposes. We might wonder why *any* property constituted by these relations would serve our purposes of explaining behavior. Set that general worry aside for a moment. We also have a worry about any particular proposed narrow meaning. Why will our semantic purposes be served by ascribing a property constituted in that way rather than any other way? What is special about that particular set of relations? The literature seems to suggest only one idea for an answer: The property we should ascribe is an epistemic one like **being confirmed if and only if *p*.** But, if Quine is anywhere near right about the holistic nature of confirmation, which he surely is, this idea leads straight to semantic holism (1.4). I have already argued against semantic holism: Our semantic purposes can be served only by ascribing a localistic property (3.10). So any narrow meaning we are interested in ascribing must be constituted by only a few of the relations of a token. But which few, and why that particular few? What is it about a property constituted out of that few that makes it serve our semantic purposes and hence be a meaning? Our purposes require a localistic meaning, and yet, on the functional-role view, we seem to lack a "principled basis" for saying what that meaning is (as so many philosophers have in effect pointed out; 1.1).

Block frankly admits that he is unable to provide identity conditions for narrow meanings but does not think that this is "an insurmountable obstacle":

My guess is that a scientific conception of meaning should do away with the crude dichotomy of same/different meaning in favor of a multidimensional gradient of similarity of meaning. (1986: 624)

Doubtless the crude dichotomy that Block has in mind is one according to which either *the* meaning of one token is the same as *the* meaning of another or it is different. If so, we should indeed do away with the dichotomy, but not in favor of mere similarities in meanings. For, as I have already argued (3.9), whenever two tokens are similar in meaning there must be some meaning that they share in virtue of which they are thus similar. So we should do away with the crude dichotomy in favor of the idea that a token may share one of its meanings with another token without sharing others. So, Block does still face the obstacle of providing identity conditions for narrow meanings. It remains to be seen if it is insurmountable.[44]

Turn next to the behavior that putative narrow meanings are alleged to explain. The behavior that NARROW PSYCHOLO-GISTS seem to have in mind is fairly brute-physical, neural impulses or mere bodily movements. In this respect, NARROW PSYCHOLOGISTS are firmly in the functionalist tradition:

functionalism . . . has typically insisted that characterizations of mental states should contain descriptions of inputs and outputs in physical language. (Block 1978: 263–4)

But what, Tyler Burge wonders, has this sort of behavior to do with psychology? He mentions specifications of behavior like the following: "She picked up the apple, pointed to the square block, tracked the moving ball, smiled at the familiar face, took the money instead of the risk." He concludes that "many relevant specifications of behavior in psychology are intentional, or relational, or both" (Burge 1986: 11). He is surely right (2.5).[45] The intentional behaviors, *actions,* that a psychology appealing to wide meanings is supposed to explain are very different from the brute-physical proximal events that NARROW PSYCHOLOGISTS seem to have in mind.

Saying exactly how actions are different is a subtle matter. I have already supported the following view (4.17). For an event to

44 Field (1977) might be seen as providing the required identity conditions. But note that he is talking only of an *intra*personal synonymy that requires *total* identity of conceptual roles. The theoretical interest of this sort of synonymy escapes me.

45 For further support see, e.g., Fodor 1987: 8–10; Papineau 1987: 59–60. Fodor nicely mocks the tendency of functionalists to brush the problem of inputs and outputs under the carpet: "Since I am very busy just now, please do not ask me what 'inputs' and 'outputs' are" (1987: 68).

be a certain intentional behavior, it is necessary that the event have a certain intention as its immediate cause. Thus, intentionally picking up the apple must be immediately caused by the intention (opaquely) to pick up the apple. That intention is a thought, an attitude to a token that means (opaquely) **PICK UP THE APPLE.** In some cases, at least, this intentional cause is not enough, for the action must have a certain *success:* You have not picked up the apple unless it ends up in your hand (or whatever). In thus relating an agent to an external object, these actions are *straightforwardly* relational. Actions that do not demand success are not so: You can hunt lions without ending up with one and hunt unicorns even though there are none to end up with. Lion hunting is, in a sense, relational in that the meaning of the intention that must cause the act relates the agent to lions. The analogous remark about unicorn hunting will not do, of course, but even unicorn hunting may be relational in that the meaning of the intention that must cause the act may relate the agent to other external things; for example, to horns and horses.

The Revisionist may, of course, accept that what Burge says is *descriptively* right but claim that it is not *normatively* so. Although psychology *does* attempt to explain behaviors that are intentional and relational in the ways described, it *should* attempt to explain something more brute physical. This extends Revisionism to cover not only the meanings alleged to explain behavior but also the behavior to be explained. It thus changes the subject: It does not claim to explain the same thing better, but a different thing.[46]

Suppose that there are intentional behaviors. Then psychology must explain them (we are taking the unrestricted view of psychology; 5.8), and this Revisionist NARROW PSYCHOLOGY would be false. Furthermore, the Representationalist properties

46 Block has pointed out a disadvantage of a psychology concerned with brute-physical outputs: It is chauvinistic (1978: 314–17). If the outputs are neural impulses, then the approach discriminates against all organisms without neurons. If the outputs are at the level of movements of arms and legs, then the approach discriminates against brains in vats, paralytics, snakes, and such like.

these intentional explanations ascribe to tokens would play one of the semantic roles I described (2.4–2.6) and hence would be meanings. In contrast, putative narrow meanings would seem not to play a semantic role and hence not to be meanings. There are, of course, levels at which brute-physical behavior is to be explained: a neuroscientific level for one; perhaps Fodor's psychological level of mental processes for another. These other levels are quite compatible with the intentional level: They *implement* the intentional level and hence cast no aspersions on it. But the properties of tokens adverted to at an implementational level explain brute-physical behavior, not intentional behavior. They are at the wrong level to be meanings. So the putative narrow meanings of this NARROW PSYCHOLOGY would not really be meanings.

So, this NARROW PSYCHOLOGY requires *the denial that there are any intentional behaviors to be explained:* Nobody ever does (intentionally) pick up an apple, point to a square block, and so on. And it requires an account of the semantic roles that make something a meaning other than the one I gave.

Such a doctrine is possible, of course. Indeed, it is not far from the Churchlands' actual doctrine. But it is a very radical one. We need a very powerful argument to convince us of it given the success of our explanations involving intentional descriptions of behavior. I do not think that there is any such argument (5.3).

In the face of this problem, suppose that NARROW PSYCHOLOGY changes its view of the behavior to be explained: There are intentional behaviors and psychology should explain them. So NARROW PSYCHOLOGY becomes the view that the psychological laws that explain these behaviors advert only to narrow meanings. The problem then is that wide meanings, not narrow functional-role ones, seem suited to this explanatory task; the relation between narrow meanings and what they are alleged to explain would be mysterious.

I am assuming that an intentional behavior is partly constituted by the intentional state that immediately causes it. So, if there is the behavior then there is the state. And such states, if there really are any, involve tokens with wide Representationalist meanings; that was the descriptive thesis established in the last chapter. So, as I pointed out (4.17), it is not hard to see how other states with similar wide meanings might cause the intention and hence explain the behavior. In contrast, how could narrow functional-role meanings explain it? The general worry we set aside earlier surfaces. How could a meaning constituted by relations between tokens, and between tokens and brute-physical inputs and outputs, explain intentional behavior? We are not going to find an answer by looking to the relations between tokens. These relations are inferential ones. Everyone agrees that inferential relations are important in explaining behavior, but they can be so only if some tokens, at least, have some other properties that are *directly* important for that purpose. So, we must look at the relations to input and output for an answer to our question. But it is hard to see how a putative meaning constituted out of these can be in the required counterfactual supporting relations to intentional behavior. The problem is, roughly, that the meaning is at the wrong level to handle the intentional nature of the behavior. Furthermore, it does not "extend far enough" to handle the relational nature of (most of) the behavior to be explained: the fact that the behavior is partly constituted by external things like apples and lions. How could meanings constituted entirely inside the head explain this behavior?

In brief, a NARROW PSYCHOLOGY committed to functional-role meanings faces a dilemma. Either it claims that psychology should explain only brute-physical behaviors, or it accepts that psychology explains intentional behaviors. If the former, then NARROW PSYCHOLOGY is committed, implausibly, to denying intentional behaviors. If the latter, then NARROW PSYCHOLOGY is committed, implausibly, to narrow meanings explaining intentional behaviors.

Stich can be seen as seeking a way out of this dilemma. On the one hand, he does not embrace the first horn, finding "no reason to expect" that "a purely physical description of movements" will be suitable for psychology. On the other hand, he does not *firmly* embrace the second horn either. He thinks, plausibily enough, that most folk descriptions of behavior – for example, 'performing its millionth weld' – are unsuitable hybrids, part psychological and part historical, social, and so on (1983: 169).[47] What then is suitable? An "autonomous behavioral description," which is such that "if it applies to an organism in a given setting, then it would also apply to any replica of the organism in that setting" (p. 167). He thinks that it may take work to forge these descriptions and offers only one example: 'performing a weld' (p. 168). It is not obvious that this is a good example. The act specified by the description is partly constituted by *the intention to* perform a weld. *Must* a replica who may share no history with the organism share that intention? I suspect not, but set that aside. If Stich's "autonomous" descriptions *are* intentional and relational, as is 'making a weld', then it is hard to see how any narrow functional-role meaning, let alone a syntactic property, could explain their application. If they *are not* intentional and relational, and yet not "purely physical" either, we lack any idea what they might be, and how we might get from them (perhaps with the help of historical facts, social facts, and so on) to the intentional and relational descriptions that Stich clearly thinks also apply to behavior. And, we would still need to be told how the application of those descriptions might be explained by narrow meanings or syntactic properties. It seems that Stich hankers after behavioral descriptions that are folk descriptions "minus a bit" and that have two properties: They are still intentional and hence can yield folk descriptions when supplemented by history, and so forth; and their application is explained by narrow functional-role meanings or syntactic properties. We have no reason to think that there are such descriptions.

47 Perhaps only what Danto (1963) has called "basic actions" – ones like *moving one's finger* – are open to a strictly psychological explanation. Other actions – like pulling the trigger – are performed *by* performing a basic one and are open to hybrid explanations. For more on basic actions, see Goldman 1970.

In sum, putative functional-role narrow meanings are unexplained and mysterious. Even if they were not, we have been given no idea how such putative meanings *could* explain intentional behaviors and hence really be meanings. If they do not explain these behaviors, then NARROW PSYCHOLOGY must deny intentional behaviors altogether. We have been given insufficient reason to believe such a denial.

These failings are very bad news for functional-role NARROW PSYCHOLOGY. For, that doctrine has a heavy onus arising from the apparently striking success of our present practice of ascribing wide meanings to explain behavior. Why do these ascriptions seem so successful if they are not really? What reason have we for thinking that the ascriptions that would be recommended by this Revisionist doctrine would do any better? In the next section, we shall see that the argument from methodological solipsism is no help to the doctrine.[48] It is hard not to see the doctrine as little more than hand waving.

5.12. Rejecting the Argument from Methodological Solipsism

NARROW PSYCHOLOGY is motivated by the argument from methodological solipsism (5.7). We distinguished three elements of this argument. First, at bottom, is a conviction that the states we need to posit for psychological explanation must supervene on the intrinsic physical states of the organism; roughly, on the brain. Second, this appealing view gets support from the consideration of duplicates. Third, it gets support from Stich's consideration of "deviants." I shall consider these elements in turn.

I have already provided some evidence of the underlying conviction. Consider, also, the following passage:

48 If this is correct, then Block's Ruritania argument for holism (1.14–1.15), which has failed already for narrow meanings as functions (n. 42), cannot be saved by taking it to be about narrow meanings as functional roles. For, there are no such meanings.

the content of an individual x's thoughts or the meaning of x's sentences is based upon their roles in the explanation of x's behavior. When that is coupled with the assumption that thoughts, etc., explain behavior as causally effective states of x (and not as states of some amalgam of x and x's environment), the conceptual role theory quite naturally imposes itself. For what appears to be essential is how such causally effective states interact with perception and each other to influence behavior. (Loar 1982: 275)

The plausibility of the claim that we need only narrow meanings to explain behavior seems to arise, as Burge points out, from certain principles of local causation:

events in the external world causally affect the mental events of a subject only by affecting the subjects's bodily surfaces;. . . nothing (not excluding mental events) causally affects behavior except by affecting (causing or being a causal antecedent of causes of) local states of the subject's body. (1986: 15)

Yet the claim does not follow from these principles. For the principles are quite compatible with mental states being *individuated* nonindividualistically in terms of their relations to the environment (pp. 16–17). States that are so individuated do not supervene on the brain alone: They partly supervene on the brain's external relations.

Fodor has an interesting and intricate response to Burge. Fodor argues that we should not individuate a mental state in terms of its relations to an environment because those relations are irrelevant to its *causal powers* (1987: 33–4). He notes a difficulty. The individuation of causal powers depends on the individuation of their output: Two states that differ in their output do differ in their causal powers. If behavior is individuated relationally, so that, for example, Oscar and Twin Oscar behave differently, then their mental states will be as well (pp. 34–8). To remove this difficulty, Fodor commits himself to a surprisingly strong and quite general assumption: Causal powers are individuated individualistically *throughout science;* hence the causal powers of mental states are;

hence behavior is (pp. 38–44). Fodor wants to establish individualism for psychology by establishing it everywhere.

What does Fodor say in favor of his assumption? He rightly claims that if the causal powers of something depend on its relations to something else, then there must be some mechanism or law to mediate that dependency. This is effective in showing that *some* relational properties are irrelevant to causal powers – in particular, the ones he ingeniously defines in terms of the position of a dime – but it does not establish that *all* are. So far as I can see, Fodor reaches his assumption by taking for granted that causal powers are "locally supervenient" (pp. 41–2), that "causal powers supervene on local microstructure" (p. 44). He seems to think that Burge would agree.[49]

I think that Burge would not agree. Burge gives some nice examples of nonindividualistic and relational individuation: continents in geology; lungs in biology. Indeed, such individuation serves many explanatory purposes. It pervades the social sciences: Someone is a capitalist in virtue of her economic relations. Think also of the parts of a car: Something is an accelerator partly in virtue of its relations to the engine. Closer to home, think of syntactic properties: Something is a conjunction symbol in virtue of its role within a language (5.5–5.6). In general, relational individuation is to be found wherever functional-structural explana-

49 Toward the end of this discussion, Fodor distinguishes what he has previously combined: individualistic and nonrelational individuation. He defines "individualism" as individuation by causal powers. He goes on: "There is nothing to stop principles of individuation from being simultaneously relational and individualistic" (p. 42). Indeed there is not, but this is only because causal powers may be individuated relationally. Fodor's example – the causal powers of a planet (p. 43) – is a good example. Fodor's discussion is puzzling: It cannot be the case *both* that the causal powers of a planet supervene on its microstructure *and* that it has those powers in virtue of its relational properties. Finally, we should note that because causal powers can be individuated relationally, Fodor's definition of "individualism" is, on the one hand, very different from Burge's (1986: 4) and, on the other hand, rather paradoxical.

tions are appropriate. Such explanations do not go against principles of local causation that Burge has enunciated. However, they do go against Fodor's assumption. Wherever a functional explanation is in order, an object has causal powers that are not supervenient on its microstructure. And whenever such an explanation is in order there is some mechanism mediating the dependency of those powers on something else.

Underlying the conviction that we need narrow meanings, particularly of the functional-role sort, to explain behavior is the view that a wide Representationalist meaning is inadequate for the job because it is not sufficiently internal to the mind. Indeed, in my discussion of narrow meanings as functions (5.10), I have raised the possibility that many wide meanings may be *largely external* to the mind: There may be very little internal that distinguishes the wide meaning of 'water' and 'gin', and there very likely is little internal that distinguishes one name from another. How then can these wide meanings explain my different behavior toward water and gin, and toward one person and another? The answer we should take from Burge is that similar internal states can have different external relations and that this difference can be crucial in explaining behaviors involving different external objects.

Two more examples may help to persuade. The first is from chess. Explanations of the behavior of pieces in a chess game typically allude to chess properties like **being a knight** or **being a bishop.** Yet chess properties are not constituted by any intrinsic internal properties of the pieces that have them. Indeed, almost anything could have a chess property. And something that has one could have any other: A knight in one game could be a bishop in another; indeed, all the chess pieces could be physically the same (even though it would then be difficult for humans to play chess). What matters to the causal powers of a chess piece are its external relations.

The second example concerns demonstratives and so is closer to home. Suppose that Flora believes that that man is dangerous (pointing to Sam) and that this leads to behavior involving Sam. Suppose next that Flora believes that that man is dangerous (point-

302

ing to Joe) and that this leads to behavior involving Joe. So the two beliefs would lead to different behavior, a difference we would like to explain. Yet, the explanation of this difference will not be found in any intrinsic difference in Flora on the two occasions, hence not in any difference in narrow meanings. The explanation is to be found in Flora's different external relations on the two occasions, relations that determine wide meanings.

According to Representationalism, a law of intentional psychology is concerned with mental states that purport to represent a world that is (mostly) external to the mind and toward which the organism's behavior is directed. The causal powers of a token depend on what it represents. We cannot settle a priori the extent to which intrinsic properties of the mind constrain this. What matters to the law is simply that the token has its representational property under a mode appropriate to the behavior it is supposed to explain. It does not matter how the token achieves this.

In sum, so far we have found nothing to support the conviction that underlies methodological solipsism. It is possible to draw boundaries anywhere and to look for explanations of the characteristics and proximal behavior of the bounded entity or system in terms of what goes on within the boundary. The view that the appropriate boundary for explaining the behavior of an organism is its skin cannot be taken for granted.

Does the underlying conviction get the support it needs from the second element of the argument, a consideration of duplicates? The claim is that people like Oscar and Twin Oscar should be psychologically the same: The psychological theory that explains their behaviors should ascribe the same properties to their mental states. Because those states differ in their wide Representationalist meanings – Oscar's referring to water, Twin Oscar's to Twin water – the theory should not ascribe those meanings. Rather it should ascribe narrow meanings that supervene on what is inside the skin and hence are shared by Oscar and Twin Oscar. We should adopt NARROW PSYCHOLOGY.

There is undoubtedly some truth in these claims about duplicates, but the truth is not enough to motivate a move away from

303

WIDE PSYCHOLOGY. First, it does not make a case for narrow meanings as functional roles. Second, insofar as it makes a case for narrow meanings as functions, that case is insufficient to justify NARROW PSYCHOLOGY.

To bring out the truth, let us start with this typical (opaque) explanation of behavior:

(1) Oscar gave water to Mary because he believed that Mary was thirsty and that water relieves thirst.

(The explanation is greatly simplified, of course, but this will not matter to the discussion.) What should we Representationalist WIDE PSYCHOLOGISTS say about explanation (1) and the laws that support it?

Concerning (1), we should say that the meanings ascribed to Mary's beliefs are wide, involving references to water and Mary. And the behavior is intentional and relational in that it must be immediately caused by an intention with a meaning that also involves reference to water and Mary. Part of the reason that (1) is a good explanation lies in the relations between the meanings in the beliefs and the intention. Concerning the supporting laws, we should say that these will quantify over token mental sentences having fully referential meanings of a certain sort and over related behaviors of a certain sort. The sorts and the relation are illustrated in (1). In specifying the sort of mental sentence, the *highest-level* law will advert to tokens having certain semantico-syntactic structures, like that of 'Mary was thirsty'. This will involve talk of tokens having general referential semantic properties like **being a proper name, being a mass term,** and so on that words in sentences having those structures must have. But it will not involve talk of tokens having any particular referential meanings, like the meaning of 'Mary' or of 'water'. And, I emphasize, *all the sorts of meanings in question are referential.*

The highest-level law will support not only (1) but many other explanations; for example:

(2) Tom gave water to Mary because he believed that Mary was thirsty and that water relieves thirst.

(3) Dick gave milk to Mary because he believed that Mary was thirsty and that milk relieves thirst.

(4) Harry gave gin to Rose because he believed that Rose was thirsty and that gin relieves thirst.

All of these explanations, hence their behaviors and beliefs, are similar in virtue of being supported by the same high-level law. These explanations are also supported by *lower-level* laws that make some explanations more similar than others. Explanations (1) and (2) are most similar – indeed, so similar that everyone would agree that they are the same – because they are supported by the low*est*-level law, varying only in the place of 'Oscar' in (1). Explanations (1) and (3) are less similar because the lowest-level law that supports them both varies also in the place of 'water' in (1); (1) and (4), less again, because the law varies also in the place of 'Mary'. Clearly, we could give other explanations supported by the highest level law that are less similar still to (1); for example, those involving relieving boredom or increasing happiness.

It is time to consider Twin Earth. Clearly, the highest level law will support the following explanation:

(5) Twin Oscar gave Twin water to Twin Mary because he believed that Twin Mary was thirsty and that Twin water relieves thirst.

So (5), and its behavior and beliefs, is similar to the other explanations. Furthermore, the lowest level law that supports both (1) and (5) is the same one that supports both (1) and (4); so, in that respect, (1) and (5) are as similar as (1) and (4). None of these similarities motivate an interest in narrow meanings.

In drawing our attention to Twin-Earth duplicates, NARROW PSYCHOLOGISTS are making two claims. First, they are insisting that (1) and (5) enjoy a different similarity from the one just noted in virtue of the fact that Twin water and Twin Mary play exactly the same "internal role" for Twin Oscar as water and Mary play for Oscar: Oscar and Twin Oscar share narrow meanings. Second, NARROW PSYCHOLOGISTS claim that psychological laws, from top to bottom, should advert only to tokens having such narrow meanings.

The WIDE PSYCHOLOGIST has no problem with the first claim about the similarity of (1) and (5) if it is taken to be about narrow meanings that are functions from contexts to wide meanings. She accepts that the same theory that will explain intentional wide meanings will explain these proto-intentional narrow meanings shared by Oscar and Twin Oscar. However, the WIDE PSYCHOLOGIST does not find any reason to accept the first claim if it is taken to be about narrow meanings that are functional roles. Duplicates must, of course, share functional roles. But we have been given no reason so far for thinking that any of these roles constitute *meanings*.

Now consider the second claim. If psychological laws should advert to narrow meanings then the psychological explanations they support should do so too. So explanations (1) to (5) must be replaced; in particular, their belief ascriptions should be replaced by ones that advert to narrow meanings instead of wide meanings. This is no problem: We resort to the *-operator introduced earlier to ascribe narrow meanings as functions (5.10). So we replace (1) and (5) by

(1*) Oscar gave water to Mary because he believed *that Mary was thirsty and *that water relieves thirst.

(5*) Twin Oscar gave Twin water to Twin Mary because he believed *that Twin Mary was thirsty and *that Twin water relieves thirst.

The narrow meanings ascribed by (1*) and (5*) are of course the same.[50]

50 Ignoring some subtle issues here because of the differences between the modes of 'Twin Mary' and 'Mary', and between 'Twin water' and 'water' (4.17). These issues could be avoided by replacing 'Twin Mary' in (5*) by

It is immediately apparent that (1*) and (5*) are inadequate explanations: They have the same explanans but different explananda. The behavior to be explained in (1*) is directed toward water and Mary in particular, that in (5*) toward Twin water and Twin Mary in particular, yet the common explanans, being narrow, concerns none of these entities. So our move to narrow meanings in the explanans must be accompanied by a corresponding move in the explananda.[51] We must modify our ascription of behavior in the same way that we modified our ascription of meaning. Part of the modification is straightforward. Giving water to Mary essentially involves the intention to give water to Mary. We need to ascribe behavior that essentially involves the intention *to give water to Mary, where '*to give water to Mary' ascribes a narrow meaning. Oscar's and Twin Oscar's behaviors will share this intention*. However, the behaviors will still differ in their relational properties: For example, Oscar's behavior successfully relates him to Mary, Twin Oscar's, to Twin Mary.[52] We need a description that abstracts from these relational differences by applying to any behavior that would count in some external context as *fulfilling* the intention*. Let us suppose that '*gave water to Mary' is such a description. So, the explanations we need are

(1**) Oscar *gave water to Mary because he believed *that Mary was thirsty and *that water relieves thirst.

(5**) Twin Oscar *gave Twin water to Twin Mary because he believed *that Twin Mary was thirsty and *that Twin water relieves thirst.

I think that these explanations are good. Indeed, how could they not be good if (1) and (5) are? So what then is the issue? If

'Mary', *as used in Twin English*; similarly, 'Twin water'. But this would be confusing.

51 This often seems to be overlooked by those who are impressed with Twin-Earth arguments for narrow meaning; e.g., Loar (1988).

52 I am indebted to Graeme Marshall for emphasizing this to me.

($1\star\star$) and ($5\star\star$) are more psychologically appropriate than (1) and (5), then psychological laws should advert to narrow meanings and NARROW PSYCHOLOGY is correct. Explanations ($1\star\star$) and ($5\star\star$) *are* more psychologically appropriate *only if* it is more psychologically appropriate to explain the "proto-intentional narrow behavior" that they advert to than the "intentional wide behavior" that (1) and (5) advert to. *The whole issue of NARROW PSYCHOLOGY comes down to this issue about the sort of behavior that psychology should explain.*

The first thing to note about this issue is that it is between the sort of behavior that we explain using wide meanings and the sort of behavior that we might explain using narrow meanings *as functions*. There is nothing here that motivates, let alone explains, narrow meanings *as functional roles*. And there is nothing that either shows how these mysterious meanings might explain intentional behaviors or, alternatively, shows that there are no such behaviors to be explained. So, *at most,* the consideration motivates a NARROW PSYCHOLOGY committed to narrow meanings as functions. If we *must* move from the wide status quo, we should move to a narrow theory that is Representationalist, close to the familiar wide one and relatively clear. We have been given no reason to move to one that is non-Representationalist, distant from the familiar one and mysterious.

The second thing to note about this issue is that it does *not* seem to be A BIG ISSUE: *This* version of NARROW PSYCHOLOGY is close to WIDE PSYCHOLOGY; its Revisionism is moderate. Every intentional explanation of wide behavior ascribing wide meanings entails a proto-intentional one of narrow behavior ascribing narrow meanings, and wherever we have a proto-intentional one, knowledge of the relevant context will yield an intentional one. Surely nothing much can hinge on whether one explanation rather than the other is more appropriate "in psychology."

Still, suppose that we have to choose which is more appropriate, which should we choose? I think we have several reasons for choosing the wide status quo, reasons that are jointly decisive.

So, at this point I part company with the initial claims that the NARROW PSYCHOLOGIST makes about duplicates; this, in my view, is the end of the truth in those claims.

The first reason is related to an earlier-mentioned objection of the sort that Block has pressed (5.10). I pointed out that many narrow meanings may well be coarse grained in that there is not much to them and promiscuous in that they can yield any of a vast range of wide meanings as values by changing the relevant external context as argument. The objection to such meanings was that they could not serve the needs of psychological explanation.[53] We can now see the correct response to this objection: The narrow meaning could serve those needs well if the behaviors that psychology needed to explain were only narrow. But then *our* objection to NARROW PSYCHOLOGY should be that *psychology does not need to explain only narrow behavior*. For that behavior is also likely to be coarse grained and promiscuous. Giving water to Mary involves giving, water, and Mary. *Giving water to Mary might involve giving and perhaps taking, kicking, and many other acts; it might involve water, *XYZ,* and perhaps many other stuffs; and it might involve Mary, Twin Mary, and perhaps any other person. We certainly want to have the more discriminating intentional behavior explained *somewhere*. I do not think that anything in the writings of the NARROW PSYCHOLOGISTS establishes that it should not be explained *in psychology*.[54]

Second, neither do I think that anything in those writings shows that we should be interested in explaining narrow behavior *as well as* the wide that we clearly want to explain.

Third, any description of narrow behavior is parasitic on a description of wide behavior. Why on earth must we go to the trouble of "subtracting" our knowledge of the context from a

---

53 Because Block is convinced by the argument for methodological solipsism, his objection to narrow meanings as functions encourages him to believe in narrow meanings as functional roles.

54 Stalnaker has some different, but related, doubts about the utility of narrow meanings as functions (1989: 293–9). See also Schiffer 1990a: 92–3.

description of behavior, using the *-operator, before applying a psychological law to it? In particular, why must we do this given that we will have to add back the knowledge we have subtracted to get a description of the wide behavior that we certainly want explained *and* that we will have to make corresponding additions to what is yielded by the psychological law in order to explain that wide behavior? This procedure seems totally misguided.

Fourth, explaining wide behavior is the status quo and we should prefer the status quo in the absence of decisive reasons against it. No such reasons have been presented.

Nevertheless, it may be thought, the status quo misses something: It misses what Oscar and Twin Oscar have in common. It need not miss this, as Field has pointed out (1990: 103). Oscar and Twin Oscar not only evince the common narrow behavior, *giving water to Mary, they evince a variety of common wide behaviors that we get by "factoring out" the differences between giving water to Mary and giving Twin water to Twin Mary; for example, both Oscar and Twin Oscar *give something that plays the role on their planets that water plays on Earth*. We can then ascribe the same wide beliefs to explain this common behavior. Aside from that, conceding that we should ascribe *common* narrow behaviors and beliefs to Oscar and Twin Oscar would be a revision of the status quo that would be both minor and quite compatible with WIDE PSYCHOLOGY. It would be minor because the status quo already identifies some behaviors and beliefs (partly) narrowly; for example, "Anne gives her father gin and so does Elizabeth" and "Anne believes that gin makes her father happy and so does Elizabeth" will usually identify behaviors and beliefs that involve different people and are, to that extent, narrow. The revision would be compatible with WIDE PSYCHOLOGY because the latter concerns psychological laws. These laws do not support narrow identifications, and so do not count them as psychological, but the laws do not outlaw the identifications either.

Finally, we must consider the third element of the argument for NARROW PSYCHOLOGY: Stich's discussion of "deviants"

(1983: 135–48). He claims that these examples show that a psychology that adverts to wide meanings will miss significant and powerful generalizations that can be captured by a narrow functional-role psychology. Stich is certainly persuasive on one score: The examples show that a person may deviate sufficiently from us for there to be no sentence in our language that can be used as the content sentence in a belief ascription to describe her belief. For, to ascribe a belief in the ordinary way, the "intimate link" (2.12, 4.11) requires that we have a sentence that means much the same as the sentence the deviant would use to express her belief. This is a *translation problem* like the one we often face when dealing with an alien (and always in dealing with nonhuman animals). We should solve it in the same way: Introduce new terms with the appropriate meanings into our language either by borrowing or by invention. It may be difficult to learn enough about the deviant to do this just as it may be difficult to learn enough about the alien. But this epistemic problem in *describing* the wide beliefs of deviants, a difficulty that would carry over to describing their wide behaviors, does *not* show that wide psychological laws do not apply to these beliefs and behaviors. Similarly, the difficulty in describing a newly discovered animal does not show that biological laws do not apply to it.

Why does Stich think otherwise? Because he assumes that wide laws will quantify over the sentences in our language that we use as content sentences to describe beliefs (1983: 132). So any belief for which there is no such sentence will not be covered by the law. But the laws will not quantify over *our content sentences*. They will quantify over beliefs, *the subjects' mental sentences*. We will *normally* be able to describe these sentences using our sentences, but deviants and aliens show that the abnormal is possible.

Of course, it *may* turn out that a deviant's belief is really not covered by our current laws: It does not have a semantico-syntactic structure adverted to in the laws. In which case, we will need new wide laws to cover it. But this does not reflect on the enterprise of providing such laws. Similarly, the fact that a newly discovered animal – a monotreme, perhaps – may not be covered by our current biological laws does not reflect on the enterprise of providing biological laws of that type.

In conclusion, Stich's argument is not intended to support the ascription of narrow meanings *as functions,* and it would not do so: Ascriptions of those meanings are parasitic on the ascription of wide ones and so would inherit any problems of the latter. The argument is intended to support a *functional-role* alternative to wide explanations and laws. Yet, despite Stich's frequent suggestions to the contrary, we have no idea what this alternative might be like, as I have pointed out.

It is time to sum up the discussion of Revisionism. A major consideration in favor of WIDE PSYCHOLOGY is that it is in accord with a successful status quo (2.9). WIDE PSYCHOLOGY would be undermined if we had strong reasons to think that wide meanings cannot be explained. But we do not have such reasons. The doctrine would be undermined also if there were a better alternative. Eliminativism about meanings and intentional behavior is not worked out nearly enough to be such an alternative. No more is a NARROW PSYCHOLOGY with meanings as functional roles. We have been given no reason for thinking that such meanings can be explained and no motivation for seeking them. I have argued that SYNTACTIC PSYCHOLOGY is false (although the computer analogy gives a persuasive argument for the more limited SYNTACTIC THOUGHT PROCESSES). Only NARROW PSYCHOLOGY with meanings as functions comes close to being an alternative at this time. But this moderately Revisionist doctrine does not come close enough. We have good reasons for preferring WIDE PSYCHOLOGY.

References

Ackerman, Felicia (Diana). 1979a. "Proper Names, Propositional Attitudes and Non-Descriptive Connotations." *Philosophical Studies* 35: 55–69.

1979b. "Proper Names, Essences and Intuitive Beliefs." *Theory and Decision* 11: 5–26.

1980. "Natural Kinds, Concepts, and Propositional Attitudes." In French, Uehling, and Wettstein 1980: 469–85.

1989. "Content, Character, and Nondescriptive Meaning." In Almog, Perry, and Wettstein 1989: 5–21.

Adams, Frederick. 1986. "Intention and Intentional Action: The Simple View." *Mind and Language* 1: 281–301.

Adams, Frederick, Robert Stecker, and Gary Fuller. 1992. "The Semantics of Thoughts." *Pacific Philosophical Quarterly* 73: 375–89.

1993. "Schiffer on Modes of Presentation." *Analysis* 53: 30–4.

Almog, Joseph. 1984. "Semantic Anthropology." In French, Uehling, and Wettstein 1984: 479–89.

1985. "Form and Content." *Nous* 19: 603–16.

1986. "Naming without Necessity." *Journal of Philosophy* 71: 210–42.

Almog, Joseph, John Perry, and Howard Wettstein, eds. 1989. *Themes from Kaplan.* Oxford: Oxford University Press.

Anderson, C. Anthony, and Joseph Owens, eds. 1990. *Propositional Attitudes: The Role of Content in Logic, Language, and Mind.* Stanford: Center for the Study of Language and Information.

Anderson, John R. 1980. *Cognitive Psychology and Its Implications.* San Francisco: W. H. Freeman and Company.

Antony, Louise M. 1987. "Naturalized Epistemology and the Study of Language." In *Naturalistic Epistemology,* ed. Abner Shimony and Debra Nails. Dordrecht: D. Reidel: 235–57.

1989. "Anomolous Monism and the Problem of Explanatory Force." *Philosophical Review* 98: 153–87.

313

Armstrong, D. M. 1973. *Belief, Truth and Knowledge*. Cambridge: Cambridge University Press.

    1978. *Nominalism and Realism: Universals and Scientific Realism*. Vol. 1. Cambridge: Cambridge University Press.

Asquith, P. D., and T. Nickles, eds. 1983. *PSA 1982*. Vol. 2. East Lansing, MI: Philosophy of Science Association.

Baker, Lynne Rudder. 1982. "Underprivileged Access." *Nous* 16: 227–42.

    1986. "Just What Do We Have in Mind?" In French, Uehling, and Wettstein 1986: 25–48.

    1987. *Saving Belief: A Critique of Physicalism*. Princeton: Princeton University Press.

Barwise, Jon, and John Perry. 1983. *Situations and Attitudes*. Cambridge, MA: MIT Press.

Bealer, George. 1992. "The Incoherence of Empiricism." *Proceedings of the Aristotelian Society,* supp. vol. 66: 99–138.

Bigelow, John, 1992. "The Doubtful A Priori." In Hanson and Hunter 1992: 151–66.

Bilgrami, Akeel. 1992. *Belief and Meaning: The Unity and Locality of Mental Content*. Oxford: Basil Blackwell.

Block, Ned. 1978. "Troubles with Functionalism." In *Minnesota Studies in the Philosophy of Science*. Vol. 9, *Perception and Cognition: Issues in the Foundations of Psychology,* ed. Wade C. Savage, 261–325. Minneapolis: University of Minnesota Press. Reprinted in Block 1980a: 268–305.

    1980a. *Readings in Philosophy of Psychology*. Vol. 1. Cambridge, MA: Harvard University Press.

    1980b. "Introduction: What Is Functionalism?" In Block 1980a: 171–84.

    ed. 1981. *Readings in Philosophy of Psychology*. Vol. 2. Cambridge, MA: Harvard University Press.

    1986. "Advertisement for a Semantics for Psychology." In French, Uehling, and Wettstein 1986: 615–78.

    1991. "What Narrow Content Is Not." In Loewer and Rey 1991: 33–64.

    1993. "Holism, Hyper-analyticity and Hyper-compositionality." *Mind and Language* 8: 1–26.

    1994–5. "An Argument for Holism." *Proceedings of the Aristotelian Society* 95: 151–69.

Block, Ned, and Sylvain Bromberger. 1980. "States' Rights." *Behavioral and Brain Sciences* 3: 73–4.

Boër, Stephen, and William G. Lycan. 1980. "Who Me?" *Philosophical Review* 89: 427–66.

Bogdan, Radu J. 1993. "The Architectural Nonchalance of Commonsense Psychology." *Mind and Language* 5: 189–205.

Boghossian, Paul A. 1990a. "The Status of Content." *Philosophical Review* 99: 157–84.

1990b. "The Status of Content Revisited." *Pacific Philosophical Quarterly* 71: 264–78.

1993. "Does Inferential Role Semantics Rest Upon a Mistake?" *Mind and Language* 8: 27–40.

1994. "The Transparency of Mental Content." In Tomberlin 1994: 33–50.

Bonjour, Laurence. 1992. "A Rationalist Manifesto." In Hanson and Hunter 1992: 53–88.

Boolos, George, ed. 1990. *Meaning and Method: Essays in Honor of Hilary Putnam.* Cambridge: Cambridge University Press.

Brandom, Robert. 1984. "Reference Explained Away." *Journal of Philosophy* 81: 469–92.

1988. "Pragmatism, Phenomenalism, and Truth Talk." In French, Uehling, and Wettstein 1988: 75–94.

Bratman, Michael. 1984. "Two Faces of Intention." *Philosophical Review* 93: 375–405.

Braun, David. 1991. "Proper Names, Cognitive Contents, and Beliefs." *Philosophical Studies* 62: 289–305.

Burge, Tyler. 1979. "Individualism and the Mental." In French, Uehling, and Wettstein 1979b: 73–121.

1986. "Individualism and Psychology." *Philosophical Review* 95: 3–45.

1988. "Individualism and Self-Knowledge." *Journal of Philosophy* 85: 649–63.

Carnap, Rudolf. 1937. *The Logical Syntax of Language.* New York: Harcourt, Brace.

Castañeda, Hector-Neri. 1966. "He★: A Study in the Logic of Self-Consciousness." *Ratio* 8: 130–57.

1967. "Indicators and Quasi-Indicators." *American Philosophical Quarterly* 4: 1–16.

Chastain, Charles. 1975. "Reference and Context." In Gunderson 1975: 194–269.

Chisholm, Roderick. 1976. "Knowledge and Belief: 'De Dicto' and 'De Re.'" *Philosophical Studies* 29: 1–20.

Chomsky, Noam. 1957. *Syntactic Structures.* The Hague: Mouton.

1965. *Aspects of the Theory of Syntax.* Cambridge, MA: MIT Press.

1980. *Rules and Representations*. New York: Columbia University Press.

Church, Alonzo. 1950. "On Carnap's Analysis of Statements of Assertion and Belief." *Analysis* 10: 97–9.

Churchland, Patricia S. 1986. *Neurophilosophy: Toward a Unified Science of the Mind-Brain*. Cambridge, MA: MIT Press.

Churchland, Patricia S., and Paul M. Churchland. 1983. "Stalking the Wild Epistemic Engine." *Nous* 17: 5–20. Reprinted in Lycan 1990b: 300–11.

Churchland, Paul M. 1979. *Scientific Realism and the Plasticity of Mind*. Cambridge: Cambridge University Press.

1981. "Eliminative Materialism and the Propositional Attitudes." *Journal of Philosophy* 78: 67–90. Reprinted in Churchland 1989: 1–22; and in Lycan 1990b: 206–23.

1989. *A Neurocomputational Perspective: The Nature of Mind and the Structure of Science*. Cambridge, MA: MIT Press.

1993. "Evaluating Our Self Conception." *Mind and Language* 8: 211–22.

Cowie, Fiona. 1987. "Meaning Holism." B.A. thesis, University of Sydney.

Crane, Tim. 1990. "The Language of Thought: No Syntax Without Semantics." *Mind and Language* 5: 188–212.

Crimmins, Mark. 1992. *Talk About Beliefs*. Cambridge, MA: MIT Press.

Crimmins, Mark, and John Perry. 1989. "The Prince and the Phone Booth: Reporting Puzzling Beliefs." *Journal of Philosophy* 86: 685–711. Reprinted in Perry 1993: 249–78.

Danto, Arthur. 1963. "What We Can Do." *Journal of Philosophy* 60: 435–45.

Davidson, Donald. 1980. *Essays on Actions and Events*. Oxford: Clarendon Press.

1984. *Inquiries into Truth and Interpretation* Oxford: Clarendon Press.

1987. "Knowing One's Own Mind." *Proceedings and Addresses of the American Philosophical Association* 60: 441–58.

1990. "The Structure and Content of Truth." *Journal of Philosophy* 87: 279–328.

Davidson, Donald, and Gilbert Harman, eds. 1972. *Semantics of Natural Language*. Dordrecht: D. Reidel.

Demopoulos, William. 1980. "A Remark on the Completeness of the Computational Model of Mind." *Behavioral and Brain Sciences* 3: 135.

Dennett, Daniel. 1978. *Brainstorms*. Cambridge, MA: Bradford Books.

Devitt, Michael. 1974. "Singular Terms." *Journal of Philosophy* 71: 183–205.

1976. "Semantics and the Ambiguity of Proper Names." *Monist* 59: 404–23.

1980. "Brian Loar on Singular Terms." *Philosophical Studies* 37: 271–80.

1981a. *Designation.* New York: Columbia University Press.

1981b. "Donnellan's Distinction." In French, Uehling, and Wettstein 1981, 511–24.

1981c. Critical notice of French, Uehling, and Wettstein 1979a. *Australasian Journal of Philosophy* 59: 211–21.

1983. "Realism and Semantics." Part 2 of a critical study of French, Uehling, and Wettstein 1980. *Nous* 17: 669–81.

1984. "Thoughts and Their Ascription." In French, Uehling, and Wettstein 1984: 385–420.

1985. Critical notice of Evans 1982. *Australasian Journal of Philosophy* 63: 216–32.

1989a. "A Narrow Representational Theory of the Mind." In *Rerepresentation: Readings in the Philosophy of Psychological Representation,* ed. Stuart Silvers, 369–402. Dordrecht: Kluwer Academic Publishers. Reprinted in Lycan 1990b: 371–98. Page references are to reprint.

1989b. "Against Direct Reference." In French, Uehling, and Wettstein 1989: 206–40.

1990a. "Meanings Just Ain't in the Head." In Boolos 1990: 79–104.

1990b. "On Removing Puzzles about Belief Ascription." *Pacific Philosophical Quarterly* 71: 165–81.

1990c. "Transcendentalism about Content." *Pacific Philosophical Quarterly* 71: 247–63.

1991a. "Why Fodor Can't Have It Both Ways." In Loewer and Rey 1991: 95–118.

1991b. *Realism and Truth.* 2d ed. rev. (1st ed. 1984). Oxford: Basil Blackwell,

1991c. "Minimalist Truth: A Critical Notice of Paul Horwich's *Truth.*" *Mind and Language* 6: 273–83.

1993a. "Localism and Analyticity." *Philosophy and Phenomenological Research* 53: 641–6.

1993b. "A Critique of the Case for Semantic Holism." In Tomberlin 1993: 281–306. Reprinted, with a new "Postscript," in Fodor and Lepore 1993a: 17–60. Page references are to reprint.

1994a. "Semantic Localism: Who Needs a Principled Basis?" In *Philosophy and the Cognitive Sciences,* ed. Roberto Casati, Barry Smith, and Graham White, 40–50. Vienna: Holder-Pichler-Tempsky.

1994b. "The Methodology of Naturalistic Semantics." *Journal of Philosophy* 91: 545–72.

Devitt, Michael, and Georges Rey. 1991. "Transcending Transcendentalism: A Response to Boghossian." *Pacific Philosophical Quarterly* 72: 87–100.

Devitt, Michael, and Kim Sterelny. 1987. *Language and Reality: An Introduction to the Philosophy of Language.* Oxford: Basil Blackwell.

1989. "Linguistics: What's Wrong with 'the Right View.' " In Tomberlin 1989: 497–531.

Donnellan, Keith S. 1966. "Reference and Definite Descriptions." *Philosophical Review* 75: 281–304.

1972. "Proper Names and Identifying Descriptions." In Davidson and Harman 1972: 356–79.

1989. "Belief and the Identity of Reference." In French, Uehling, and Wettstein 1989: 275–88.

Dretske, Fred I. 1981. *Knowledge and the Flow of Information.* Cambridge, MA: MIT Press.

1990. "Does Meaning Matter?" In Villanueva 1990: 5–17.

Dummett, Michael. 1973. *Frege: Philosophy of Language.* London: Duckworth.

1975. "What Is a Theory of Meaning?" In Guttenplan 1975: 97–138.

1978. *Truth and Other Enigmas.* Cambridge, MA: Harvard University Press.

1981. *The Interpretation of Frege's Philosophy.* Cambridge, MA: Harvard University Press.

Evans, Gareth. 1982. *The Varieties of Reference,* ed. John McDowell. Oxford: Clarendon Press.

Field, Hartry. 1972. "Tarski's Theory of Truth." *Journal of Philosophy* 69: 347–75.

1973. "Theory Change and the Indeterminacy of Reference." *Journal of Philosophy* 70: 462–81.

1977. "Logic, Meaning, and Conceptual Role." *Journal of Philosophy* 74: 379–409.

1978. "Mental Representation." *Erkenntnis* 13: 9–61. Reprinted with Postscript in Block 1981: 78–114. Page references are to reprint.

1980. *Science Without Numbers: A Defense of Nominalism.* Princeton: Princeton University Press.

1990. " 'Narrow' Aspects of Intentionality and the Information-Theoretic Approach to Content." In Villanueva 1990: 102–16.

Fodor, Jerry A. 1975. *The Language of Thought.* New York: Thomas Y. Crowell Company.

1980a. "Methodological Solipsism Considered as a Research Strategy in

Cognitive Psychology." *Behavioral and Brain Sciences* 3: 63–73. Reprinted in Fodor 1981.

1980b. "Methodological Solipsism: Replies to Commentators." *Behavioral and Brain Sciences* 3: 99–109.

1981. *Representations: Philosophical Essays on the Foundations of Cognitive Science.* Cambridge, MA: MIT Press.

1982. "Cognitive Science and the Twin-Earth Problem." *Notre Dame Journal of Formal Logic* 23: 98–118.

1983. *The Modularity of Mind: An Essay on Faculty Psychology.* Cambridge, MA: MIT Press.

1985. "Fodor's Guide to Mental Representation: The Intelligent Auntie's Vade-Mecum." *Mind* 94: 76–100.

1987. *Psychosemantics: The Problem of Meaning in the Philosophy of Mind.* Cambridge, MA: MIT Press.

1990. *A Theory of Content and Other Essays.* Cambridge: MIT Press.

1991. "Replies." In Loewer and Rey 1991: 255–319.

1994. *The Elm and the Expert: Mentalese and Its Semantics.* Cambridge, MA: MIT Press.

Fodor, Jerry A., and Ernest Lepore. 1992. *Holism: A Shopper's Guide.* Oxford: Basil Blackwell.

eds. 1993a. *Holism: A Consumer Update. Grazer Philosophische Studien* 46. Amsterdam: Rodopi, B.V.

1993b. "Replies." In Fodor and Lepore 1993a: 303–22.

Fodor, Jerry A., and Zenon W. Pylyshyn. 1981. "How Direct Is Visual Perception? Some Reflections on Gibson's 'Ecological Approach.' " *Cognition* 9: 139–96.

1988. "Connectionism and Cognitive Architecture: A Critical Analysis." *Cognition* 28: 3–71.

Frege, Gottlob. 1952. *Translations from the Philosophical Writings of Gottlob Frege,* ed. Peter Geach and Max Black. Oxford: Basil Blackwell.

French, Peter A., Theodore E. Uehling, Jr., and Howard K. Wettstein, eds. 1979a. *Contemporary Perspectives in the Philosophy of Language.* Minneapolis: University of Minnesota Press.

eds. 1979b. *Midwest Studies in Philosophy.* Vol. 4, *Studies in Metaphysics.* Minneapolis: University of Minnesota Press.

eds. 1980. *Midwest Studies in Philosophy.* Vol. 5, *Studies in Epistemology.* Minneapolis: University of Minnesota Press.

eds. 1981. *Midwest Studies in Philosophy.* Vol. 6, *The Foundations of Analytic Philosophy.* Minneapolis: University of Minnesota Press.

eds. 1984. *Midwest Studies in Philosophy*. Vol. 9, *Causation and Causal Theories*. Minneapolis: University of Minnesota Press.

eds. 1986. *Midwest Studies in Philosophy*. Vol. 10, *Studies in the Philosophy of Mind*. Minneapolis: University of Minnesota Press.

eds. 1988. *Midwest Studies in Philosophy*. Vol. 12, *Realism and Antirealism*. Minneapolis: University of Minnesota Press.

eds. 1989. *Midwest Studies in Philosophy*. Vol. 13, *Contemporary Perspectives in the Philosophy of Language II*. Notre Dame: University of Notre Dame Press.

Gasper, Philip. 1986. Review of 1st. ed. of Devitt 1991b. *Philosophical Review*. 95: 446–51.

Goldman, Alvin I. 1970. *A Theory of Human Action*. Englewood Cliffs, NJ: Prentice-Hall.

1989. "Interpretation Psychologized." *Mind and Language* 4: 161–85.

Goodman, Nelson. 1979. "Predicates Without Properties." In French, Uehling, and Wettstein 1979a: 347–8.

Gordon, Robert M. 1986. "Folk Psychology as Simulation." *Mind and Language* 1: 158–71.

Grice, Paul. 1989. *Studies in the Way of Words*. Cambridge, MA: Harvard University Press.

Gunderson, Keith, ed. 1975. *Minnesota Studies in the Philosophy of Science*. Vol. 7, *Language, Mind and Knowledge*. Minneapolis: University of Minnesota Press.

Guttenplan, Samuel, ed. 1975. *Mind and Language*. Oxford: Clarendon Press.

Hannan, Barbara. 1993. "Don't Stop Believing: The Case Against Eliminative Materialism." *Mind and Language* 8: 165–79.

Hanson, Philip, and Bruce Hunter, eds. 1992. *Return of the A Priori: Canadian Journal of Philosophy,* supp. vol. 18. Calgary: The University of Calgary Press.

Harman, Gilbert. 1973. *Thought*. Princeton: Princeton University Press.

1975. "Language, Thought, and Communication." In Gunderson 1975: 270–98.

1987. "(Nonsolipsistic) Conceptual Role Semantics." In *New Directions in Semantics,* ed. Ernest Lepore, 55–81. London: Academic Press.

1993. "Meaning Holism Defended." In Fodor and Lepore 1993a: 163–71.

Haugeland, John. 1978. "The Nature and Plausibility of Cognitivism." *Behavioral and Brain Sciences* 1: 215–26. Reprinted in Haugeland 1981: 243–81. Page references are to reprint.

1980. "Formality and Naturalism." *Behavioral and Brain Sciences* 3: 81–2.

ed. 1981. *Mind Design: Philosophy, Psychology, Artificial Intelligence.* Cambridge, MA: MIT Press.

1985. *Artificial Intelligence: The Very Idea.* Cambridge, MA: MIT Press.

Heidelberger, Herbert. 1980. "Understanding and Truth Conditions." In French, Uehling, and Wettstein 1980: 401–10.

Higginbotham, James. 1991. "Truth and Understanding." *Iyyun, the Jerusalem Quarterly* 40: 271–88.

Horgan, Terence. 1993. "The Austere Ideology of Folk Psychology." *Mind and Language* 8: 282–97.

Horgan, Terence, and James Woodward. "Folk Psychology Is Here to Stay." *Philosophical Review* 94: 197–226. Reprinted in Lycan 1990b: 399–420. Page references are to reprint.

Horwich, Paul. 1990. *Truth.* Oxford: Basil Blackwell.

Jones, Todd, Edmond Mulaire, and Stephen Stich. 1991. "Staving Off Catastrophe: A Critical Notice of Jerry Fodor's *Psychosemantics.*" *Mind and Language,* 6: 58–82.

Kaplan, David. 1968. "Quantifying In." *Synthese* 19: 178–214.

1986. "Opacity." In *The Philosophy of W. V. Quine,* ed. Lewis E. Hahn and Paul A Schilpp, 229–89. La Salle, IL: Open Court.

1989a. "Demonstratives: An Essay on the Semantics, Logic, Metaphysics, and Epistemology of Demonstratives and Other Indexicals." In Almog, Perry, and Wettstein 1989: 510–92.

1989b. "Afterthoughts." In Almog, Perry, and Wettstein 1989: 565–614.

Katz, Jerrold J. 1972. *Semantic Theory.* New York: Harper and Row.

1984. "An Outline of a Platonist Grammar." In *Talking Minds: The Study of Language in Cognitive Sciences,* ed. Thomas G. Bever, John M. Carroll, and Lance A. Miller, 17–48. Cambridge, MA: MIT Press. Reprinted in Katz 1985.

ed. 1985. *The Philosophy of Linguistics.* Oxford: Oxford University Press.

1990. "Has the Description Theory of Names Been Refuted?" In Boolos 1990: 31–61.

Kirkham, Richard L. 1989. "What Dummett Says about Truth and Linguistic Competence." *Mind* 98: 207–24.

Kitcher, Patricia. 1984. "In Defense of Intentional Psychology." *Journal of Philosophy* 81: 89–106.

1985. "Narrow Taxonomy and Wide Functionalism." *Philosophy of Science* 52: 78–97.

Kitcher, Philip. 1980. "A Priori Knowledge." *Philosophical Review* 76: 3–23.

321

Kripke, Saul A. 1979a. "Speaker's Reference and Semantic Reference." In French, Uehling, and Wettstein 1979a: 6–27.

1979b. "A Puzzle about Belief." In *Meaning and Use,* ed. A. Margalit, 239–83. Dordrecht: D. Reidel.

1980. *Naming and Necessity.* Cambridge, MA: Harvard University Press. [This is a corrected version of an article of the same name (plus an appendix) in Davidson and Harman 1972, together with a new preface.]

Kuhn, Thomas S. 1962. *The Structure of Scientific Revolutions.* Chicago: Chicago University Press. 2d. ed. 1970.

Larson, Richard K., and Peter Ludlow. 1993. "Interpreted Logical Forms." *Synthese* 95: 305–57.

Lepore, Ernest, and Jerry Fodor. 1993. "Reply to Critics." *Philosophy and Phenomenological Research* 53: 673–82.

Lepore, Ernest, and Barry Loewer. 1986. "Solipsistic Semantics." In French, Uehling, and Wettstein 1986: 595–614.

Levine, Joseph. 1993. "Intentional Chemistry." In Fodor and Lepore 1993a: 103–34.

Lewis, David K. 1972. "General Semantics." In Davidson and Harman 1972: 169–218.

1973. *Counterfactuals.* Oxford: Basil Blackwell.

1983. *Philosophical Papers.* Vol. 1. New York: Oxford University Press.

1986. *On the Plurality of Worlds.* Oxford: Basil Blackwell.

1994. "Reduction of Mind." In *A Companion to Philosophy of Mind,* ed. Samuel Guttenplan, 412–31. Oxford: Basil Blackwell.

Loar, Brian. 1976. "The Semantics of Singular Terms." *Philosophical Studies* 30: 353–77.

1980. "Syntax, Functional Semantics, and Referential Semantics." *Behavioral and Brain Sciences* 3: 89–90.

1981. *Mind and Meaning.* Cambridge: Cambridge University Press.

1982. "Conceptual Role and Truth-Conditions." *Notre Dame Journal of Formal Logic* 23: 272–83.

1983a. "Must Beliefs Be Sentences?" In Asquith and Nickles 1983: 627–43.

1983b. "Reply to Fodor and Harman." In Asquith and Nickles 1983: 662–6.

1987. "Subjective Intentionality." *Philosophical Topics* 15: 89–124.

1988. "Social Content and Psychological Content." In *Contents of*

Thought, ed. D. Merrill and R. Grimm, 99–110. Tucson: University of Arizona Press.

Loewer, Barry, and Georges Rey, eds. 1991. *Meaning in Mind: Fodor and His Critics.* Oxford: Basil Blackwell.

Lormand, Eric. 1995a. "How to Be a Meaning Holist." Unpublished.

1995b. "How to Be a Meaning Atomist." Unpublished.

Lycan, William G. 1984. *Logical Form in Natural Language.* Cambridge, MA: MIT Press.

1985. "The Paradox of Naming." In *Analytical Philosophy in Comparative Perspective,* ed. B. K. Matilal and J. L. Shaw, 81–102. Dordrecht: D. Reidel.

1988. *Judgement and Justification.* Cambridge: Cambridge University Press.

1990a. "On Respecting Puzzles About Belief Ascriptions [A Reply to Devitt]." *Pacific Philosophical Quarterly* 71: 182–8.

ed. 1990b. *Mind and Cognition: A Reader.* Oxford: Basil Blackwell.

1991. "Definition in a Quinean World." In *Definitions and Definability: Philosophical Perspectives,* ed. J. H. Fetzer, D. Shatz, and G Schlesinger, 111–31. Dordrecht: Kluwer Academic Publishers.

McClamrock, Ron. 1989. "Holism Without Tears." *Philosophy of Science* 56: 258–74.

MacDonald, G., and Philip Pettit. 1981. *Semantics and Social Science.* London: Routledge and Kegan Paul.

McGinn, Colin. 1980. "Truth and Use." In *Reference, Truth and Reality: Essays on the Philosophy of Language,* ed. Mark Platts, 19–40. London: Routledge and Kegan Paul.

1982. "The Structure of Content." In *Thought and Object,* ed. A. Woodfield, 207–58. Oxford: Clarendon Press.

McKinsey, Michael. 1994. "Individuating Belief." In Tomberlin 1994: 303–30.

Malcolm, Norman. 1968. "The Conceivability of Mechanism." *Philosophical Review* 77: 45–72.

Marcus, Ruth Barcan. 1981. "A Proposed Solution to a Puzzle about Belief." In French, Uehling, and Wettstein 1981: 501–10.

Mates, Benson. 1952. "Synonymity." In *Semantics and the Philosophy of Language,* ed. L. Linsky, 111–36. Champaign: University of Illinois Press.

Millikan, Ruth. 1984. *Language, Thought, and Other Biological Categories: New Foundations for Realism.* Cambridge, MA: MIT Press.

1993. *White Queen Psychology and Other Essays for Alice.* Cambridge, MA: MIT Press.

Neale, Stephen. 1990. *Descriptions.* Cambridge, MA: MIT Press.

Oppy, Graham. 1992. "Why Semantic Innocence?" *Australasian Journal of Philosophy* 70: 445–54.

Owens, Joseph I. 1989. "Contradictory Belief and Cognitive Access." In French, Uehling, and Wettstein 1989: 289–316.

1990. "Cognitive Access and Semantic Puzzles." In Anderson and Owens 1990: 147–73.

Papineau, David. 1984. "Representation and Explanation." *Philosophy of Science* 51: 550–72.

1987. *Reality and Representation.* Oxford: Basil Blackwell.

Pastin, Mark. 1974. "About *De Re* Belief." *Philosophy and Phenomenological Research* 24: 569–75.

Patterson, Sarah. 1990. "The Explanatory Role of Belief Ascriptions." *Philosophical Studies* 59: 313–32.

Pelletier, Francis Jeffry. 1989. "Another Argument Against Vague Objects." *Journal of Philosophy* 86: 481–92.

Perry, John. 1993. *The Problem of the Essential Indexical and Other Essays.* New York: Oxford University Press.

Putnam, Hilary. 1975. *Mind, Language and Reality: Philosophical Papers.* Vol. 2. Cambridge: Cambridge University Press.

1983. *Realism and Reason: Philosophical Papers.* Vol. 3. Cambridge: Cambridge University Press.

1988. *Representation and Reality.* Cambridge, MA: MIT Press.

Pylyshyn, Z. 1980a. "Computation and Cognition: Issues in the Foundations of Cognitive Science." *Behavioral and Brain Sciences* 3: 111–32.

1980b. "Cognitive Representation and the Process-Architecture Distinction." *Behavioral and Brain Sciences* 3: 154–69.

1984. *Computation and Cognition.* Cambridge, MA: MIT Press.

Quine, W. V. 1953. *From a Logical Point of View.* Cambridge, MA: Harvard University Press.

1960. *Word and Object.* Cambridge, MA: MIT Press.

1966. *Ways of Paradox and Other Essays.* New York: Random House.

1969. *Ontological Relativity and Other Essays.* New York: Columbia University Press.

1975. "Mind and Verbal Dispositions." In Guttenplan 1975: 83–95.

1979. "Intentions Revisited." In French, Uehling, and Wettstein 1979a: 268–74.

1981. *Theories and Things*. Cambridge, MA: Harvard University Press.

1991. "Two Dogmas Revisited." *Canadian Journal of Philosophy* 21: 265–74.

Rey, Georges. 1980. "The Formal and the Opaque." *Behavioral and Brain Sciences* 3: 90–2.

1993. "The Unavailability of What We Mean: A Reply to Quine, Fodor and Lepore." In Fodor and Lepore 1993a: 61–101.

Richard, Mark. 1983. "Direct Reference and Ascriptions of Belief." *Journal of Philosophical Logic* 12: 425–52.

1990. *Propositional Attitudes: An Essay on Thoughts and How We Ascribe Them*. Cambridge: Cambridge University Press.

Salmon, Nathan. 1981. *Reference and Essence*. Princeton: Princeton University Press.

1986. *Frege's Puzzle*. Cambridge, MA: MIT Press.

1990. "A Millian Heir Rejects the Wages of *Sinn*." In Anderson and Owens 1990: 215–47.

Schiffer, Stephen. 1979. "Naming and Knowing." In French, Uehling, and Wettstein 1979a: 61–74.

1981. "Truth and the Theory of Content." In *Meaning and Understanding*, ed. Herman Parret and Jacques Bouveresse, 204–22. Berlin: Walter de Gruyter.

1987. *Remnants of Meaning*. Cambridge, MA: MIT Press.

1990a. "Fodor's Character." In Villanueva 1990: 77–101.

1990b. "The Mode-of-Presentation Problem." In Anderson and Owens 1990: 249–68.

1992. "Belief Ascription." *Journal of Philosophy* 89: 499–521.

Searle, John R. 1958. "Proper Names." *Mind* 67: 166–73.

1983. *Intentionality: An Essay in the Philosophy of Mind*. Cambridge: Cambridge University Press.

Sellars, Wilfrid. 1963. *Science, Perception, and Reality*. New York: Humanities Press.

Sleigh, R. C. 1967. "On Quantifying into Epistemic Contexts." *Nous* 1: 23–31.

Soames, Scott. 1985a. "Semantics and Psychology." In Katz 1985: 204–26.

1985b. "Lost Innocence." *Linguistics and Philosophy* 8: 59–71.

1987. "Direct Reference, Propositional Attitudes, and Semantic Content." *Philosophical Topics* 15: 47–87. [A condensed version, "Direct Reference and Propositional Attitudes," is in Almog, Perry, and Wettstein 1989: 393–419.]

1988. "Substitutivity." In *On Being and Saying: Essays for Richard Cartwright,* ed. J. J. Thomson, 99–132. Cambridge: MIT Press.

Sosa, Ernest. 1970. "Propositional Attitudes *de Dictu* and *de Re.*" *Journal of Philosophy* 67: 883–86.

Stalnaker, Robert. 1989. "On What's in the Head." In Tomberlin 1989: 287–316.

Stampe, Dennis. 1979. "Toward a Causal Theory of Linguistic Representation." In French, Uehling, and Wettstein 1979a: 81–102.

Stich, Stephen P. 1978. "Autonomous Psychology and the Belief-Desire Thesis." *Monist* 61: 573–91. Reprinted in Lycan 1990b: 345–61.

1979. "Do Animals Have Beliefs?" *Australasian Journal of Philosophy* 57: 15–28.

1980. "Paying the Price for Methodological Solipsism." *Behavioral and Brain Sciences* 3: 97–8.

1983. *From Folk Psychology to Cognitive Science: The Case Against Belief.* Cambridge, MA: MIT Press.

1986. "Are Belief Predicates Systematically Ambiguous?" In *Belief: Form, Content and Function,* ed. Radu Bogdan, 119–147. Oxford: Oxford University Press.

1991. "Narrow Content Meets Fat Syntax." In Loewer and Rey 1991: 239–54.

Stich, Stephen P., and Shaun Nichols. 1992. "Folk Psychology: Simulation or Tacit Theory?" *Mind and Language* 7: 35–71.

Strawson, P. F. 1959. *Individuals: An Essay in Descriptive Metaphysics.* London: Methuen.

Tarski, Alfred. *Logic, Semantics, Metamathematics.* Trans. J. H. Woodger. Oxford: Oxford University Press.

Taschek, William W. 1987. "Content, Character, and Cognitive Significance." *Philosophical Studies* 52: 161–89.

Taylor, Kenneth A. 1990. Review of Devitt and Sterelny 1987. *The Philosophical Review* 99: 260–3.

1994. "How Not to Refute Eliminative Materialism." *Philosophical Psychology* 7: 101–25.

Tomberlin, James E., ed. 1987. *Philosophical Perspectives, 1: Metaphysics.* Atascadero, CA: Ridgeview Publishing Company.

ed. 1989. *Philosophical Perspectives, 3: Philosophy of Mind and Action Theory.* Atascadero, CA: Ridgeview Publishing Company.

ed. 1993. *Philosophical Perspectives, 7: Language and Logic.* Atascadero, CA: Ridgeview Publishing Company.

ed. 1994. *Philosophical Perspectives, 8: Logic and Language*. Atascadero, CA: Ridgeview Publishing Company.

Villanueva, Enrique, ed. 1990. *Information, Semantics and Epistemology*. Oxford: Basil Blackwell.

Von Eckardt, Barbara. 1984. "Cognitive Psychology and Principled Skepticism." *Journal of Philosophy* 81: 67–88.

Wagner, Steven J. 1986. "California Semantics Meets the Great Fact." *Notre Dame Journal of Formal Logic* 27: 430–55.

Wettstein, Howard. 1981. "Demonstrative Reference and Definite Descriptions." *Philosophical Studies* 40: 241–58.

1986. "Has Semantics Rested on a Mistake?" *Journal of Philosophy* 83: 185–209.

1989a. "Cognitive Significance Without Cognitive Content." In Almog, Perry, and Wettstein 1989: 421–54.

1989b. "Turning the Tables on Frege or How Is It that 'Hesperus Is Hesperus' Is Trivial?" In Tomberlin 1989: 317–39.

White, Morton G. 1950. *John Dewey: Philosopher of Science and Freedom*. New York: The Dial Press.

White, Stephen L. 1982. "Partial Character and the Language of Thought." *Pacific Philosophical Quarterly* 63: 347–65.

Wilson, G. 1978. "On Definite and Indefinite Descriptions." *Philosophical Review* 87: 48–76.

1991. "Reference and Pronominal Description." *Journal of Philosophy* 88: 359–87.

Wilson, N. L. 1959. "Substances without Substrata." *Review of Metaphysics* 12: 521–39.

1967. "Linguistic Butter and Philosophical Parsnips." *Journal of Philosophy* 64: 55–67.

Wittgenstein, Ludwig. 1953. *Philosophical Investigations*. Trans. G. E. M. Anscombe. 2d ed. rev. 1958. Oxford: Basil Blackwell.

Wright, Crispin. 1976. "Truth Conditions and Criteria." *Proceedings of the Aristotelian Society,* supp. vol. 50: 217–45.

Yagasawa, Takashi. 1993. "A Semantic Solution to Frege's Puzzle." In Tomberlin 1993: 135–54.

Index

informativeness and cognitive significance of identity statements, 2, 8,
172–3, 176–180, 238
intentional behaviors or actions,
basic, 298n
denial of, 9, 249–55, 258, 295–9,
308, 312
nature of, 230–1, 294–5
intimate link, 8, 82–3, 86, 116, 118,
121, 123, 193, 198–208, 215–6,
247n, 311
intuitions, role of, 1, 5, 42, 48–54, 65,
72–85, 184n, 242; *see also* methodology of philosophy; naturalism
IT (illustrative theory of referential
meanings), 163–71, 173, 177–8,
218, 223, 226–8, 239–40, 288–9

Jackson, Frank, 150n
Jones, Todd, 15–16

Kant, Immanuel, 250
Kaplan, David, 141n, 143n, 170n,
179n, 180n, 185n, 186, 222–3n
Katz, Jerrold J., 18n, 55, 56n, 169n
Kirkham, Richard L.
Kitcher, Patricia, 254n, 255n, 257n
Kitcher, Philip, 50n
Kripke, Saul A., 8, 82n, 114–15, 118,
139, 161, 163, 164n, 170n, 172,
189n, 198n, 203, 222, 228n,
228–41, 242n
Kuhn, Thomas S., 88

language-of-thought hypothesis, 13,
56n, 95n, 139, 154–8, 248, 254,
266
Larson, Richard K., 67n, 166n
Lepore, Ernest, 11n, 15n, 18n, 23n,
24–5n, 35n, 53n, 64n, 87, 93n,

94, 124n, 133n, 134n, 169n,
173n, 250n, 257n
Levine, Joseph, 33–6, 134n
Lewis, David K., ix, 43, 45, 65n,
109n, 158n, 210
linguistic-conceptual competence, 2,
5, 25, 26–8, 32, 51–3, 65, 66n,
78–83, 94, 160n, 172–3, 176,
178–9, 185n, 227, 238
Loar, Brian, 17n, 20n, 52n, 169n,
187n, 191n, 192n, 236n, 249n,
256, 264n, 273, 274n, 275n,
292n, 300, 307n
localism, *see* artifactual holism and localism; astronomical holism and
localism; biological holism and
localism; economic holism and
localism; LOCALISM doctrines
defined; psychological holism
and localism; semantic localism
cluster, 11n, 19n, 97–100
LOCALISM doctrines defined,
DESCRIPTIVE SEMANTIC, 100
NORMATIVE SEMANTIC, 99
SEMANTIC, 98
Loewer, Barry, 53n, 169n, 173n,
257n
logical necessity, 22–3, 25, 28, 33,
172, 176
logical truth, 22–3, 25–9, 32, 50, 51–
2
Lormand, Eric, ix, 69n, 161n, 216n
Ludlow, Peter, ix, 67n, 166n
Lycan, William G., ix, 20n, 28, 44,
55, 56n, 63, 67n, 77n, 169n,
170n, 180n, 186, 187n, 188–9,
192, 208, 224, 225n, 257n

McClamrock, Ron, 16, 43, 121
MacDonald, G., 67n
McGinn, Colin, 20n, 53n, 169n,
187n, 192n, 257n, 272, 292n

McKinsey, Michael, 52n
Malcolm, Norman, 250n
Marcus, Ruth Barcan, 169n
Marshall, Graeme, 307n
Mates, Benson, 242n
meaning, tokens having more than
    one, viii, 3–4, 68–9, 79n, 85, 89,
    91, 94, 95–6, 139, 143–154, 239,
    242
meaning holism, *see* semantic holism
meaning localism, *see* semantic localism
meanings, *see* attitude ascriptions,
    meanings of; coarse-grained
    meanings; complexity of mean-
    ings; fine-grained meanings; first-
    and second-level meanings distin-
    guished; function of meanings;
    meaning, tokens having more
    than one; modes of reference
    or (re)presentation as meanings;
    narrow meanings (contents);
    promiscuous meanings; proto-
    intentional meanings and behav-
    ior; semantic roles, nature of;
    senses, Fregean; similarities in
    meanings; vagueness of meaning;
    wide meanings (contents) (in
    contrast to narrow)
methodological proposals,
    first, 5, 62, 70, 84, 140
    second, 5, 71, 84, 140, 252–3
    third, 5, 77, 84, 140
    fourth, 6, 83–5, 140, 208–15
    see also methodology of semantics
methodological solipsism, 8–9, 255–6,
    268n, 272–7, 285, 291, 292,
    299–312
methodology,
    of linguistics, 53n, 77, 81n
    of philosophy, 1, 48, 54, 75–6; *see
    also* conceptual analysis
    of psychology, 63n, 85n

of science, 1, 48–9, 70–6, 78–9,
    244–5
of semantics, viii–ix, 1–6, 8, 47, 48–
    86, 87, 100–1, 122, 140, 173–4,
    176, 179, 183–4, 186, 197, 208–
    15, 218n, 251–2
Millian theory, *see* 'Fido'-Fido theory
Millikan, Ruth, 161
modes of reference or (re)presenta-
    tion,
    causal, ix, 4, 7–8, 99, 116, 129,
    133–4, 138, 139, 160–70, 176–8,
    183n, 185–6, 218, 226–8, 267,
    288–91
    demonstrative, 142–3, 218–223,
    231, 232, 234, 236, 241
    descriptive, 4, 7, 139, 159–65, 176,
    185, 234, 242–3, 270, 274, 290
    disjunctive, for names, 233–5, 292
    en rapport (designational), 7, 143–
    8, 147n, 151, 153–4, 163–6,
    200–3, 216, 222
    first-person, 223–5
    as meanings, 4, 7, 64, 85–6, 128–9,
    133–4, 139, 142–5, 148–54,
    161–3, 165–71, 174–86, 188,
    195, 200–6, 216–44, 267, 285,
    288–91, 303, 306n; *see also*
    senses, Fregean
    one a species of another, 231–2,
    236–7
    unified, 231–2, 234, 236–7
Mrs. T, 36–7n, 119–20, 190, 273
Mulaire, Edmond, 15–16

names, *see* proper names, theories of
narrow behavior, 307–10
narrow meanings (contents), 3, 9,
    14n, 16, 39–42, 48, 60, 128,
    255n, 256, 258, 273–7, 278, 285,
    299–312
    as functional roles, 9, 20, 42, 255n,

258, 274, 275–6, 292–9, 302,
304–12
as functions, 9, 41–2, 128, 255n,
258, 280, 285–292, 302, 304–
12
NARROW PSYCHOLOGY, 9, 60,
256–8, 272–7, 285–312
naturalism, ix, 1–2, 5–6, 23–38, 46,
48–86, 90, 160–4, 172, 194,
249–53
Neale, Stephen, 164n
networks for proper names, 164, 167–
9, 173, 177, 226–7, 239
new theory, *see* 'Fido'-Fido theory
Nichols, Shaun, 79–80n
nominalism, 66n, 246n
no-principled-basis consideration, vii-
ix, 3, 183, 293
appeal of, 93–5, 134–5
a case against, 6–7, 87–135
rejection of the case for, 4–5, 11–
47, 290–1n, 299n

Occam, William of, 210
Opacity Problem, 171, 175–7, 180–5,
240–3
opaque ascriptions,7, 69, 117–8, 141–
54, 161, 166–8, 171, 174–8, 180,
184, 188–92, 195–203, 217–26,
230–38, 276n, 285, 287–91, 295,
304
Oppy, Graham, ix, 203n
Owens, Joseph I., 53n, 238n

Papineau, David, 16, 21, 38, 161,
294n
paradox of analysis, 173n
partial reference, 225–8
Pastin, Mark, 145n
Patterson, Sarah, 236n
Pelletier, Francis Jeffry, 76n

Perry, John, 170n, 180n, 201n, 202n,
203n, 205, 206n, 223–4, 236n
Pettit, Philip, 67n
physicalism (materialism), 265, 268–9,
272, 276–7
Platonism, 8, 55n, 83–4, 210–15
possible worlds semantics, 56n, 208,
210
pragmatics, 179–85
principles of charity and rationality,
15, 67, 192n
promiscuous meanings, 287–92, 309
proper names, theories of, ix, 8, 85,
129, 130, 138, 142–54, 159–61,
163–87, 222, 224–44, 261, 286n,
288–92, 302
propositions, 8, 13, 32–3, 56n, 57,
83–4, 155n, 180–2, 186n, 192n,
202n, 210–15, 224, 237n, 239n
proto-intentional meanings and behavior, 280, 286, 292, 306–10
psychological holism and localism,
43–6, 90, 104–13, 124
Putnam, Hilary, ix, 5, 15n, 17n, 18n,
19n, 20n, 25n, 32, 39, 99, 114–
5, 159, 161, 173n, 189, 256,
273,
Pylyshyn, Z., 255n, 257, 264n, 265,
280n, 282n

quantifying in, 141, 147n
Quine, W. V., vii, ix, 7, 15, 17–38,
50, 52n, 54, 66–7, 69, 87, 93n,
94, 117–20, 141–8, 166, 175,
197, 199–208, 210–15, 220, 222,
229, 235, 237, 247, 293

Ramsey sentences, 109–10, 124
Ray, Greg, ix
realism about the external world, 2,
21, 102–3, 130, 194
Reddam, Paul, 202n

335

possible worlds semantics; Representationalism; revisionism, semantic; truth-referential semantics; two-factor theories; use theories; verificationism
semi-Representationalism, 8, 132, 138, 187–92, 196, 243
senses, Fregean, ix, 82n, 134n, 161, 165, 180–1, 198n
similarities in meanings, 46–7n, 65, 77, 119n, 120–1, 293–4
simulation theory, 79–80n
Slater, Carol, 83n
Sleigh, R. C., 143n
slippery-slope or sorites arguments, 11n, 119–20n
Slote, viii–ix
Soames, Scott, 53n, 170n, 180n, 181n, 203n, 223n, 233, 241n, 242–3
Sosa, Ernest, 145n, 225n
speaker meaning, 59n, 65, 68n, 154–8, 193n, 225–8, 232–9; see also conventional meaning
Stalnaker, Robert, 309n,
Stampe, Dennis, 161
Stecker, Robert, 162n, 163n, 168n, 182–3n, 242n
Sterelny, Kim, ix, 2, 15n, 28n, 51n, 53n, 65n, 81n, 147n, 157n, 163, 165n, 169n, 260n
Stich, Stephen P., 15–16, 43, 46–7n, 79n, 119–20, 123n, 147n, 190–1, 207n, 208, 254n, 256–7, 264n, 266–7, 272–3, 275–6, 278–80, 297–8, 299, 310–12
STM (Syntactic Theory of the Mind), 256–7, 263, 266, 275–80; see also FORMAL IMPLEMENTATION, NARROW PSYCHOLOGY, SYNTACTIC PSYCHOLOGY
Strawson, P. F., 52n, 97

substitutivity of identity, 142, 147, 171, 175–7, 181n, 184, 235, 240–3
success of our ascriptions, argument from for the status quo, 70–1, 76, 81, 84, 85, 101, 112, 126, 132–3, 150–1, 154, 174, 244, 252–3, 312
against direct reference, 184
against eliminativism, 254
against NARROW PSYCHOLOGY, 7, 296, 299
against semantic holism, 6, 100–1, 113, 122, 127, 132, 135
against two-factor, use, and verificationist theories, 86, 187, 196
Swain, Corliss, ix
synonymy, 23, 65, 77, 162–3, 173, 242–3, 294n
syntactic properties, nature of, 123, 258–65, 275–6; see also formal properties, nature of
SYNTACTIC PSYCHOLOGY, 9, 60, 256–85, 312; see also STM (Syntactic Theory of the Mind)
SYNTACTIC THOUGHT PROCESSES, 268–72, 275–7, 281, 312

tacit (implicit) beliefs, theories, or knowledge, 2, 27, 51, 73–4, 79–80, 83, 140, 149, 160n, 248–9
Tarski, Alfred, 157
Taschek, William W., 172, 179n, 239n
Taylor, Kenneth A., ix, 165n, 250n
thought experiments, 1, 5, 48, 54, 72, 74–5, 80, 84–5, 114, 141; see also methodology of philosophy; naturalism
transcendentalism, 8, 249–53

transparent ascriptions, 7, 69, 117–18, 120, 142–4, 149–50, 192, 201–2, 220, 223n, 225, 241, 286n

rapport-, 7, 144–8, 151, 153–4, 200–2, 222

simply-, 7, 144–8, 151–4, 161, 176, 184, 188, 195–202, 217–8, 222, 232, 285, 291–2

truth-referential semantics, viii, 1, 20, 43, 83, 128, 162, 248, 254; *see also* Representationalism

Twin Earth, 159–60, 189, 273, 286n, 287–9, 300, 303, 305–10

two-factor theories, viii, 3, 8, 20, 48, 64, 69, 86, 96, 129n, 132, 134–5, 138, 187–92, 194, 243, 256

"ultimate" method, nature of, 5, 72–8, 104, 113–4, 140–1, 215

use theories, 1, 3, 64, 132, 139, 187, 193–6, 243

vagueness,
of meaning, 14, 55, 61, 63, 80, 116, 233n, 246–7
of reality, 76, 80, 105, 116, 246

verificationism, viii–ix, 1, 3, 4, 8, 17–18, 20–1, 46, 48, 64, 86, 132, 187, 193–6, 243, 256n

Von Eckardt, Barbara, 255n, 278n

Wagner, Steven J., 169n

warranted assertability, 1, 20–1

Wettstein, Howard, 53n, 164n, 169n, 170n, 180n, 181n, 185n

White, Morton G., 29n

White, Stephen L., 286n

wide behavior (in contrast to narrow), 307–10

wide meanings (contents) (in contrast to narrow), 9, 14n, 20, 39, 41, 48, 128, 255n, 256–8, 273–5, 278, 279–80, 285, 286n, 286–312

WIDE PSYCHOLOGY, 9, 275, 303–12; *see also* NARROW PSYCHOLOGY

Wiggins, David, 52n

Wilson, G., 147n, 164n

Wilson, N. L., 18n, 97

Wittgenstein, Ludwig, 52n, 97

Woodward, James, 254n

Wright, Crispin, 53n

Yagasawa, Takashi, 177n